CW01188094

ESCAPE FROM BERLIN

The incredible journey of the Latvian 15th SS Janums Battle Group, April 1945

Vincent Hunt

Helion & Company Limited

Helion & Company Limited
Unit 8 Amherst Business Centre
Budbrooke Road
Warwick
CV34 5WE
England
Tel. 01926 499 619
Email: info@helion.co.uk
Website: www.helion.co.uk
Twitter: @helionbooks
Visit our blog https://helionbooks.wordpress.com/

Published by Helion & Company 2025
Designed and typeset by Mach 3 Solutions (www.mach3solutions.co.uk)
Cover designed by Paul Hewitt, Battlefield Design (www.battlefield-design.co.uk)

Text © Vincent Hunt 2024
Images © Vincent Hunt unless otherwise credited
Maps by George Anderson © Helion & Company 2024

Cover: Colonel Vilis Janums leads men of the 15th SS Division Latvian Legion through the streets of Calbe, Germany, after surrendering to the Americans at Güterglück on 27 April 1945. Still picture by author from newsreel footage in the collection of the United States Holocaust Memorial Museum at <https://collections.ushmm.org/search/catalog/irn1004700>. Used with permission.

Back cover: The river Elbe at Güterglück, spanned by the US Army on 13 April 1945 using a pontoon bridge. This bridgehead was 'The Gateway to Berlin' but Allied supreme commander Dwight D. Eisenhower stopped the American advance here. The sight of this river meant safety and survival for the Latvians. Picture: author.

Every reasonable effort has been made to trace copyright holders and to obtain their permission for the use of copyright material. The author and publisher apologize for any errors or omissions in this work and would be grateful if notified of any corrections that should be incorporated in future reprints or editions of this book.

ISBN 978-1-804516-29-4

British Library Cataloguing-in-Publication Data.
A catalogue record for this book is available from the British Library.

All rights reserved. No part of this publication may be reproduced, stored in a retrieval system, or transmitted, in any form, or by any means, electronic, mechanical, photocopying, recording or otherwise, without the express written consent of Helion & Company Limited.

For details of other military history titles published by Helion & Company Limited contact the above address or visit our website: http://www.helion.co.uk.

We always welcome receipt of book proposals from prospective authors.

Contents

List of Maps	v
Preface	vi
Acknowledgements	vii

Part One: Across the Oder — 9
1. Introduction — 11
2. Crossing the Oder — 16
3. The Medal Ceremony at Cölpin Manor — 25
4. Himmler's Hospital at Hohenlychen — 34
5. 'If There is an Order to Move, Try to Break Through to the Allied Front.' — 45
6. 19 April 1945 — 55
7. The Janums Battle Group Abandons its Positions — 68

Part Two: The Incredible Journey — 73
8. The Decision to Desert — 75
9. Edvīns Bušmanis, 21 April 1945 — 82
10. On the Trail of the Janums Battle Group — 95
11. Fiat 500 in Beelitz — 101
12. Alarm! — 103
13. By Compass Through the Forest — 116
14. Edvīns Bušmanis at Verlorenwasser — 124
15. Fiat 500 at Werbig — 131
16. The 'Going Over' — 137
17. Fiat 500 in Schora — 148
18. The Surrender — 151
19. 78 Years Later — 154

Part Three: Janums' Captivity — 159
20. 'We are Latvians, and we consider that the war has finished' – the Handwritten Diary of Colonel Janums — 161

Part Four: Zerbst — 173
21. The Bombing of Zerbst — 175
22. A Meeting with the Mayor of Zerbst — 190

iii

Part Five: Postscript 205
23 One of Janums' Men: Henry Vītols 207
24 The Post-Surrender Diary of Edvīns Bušmanis 211
25 The Life and Legacy of Colonel Janums 221

Bibliography 231
Index 236

List of Maps

1. The incredible journey of the Janums Battle Group 20.4.45–27.4.45   10
2. Crossing the Oder March 1945   15
3. The Latvian 15th SS in Mecklenburg   35
4. The Soviet crossing of the Oder-Neisse   53
5. The parting of the ways, 19 April 1945   58
6. Latvian positions south-east of Berlin 20.4.45 and 21.4.45   69
7. The Soviet thrust towards Berlin   72
8. The bridge at Schmöckwitz   80
9. The route of the Janums Battle Group south of Berlin   89
10. From Dahlewitz to Fichtenwalde   108
11. Fichtenwalde to Verlorenwasser 22.4.45–24.4.45   110
12. Swamps and forests: Golzow to Verlorenwasser   118
13. The 'Going Over': the Mexican standoff on the night of 26.4.45   136
14. The American advance across the Elbe, April 1945   174

Preface

This book is the latest in a series bringing a Latvian perspective to combat during the Red Army's Vistula–Oder offensive of January to March 1945, the Battle of Berlin and the end of the war in Germany in 1945.

The stories come from the diaries and eyewitness accounts of soldiers involved. They chart – in their own words – daring escapes and defiance not told before in English which bring new insight into the relationship between the Latvians and their German commanders as well as their motivation for fighting.

In this book, the accounts of senior officers and many soldiers serving with the Janums Battle Group (Kampfgruppe *Janums*) offer a gripping and detailed account of the incredible escape of the 800-strong Latvian unit and its surrender to the Americans on the Elbe. The diary of First Lieutenant Edvīns Bušmanis is a wonderfully descriptive and sharply observed hour-by-hour document of their astonishing evasion of both Soviet and German troops through the swamps and forests of Brandenburg, while Captain Vilis Akermanis was the officer who actually negotiated the surrender at Güterglück. Astonishing newsreel footage of the Janums battle group in captivity was discovered during the research for this book.

In the next volume – *Sent to Die in Berlin* – the memories of the men who fought in the 15th SS Division 'Recce' Battalion in the ruins of central Berlin will add dramatic new episodes to the existing accounts of the last days of Hitler's Third Reich.

Also by this author

Fire and Ice – the Nazis' scorched earth campaign in Norway (The History Press, 2014)

Blood in the Forest – the end of the Second World War in the Courland Pocket (Helion, 2017)

Up Against the Wall – the KGB and Latvia (Helion, 2019)

The Road of Slaughter – the Latvian 15th SS Division in Pomerania, Jan-March 1945 (Helion, 2023)

Acknowledgements

This book began with, and has been built around, the unpublished diary of 15th Division Adjutant First Lieutenant Edvīns Bušmanis, passed to the author by the WWII curator of the Latvian War Museum in Rīga, Jānis Tomaševskis. Translated into English by Daina Vītola, it is an amazingly detailed and gripping read – testimony both to the writer's ability with words, and to Daina's skill in recreating the meaning in English.

The tenacious research of Aivars Sinka, worldwide head of the Daugavas Vanagi veterans' group, has uncovered several key texts for this book, including that of Arvīds Kalupnieks and the officer sent to negotiate the surrender to the Americans, Captain Vilis Akermanis. The many hours of translation and archive research Aivars has dedicated to telling the story of the 15th Division has enabled the writing of this book in this form. The incredible film of the Janums' battle group in Calbe hours after surrendering to the Americans was discovered during research for this book at the United States Holocaust Memorial Museum online. I would urge readers to view it and see the expressions on the soldiers' faces at the end of their week-long marathon journey. There are stills from the film between pp.166–170.

I am very grateful to Sarmīte Ērenpreiss-Janovskis, the wife of novelist Gunars Janovskis, who generously allowed me to use extracts from his book about his experiences in Pomerania, *After Doomsday*. It is vivid and compelling, and very readable but tragic literature.

Māra Walsh-Sinka translated the account of Peteris Krievs, which is used with permission of Latvian military historian Aivars Petersons who interviewed him originally for his excellent title Mums Japarnak. I am very grateful to Mr Petersons for allowing me to use this material, which forms the basis for my forthcoming volume *Sent to Die in Berlin*. The memoirs of Arvīds Kalupnieks and Vilis Akermanis were also translated by Māra.

I am very grateful to Zerbst city archivist Juliane Bruder and Professor Herbert Witte for their research and help, and to town mayor Andreas Dittmann and Andreas Baumgart who helped me piece together what happened in Zerbst as the Latvians passed through that region.

I am indebted to Matthias Hille in Calbe for identifying the locations of the Janums Battle Group in the photographs, and to Doreen Ryssmann in Fichtenwalde and her history group for further information about events in Beelitz and around. I am grateful to Aija Ebden – who lived in the same DP camp as Colonel Janums in

Germany after the war – for her help summarising his post-war years and to Tania Kibermanis for her help with the finer points of German vocabulary.

I must thank Duncan Rogers and the team at Helion once again for allowing me to write this book as I saw it, and for their excellent work making it a reality.

I must thank my son Martins Vitolins-Hants and his partner Leigh Titterton as well as my friends David Ford, Derek Ivens, Geoff Walton, Sam Heitzman, Rob Jones, Lawrence Brannon and Simon Price for providing welcome distractions as I assembled the pieces of this story.

Finally, special thanks are due to Natalie Carragher, my road partner, navigator and photographer on the trip to the Elbe and a source of ongoing support throughout the writing of this book.

Vincent Hunt
Manchester, January 2025
www.vincenthunt.co.uk

Part One

Across the Oder

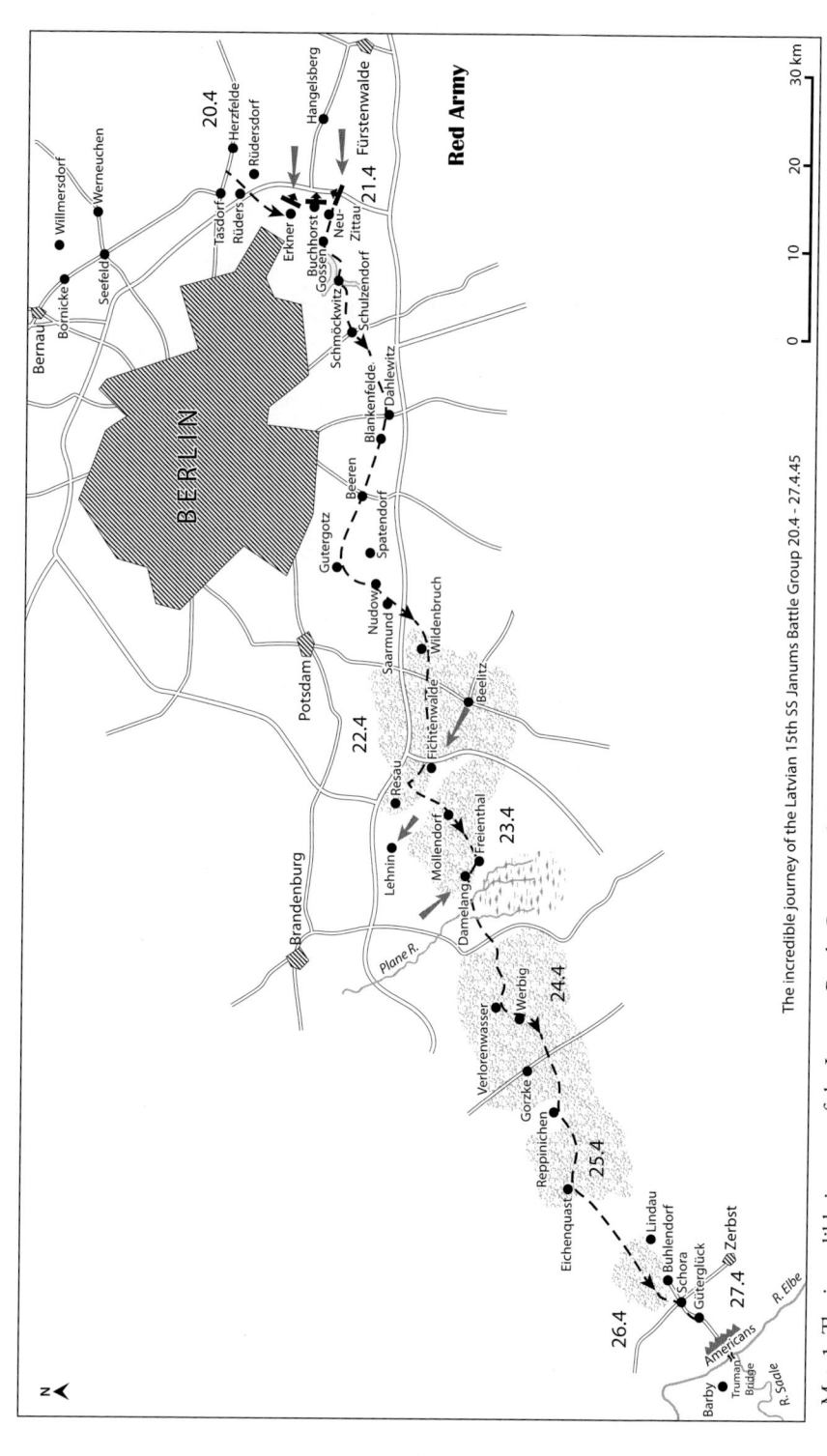

Map 1 The incredible journey of the Janums Battle Group 20.4.45–27.4.45. The escape of the Latvian 15th SS Janums Battle Group from the south-east of Berlin: an epic week-long journey through forests and swamps, evading both German patrols and Red Army advance units to surrender to the Americans at Güterglück.

1

Introduction

Shortly after midnight on the night of 26 April 1945, a column of 800 well-armed soldiers in German uniform moved across a bridge over a river around 150 kilometres south-west of Berlin. These were the final moments of the incredible escape of the Janums Battle Group, two regiments of men from the 15th Latvian SS Division about to surrender to the Americans. Flares fired from the positions of the US Army's Eighth Armoured Group kept them on track in the darkness, their boots echoing off the cobbles of the country village road.

The commanding officer, a thin, wiry, bird-like figure dressed in a knee-length coat, turned to his men carrying Panzerfausts, the shoulder-fired bazookas that destroyed so many Red Army tanks. Among them was 20 year-old Henrijs (Henry) Vītols.

'You can throw them in the river, lads,' he said. 'You won't be needing them anymore.'

And with that, Colonel Vilis Janums marched on into captivity, saving his men from dying a needless, pointless death for a fanatical dictator and a lost cause.

In this book the diaries of 15th Division adjutant First Lieutenant (*Virsleitnants*) Edvīns Bušmanis give a gripping hour-by-hour account of their escape from the frontlines south-east of Berlin. Archive US Army film footage of the Latvians going into captivity in Calbe has emerged during the writing of it. The author followed the journey of the Latvians around the south of Berlin and through the forests to the Elbe to see if their brief passage through these German villages during this incredible escape has been remembered. Surprisingly enough, during a time of such turmoil and through the eighty years since, it has.

The Latvian 15th SS Division was formed in 1943 after a call-up of men of fighting age during the Nazi occupation of Latvia. Most were conscripts, not volunteers: trained and sent to the Russian Front in November that year to bolster the German lines around Moscow and Leningrad. On the other side of the front, ten thousand Latvians fought in the defence of Moscow in the 201st Latvian Rifleman Division – a mix of around 3,000 survivors of the Latvian pre-war army pressed into service (those that weren't killed, deported, deserted or demobilised); 4,000 Russians introduced into the army in 1940 to make it less Latvian; Latvian communists from Russia, and Latvian communists and Jewish volunteers who escaped Latvia as the Germans advanced in 1941.

The river Elbe at Güterglück, spanned by the US Army on 13 April 1945 using a pontoon bridge. This bridgehead was 'The Gateway to Berlin' but Allied supreme commander Dwight D. Eisenhower stopped the American advance here. The sight of this river meant safety and survival for the Latvians. Picture: author.

Their bravery stopping Hitler's strike into the Soviet Union was recognised with their unit being given the honorific 'Latvian Guards Division'.

In 1942 the 201st Rifleman Division became the 43rd Guards Latvian Riflemen Division. This was an elite infantry unit which fought at Velikie Luki and Leningrad and later became part of the 130th Latvian Rifle Corps, taking Riga and fighting in the Courland Pocket. From 1944 the make-up of the nominally Latvian Soviet units became more ethnically Latvian as around 60,000 conscripts from the Soviet-occupied eastern regions of Vidzeme, Latgale and Zemgale were added to the mix.

These men suffered a 50 percent casualty rate: of 4,000 Jews who fought in the Red Army after being evacuated from Latvia, 2,000 died. Among them were men already in Russia who joined up and soldiers from the pre-war Latvian Army forcibly absorbed into the Red Army. Of the 10,000 Latvians who fought in the Red Army in 1941, some 6,000 died.[1]

---

1 Figures from Museum of the Occupation of Latvia conference, 20.07.2022. *Latvian Losses in the Second World War: the fates of soldiers and civilians* (Latvijas tautas zaudējumi Otrajā pasaules karā: karavīru un civilistu likteņu summa) online at <https://vecais.okupacijasmuzejs.lv/lv/aktualitates/aicinam-uz-konferenci-latvijas-tautas-zaudejumi-otraja-pasaules-kara-karaviru-un-civilistu-liktenu-summa-1148/>. Guards Division details from Max Kaufmann (2010) in *Churbn Lettlands – the Destruction of the Jews of Latvia*, pp.273–274. He writes: 'They fought and died like heroes. Because this division was generally regarded as a Latvian unit, the world, of course, knows little of the Jewish fighters. But we Latvian Jews cannot, and never will, forget them!'

When the Red Army launched its summer 1944 offensive westward, the 15th Division bore the brunt of it. Stricken from the losses it had sustained, the 15th was withdrawn to Rīga while the 19th Division – strengthened by the heavy weapons their fellow soldiers left behind and the transfer of an artillery regiment, sapper battalion and some battle-capable NCOs and soldiers – held back the Red Army advance as long as possible.

As the fall of Rīga became inevitable, the survivors from the 15th on the Russian Front were shipped to Pomerania to re-group with a fresh intake of conscripts. Another 25,000 young men were called up for military service: 15,684 went into the Legion, 5,543 became Luftwaffe *flakhelfer* – in effect, teenagers aged 14–17 used as anti-aircraft gun crew – and 3,614 were sent to the *Reichsarbeitsdienst* labour battalions (RAD).[2]

In Pomerania these inexperienced soldiers trained in the West Prussian training ground west of Danzig with whatever weapons and equipment they had. They had been told they would be shipped back to Courland to defend their homeland. Instead they were sent to stop the Red Army's powerful Vistula to Oder offensive in the sub-zero blizzards of January 1945. Those who survived battles at Nakel, Vandsburg, Kujan, Sparsee, Jastrow, Flederborn, Landeck and Domslaff through January and February 1945 then fought their way along the Baltic coast at Hoff and Horst in March before crossing the Oder to the relative safety of Germany proper.

Pomerania was a battlefront where many foreign SS units saw active service: the French volunteers of the 33rd SS Charlemagne Division, the 31st SS German-Hungarians and Generalleutnant Günther Krappe's X SS Corps were all effectively smashed during this seven-week period. The patched-up Latvian 15th SS – built around a core of Latvian Army officers and experienced soldiers – was repeatedly put into the frontlines by German commanders. Constant Red Army encirclements meant thousands of Latvians died in the seven-week retreat to the Oder, with as many as 5,000 killed along a stretch of road between Jastrow and Landeck in early February – a period veterans describe as the 15th Division's 'Golgotha'.[3]

This book follows the story of the men of the 15th Division once across the Oder in March 1945 until 19 April 1945. On that day German orders sent 1,200 Latvians to Berlin as the Janums Battle Group to stop the Russian encirclement of the capital. The three battalions involved became split up on the way and Colonel Janums took advantage of the confusion to lead his 850 men to the south-west. The Recce, or Reconnaissance Battalion, comprising around 300 of the best and most decorated fighters was sent into the centre of Berlin to 'stiffen resistance' there. This was, in effect, a death sentence.

A third group of about 4,500 men were sent to the lakes and forests of Mecklenburg north of Berlin, where they eventually refused to fight, double-crossed their SS commanders in their forest HQ and marched away through the night to surrender to the Americans at Schwerin on 2 May.

This book focuses on the daring escape – or outrageous desertion – of Colonel Vilis Janums, a regimental commander in the division, who abandoned his positions

---

2   Figures from *Latvian losses in the Second World War*: the fates of soldiers and civilians, details as above.
3   See the author's previous book *The Road of Slaughter* (Helion, 2023).

south-east of Berlin and marched his men 125 km through forests and swamps to surrender to the Americans at the Elbe. However, he left behind the Recce Battalion because he did not trust its German commander, SS-Hauptsturmführer Eldon Walli – with good reason – and did not risk sharing his escape plan with him.

As an officer with a reputation for courage, stamina and military skills who saved his men on many occasions, Janums commanded absolute loyalty from those who served under him – to their dying day, as the author discovered on several occasions.

Following the journey of the Janums Battle Group around Berlin using modern methods is not as straightforward as might be assumed, as the route they took is – understandably – off-road through swamps and forests. But astonishingly their brief passage through this belt of marshes and woods between the southern Berlin autobahn and the river Elbe is the subject of several German historical accounts highlighted here – and the battle group was captured on film shot by the Americans post-surrender.[4] As a counterpoint to the incredible escape of the 824 Latvians, the reduction to rubble by the USAF of a town considered a 'medieval jewel' also features, as part of the wider story of the end of the Second World War and the lasting consequences of Nazi fanaticism.

Colonel Vilis Janums in the forest near Kalininko, Russia, 12 July 1944. Kalininko was a shambolic retreat from the Red Army brought about by poor German strategy and command, and is covered in more detail in Chapter 25. Picture courtesy of the Latvian War Museum in Riga, ref: LKM 5-190-FT/p.

Zerbst in Brandenburg will never return to what it once was – a beautifully preserved and charming settlement dating back to the Middle Ages. It will be scarred forever by the high explosives and incendiaries dropped by the US Air Force on 16 April 1945, ten days before the Latvians reached the area. Less than a month later, the town and its citizens came under the control of the Red Army, and Zerbst spent the next half-century on the Soviet side of the Iron Curtain.

4 Latvian prisoners in Calbe, May 1945: US Army film in the collection of the United States Holocaust Memorial Museum at <https://collections.ushmm.org/search/catalog/irn1004700>

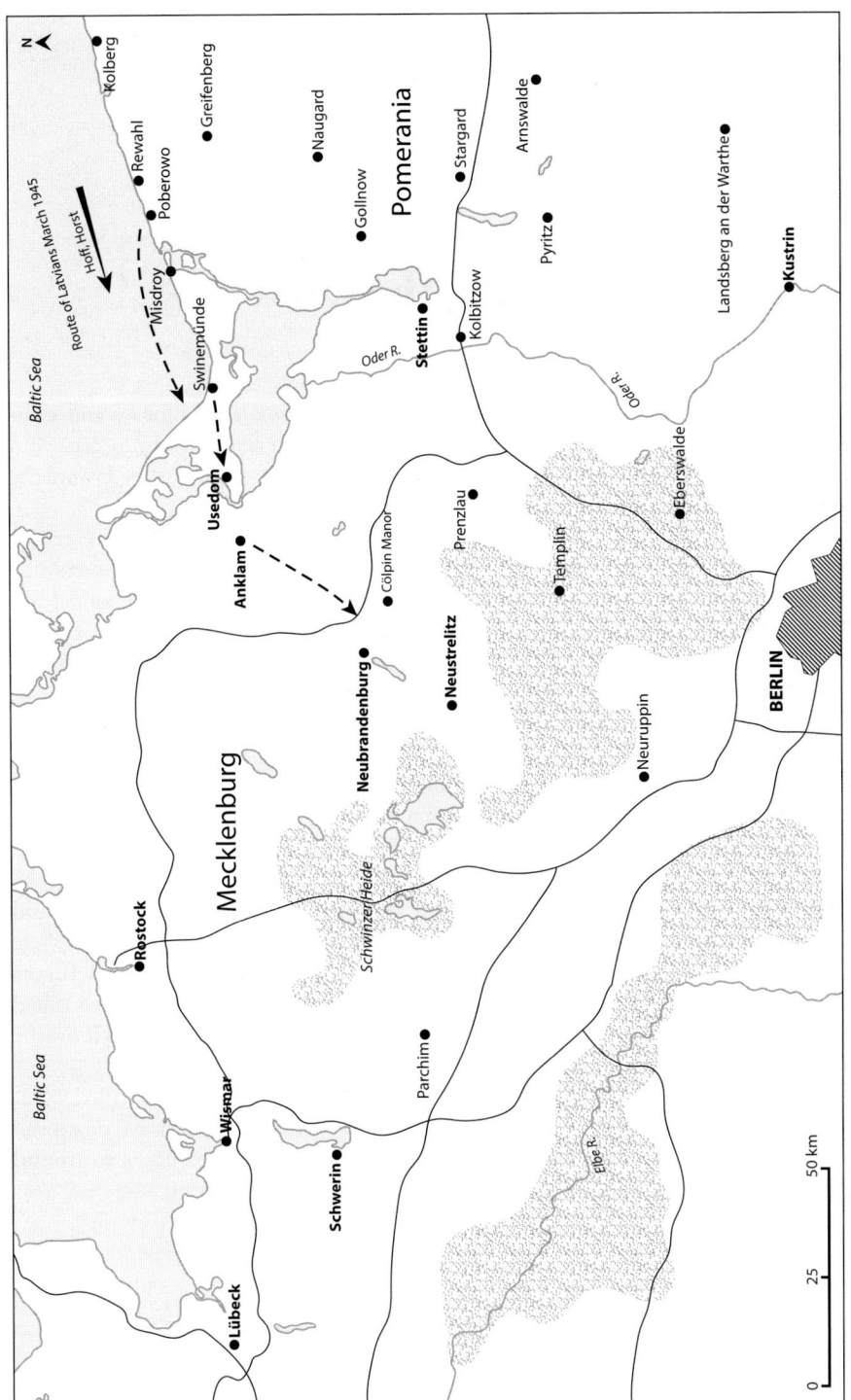

Map 2 The Latvian 15th SS escaped from Pomerania in March 1945 from the bridgehead at Dievenow to Wolin and then Swinemünde, where they were disarmed. They were then sent south to re-group around Neubrandenburg, Feldberg, Lychen and Fürstenberg.

2

Crossing the Oder

Swinemünde in 1945 was one of the most important German naval bases and military supply hubs on the Baltic Sea: a fuel and ammunition centre, training base and shipyard. It had become the focus of the evacuation from the Russian Front, the Baltics and East Prussia, and the city was full of refugees.

Four days before the Latvians crossed the Oder, on 7 March 1945, the German Navy's armoured cruisers *Lutzow* and *Admiral Scheer* had been moved to Swinemünde (now Świnoujście) to support the ongoing evacuation of 350,000 military personnel and 800,000–900,000 civilians from the Eastern Front through Gotenhafen and Danzig in Operation Hannibal, one of the largest seaborne evacuations in history. Several destroyers, torpedo boats and 12 Kriegsmarine transport ships docked there too.

The *Lutzow*, *Admiral Scheer* and *Prinz Eugen* were re-fuelled and re-armed in Swinemünde before going back to bombard Soviet forces in East Prussia and Pomerania. Their guns posed a considerable threat to the Soviet forces close to the Oder at Wolin preparing to advance further west so the chief of the Russian air force asked the Allies to bomb the city.[1]

On 12 March 1945, 600 B-17 Flying Fortresses and B-24 Liberators from the 392nd Group of the 8th US Army Air Force were sent to target the naval base and railway marshalling yards at Swinemünde. Instead they hit the city centre, where between 70,000 and 100,000 local residents and half-starved, exhausted refugees from East Prussia and Pomerania were sheltering. Thousands of people were killed and more than half the city's buildings destroyed as 1,500 tons of bombs fell on the city in less than an hour.

Six ships packed with refugees were sunk. More than 570 people were killed when the *Androsie* was hit, mostly women and children from the east. The official death toll at the time was given as 23,000 people, which has since been revised down to around 5,000.[2] The Latvians passed through Swinemünde shortly afterwards.

---

1 Blank, Fings and Echtemkamp, *Germany and the Second World War* Vol IX–1, p.472, and Koop, and Schmolke, *Pocket Battleships of the Deutschland Class: Warships of the Kriegsmarine* (Barnsley: Seaforth Publishing, 2014), p.58.
2 Blank, Fings and Echtemkamp, p.472, and Swinousjcie city website at <https://www.swinoujskie.info/2017/03/10/amerykanskie-bombowce-zrzucily-na-swinoujscie-3218-bomb/>

One veteran, Legion machinegunner Jānis Čevers, served on the Russian Front through 1944 with the 15th Division and was shipped to Pomerania in 1945 to help rebuild the unit. As we talk in the front room of his home in the Allenton district of Derby seven and a half decades later, his memories are razor sharp and detailed.

> We came to the Oder. It's a big wide river and a ship was waiting. The Russians were coming and everybody wanted to get on that ship [away]. The German SS officers were saying 'We should be on the boat' and they were shooting each other!
> But – for some reason, I can't understand why – they kept the Germans behind and put the Latvian 15th Division on that boat. Why did they do that? There were SS, Wehrmacht, Latvians … all waiting to get this boat across to Swinemünde, and the boat couldn't take everybody. There were thousands of soldiers, but for some reason we were selected to get on.[3]
> Our battalion stayed about three kilometres outside Swinemünde in the forest, and that night about 700 planes bombed the city. We heard the bombing but we were outside the town: the centre was full of refugees. The next morning we marched through and there were bodies everywhere, hanging in trees, heads everywhere, dead horses too. There was a field that was full of thousands of dead people, covered by white sheets.
> Oh, the sights. Hands, heads; in trees that were just stubs, and parts of bodies everywhere. We just walked through, like nothing. That was like a daily routine. It was normal, like going for a picnic. That was the biggest attack we saw from Western aeroplanes. Swinemünde was hammered. We weren't bothered, we just walked on.[4]

At the end of the war, 25,000 Legionnaires, mostly from the 15th Division, surrendered to the Allies in Germany. Mr Čevers was one of 10,000 veterans who relocated to the UK in 1947, taking jobs as part of the post-war European Voluntary Workers' scheme. He settled in Derby and lived the rest of his life in the UK. Another veteran, Žano Mūsiņš, settled in Coventry in the west Midlands of the UK. He too came to the UK through the EVW, and even at the age of 95 had vivid memories of the destruction of Swinemünde.

> At that time Swinemünde had been destroyed because of the V2 base not far away. The whole town was like a desert with a few chimneys sticking up here and there. There was nothing standing above chest height. That's the first time I saw half a horse hanging in the telephone wires. I think that was practically the end of the hostilities.

(accessed 26 August 2019). Many of those who died in the bombing are buried at Golm war cemetery on the island of Usedom. Source: The 2011 Golm Book at <https://www.volksbund.de/seite-nicht-gefunden.html>.
3   Apparently due to string-pulling by Latvian Legion Inspector-General Rūdolfs Bangerskis.
4   Interview with author, 2017.

After weeks of constant fighting, narrow escapes and the relief of repeatedly cheating death, the Latvians were mentally and physically exhausted. At that point in the war, Mr Mūsiņš feels the German Army was on the verge of collapse.

> ZM: Once we crossed [the Oder] we disarmed. All our arms were…

He searches for the words.

> ZM: …our 1st Battalion had the full armament that we had, and what we had was … bits and bobs, the dregs, you know? There was bugger all. At that particular time we weren't an army any more.
> VH: [The Legion chief of staff and historian Arturs] Silgailis mentions that you had your weapons taken off you and they were given to the frontline troops. He says everyone was fed up because you'd carried them half way across Europe.
> ZM: Well, that's what it was. See, the German Army was in total disarray at that time and we didn't have any information from them. So that was it. It was every man for himself.[5]

The Latvians were taken by boat to the island of Usedom on 14 March and disarmed. They had to wait until 16 March to get their first food for some time, during which time the troops 'were literally starving'.[6] Silgailis writes of this period: 'On 14 March the division was ordered to turn its weapons over to German units engaged in frontlines. This order exasperated the men. During the past weeks of strenuous marches and battles the men had literally carried the weapons on their backs in order to safeguard them, and now they were ordered to give them away. They felt insulted.'[7]

The German high command planned to disband the division and use the Latvians as reinforcements, but Legion Inspector-General Bangerskis argued successfully for them to remain as one unit and bring in reinforcements from the reserves that had escaped from the Field Replacement Depot at Toruń, a city on the Vistula river to the south-west of Pomerania. These reserves were drafted into the 32nd Regiment, which was being rebuilt around the 2nd Battalion of the 33rd Regiment. On 30 March the division was moved to the area around Fürstenberg, Feldberg and Lychen, working round the clock to build a new defensive line – the C Line – as the Red Army crossed the Oder on 11 April.

At this time rumours began to circulate that the Latvians were to be sent back to Kurzeme without weapons – a move that would mean certain captivity and probably years in Siberian labour camps, if not worse. Silgailis writes: 'Some unit commanders

---

5 Interview with author, Coventry, September 2018. The Latvian Legion Inspector-General Rūdolfs Bangerskis and his senior officers were concerned that the discipline of the units would slacken and they would drift away, at which point their chances of survival would reduce dramatically. Bangerskis had discussions with Janums and his commanders about dashing west as a division, which were scuppered when on 19 April 1945 Colonel Janums was sent to Berlin.
6 A. Brombergs, *The Latvian Encyclopaedia* (Hazners, Vilis vol.1_0004, 1952), p.32.
7 Silgailis, *Latvian Legion*, p.182.

had decided not to comply with such an order. The plan was, should it become fact, to retreat to the west under the leadership of *Staf.* Janums, and to surrender to the Western Allies, with force if necessary.'

The Inspector-General of the Latvian Legion (Bangerskis) was finally assured by the German high command that the division would not be transferred to Kurzeme. The divisional commander SS-Oberführer Karl Burk also promised to do everything possible on his part to prevent Latvians from becoming prisoners of the USSR.[8]

The Latvians were moved south in an almost-continuous 50 km route march until the column was eight kilometres from Neubrandenburg. Then they turned off the main road for the final stages to their destination – a country manor house. Sapper Imants Jansons wrote: 'Some of the boys are no longer able to keep up and stop to sleep in roadside houses. I continue with my last energy, knowing that tomorrow this path will not be any easier to walk. We reach the manor house indicated for our battalion at midnight. We have managed 58 km. I fall on the straw in the shed and no longer feel anything.'[9]

By mid-March 1945 Jānis Urpens had been in the 15th Division for a month. He had been automatically re-assigned to the Legion from the Reich Labour Service (RAD or *Reichsarbietsdienst*) and sent to the 15th Division at the front after the battle of Kamin in mid-February. After the war he came to the UK as an EVW worker, settled in the Cambridge area and worked for the council until he retired. At his home in Fenstanton 74 years later, he remembered that time:

> I really didn't see much because I was very lucky: I lost the regiment. They left me in a barn sleeping.[10] No-one woke me up. When I woke up I was standing there outside and then someone else came out of the straw. He was from the RAD too – I knew him. I said, 'What are we going to do? They're all gone!' And he said, 'Well, let's see on the road.'
>
> There were soldiers on the road; one German with a bag of tobacco, and he gave everyone going by a bag of tobacco! I don't know why he did that. So we started walking and after a few kilometres we came to a village.
>
> I noticed there were two ambulances that had our divisional emblem on them – two swans – so I said, 'Let's go and talk to those ambulancemen, because they're from our regiment. They'll know where our unit is.'
>
> So we went over, and believe it or not, that ambulance driver was the brother of my brother-in-law. I said, 'Juri, do you remember me?' I must have looked terrible because I hadn't shaved for weeks, I hadn't had a wash and I was wounded and so on. He looked at me and said, 'You do look familiar. Where have I seen you before?'

---

8   Silgailis, pp.182–183. *Staf* is a short form for Standartenführer, the Waffen-SS equivalent of a colonel.
9   Jansons, p.174.
10   Coincidentally the starting point for the 1968 Gunars Janovskis novel *After Doomsday*, translated by Janovskis's third wife Sarmīte Ērenpreiss-Janovskis and reproduced here with her permission.

I said, 'I'm Jānis!' And he looks again and says, 'Jānis! What are you doing here?!'

I said, 'Can I join you?' And he says, 'If you don't mind sitting on the wing outside, then you can join me. I have a wounded woman inside the ambulance.'

So all the way on the journey there I was sitting on the wing of the ambulance with my friend on the other wing. The German forces broke through so we had to go with the ambulance and all the time they [the Russians] bombarded the road with shells.

My friend on the other side of the ambulance shouted over, 'Let's promise each other if one of us is wounded we'll help each other out until we get through this.' So we reached across the bonnet to hold each other on the wings of the ambulance, and we weren't wounded at all. We arrived alive![11]

The German army was by now engaged in a desperate defence of the approaches to Berlin from the Oder river. Around 100 km east of Neubrandenburg fierce fighting raged for control of the port city of Stettin (Szczecin). Frontal infantry assaults and mass tank attacks were launched against the German frontline in the Stettin suburbs of Altdamm and Finkenwalde (now Dabie and Zdroje).

Accounts of the ferocity of the battle for Stettin come from survivors of another foreign legion fighting for Adolf Hitler, the 28th SS Grenadier Division *Walloonien*. They were Belgian volunteers, led by the Nazi collaborator and fascist political leader Leon Degrelle. The Walloon Legion arrived in Pomerania in February 1945 as badly-mauled veterans of the defence of Estonia against the Red Army, having survived the fighting in the Cherkassy Pocket which claimed the lives of 1,300 of its 2,000 men.[12] Degrelle wrote of the fighting at Stettin:

> The casualties were terrible. In three days our sector lost sixty percent of its defenders, who had either been killed or wounded. Dug in their foxholes, only their heads or arms sticking out, they got hit by shrapnel from shells or mortars, mostly in the face. They would then run to my tiny command post with terrifying bloody holes where their jaws used to be. Twenty-five or thirty wounded men would run to me at a time.
>
> Some of them, who were hit on the run, had metal shrapnel in their groins. They would convulse horribly, screaming in agony. But I had to command, had to keep an eye on everything, despite the stench of curdling blood and excrement that floated over wet trenches.[13]

---

11 Interview with author, March 2019. The story may be from the division's escape along a narrow corridor on the Baltic coastline, under constant Soviet shellfire.
12 R. Rule, *Leon Degrelle, Traitor of Belgium* in Warfare History Network, 9 January 2019. Degrelle and his men were desperate to avoid Soviet captivity at the end of the war so headed for Lübeck to surrender to the British. Degrelle went on to Denmark and Norway where he commandeered a Heinkel 111 and flew to Spain, then controlled by General Franco. Franco refused Belgian requests to extradite him and granted him citizenship. He died in 1994.
13 T. Borowski, *Last Blood on Pomerania*, p.103.

By contrast, in mid-March 1945, the 32nd Regiment of the Latvian 15th SS Division were in the Neustrelitz area, near to Rollenhagen at the southern end of the Tollensesee lake at Neubrandenburg. Major Jūlijs Ķīlītis issued orders for the men to assemble and gave instructions as to their behaviour. Uniforms were to be mended and there should be 'correct behaviour' towards civilians. The order was 'to take nothing without their permission' and there was to be no 'loafing around'.[14] This period of rest was in striking contrast to the scenes developing across the rest of Germany.

Among the Latvian soldiers in the retreat from Pomerania was Gunārs Janovskis, an interpreter for the German Army and later a well-known Latvian writer. His 1968 book *Pēc pastardienas* (*After Doomsday*) was translated into English by his third wife Sarmīte Ērenpreiss-Janovskis. Janovskis paints grim scenes of the reality of those final days of war through the eyes of his narrator.

As he comes to a manor house he calls 'Blidow,' west of the Oder in the region around Neubrandenburg, he describes the last-ditch defences against the oncoming tanks and mass infantry of the Red Army, and the ruthless discipline applied to those in German uniform.

> On the main road [past the manor house] a tank barrier had been constructed: four pine trunks dug into the ground. Four more tree trunks were craftily balanced on their ends ... The purpose of this fence was to arrest the progress of the tank divisions of the armies of Zhukov, Konev and Rokossovsky. What had been impossible for the Dnieper, the Donau, the Visla and the Oder should now be achieved by this eight-trunked contraption.
>
> At this barrier a guard stood there day and night: three old men and two boys. Their armaments were two hunting guns, two muck forks and a French carbine with a very obvious engraving: *Anno 1871*. It was to be loaded with one fairly large, bright yellow cartridge. In total, this armament amounted to fifteen shots.[15]

Janovskis describes masses of refugees streaming along a road lined with oak trees which had seen much conflict down the years. Wallenstein mercenaries marched along here in the Thirty Years War of 1618–1648 hanging everyone who wasn't Catholic.[16] Then the Swedes came and hanged everyone who *was* Catholic. There were Napoleon's Grenadiers and after them the German regiments marching to the battlefields of Verdun, Marne and the Somme. More recently, English and American prisoners of war shuffled along this road in the 'Long March' after being freed from Nazi camps in the east. Janovskis continues:

---

14 Ķīlītis: Order No.1 to the 32nd Waffen SS Regiment, 16 March 1945 at Rollenhagen.
15 Janovskis, *After Doomsday*, pp.85–86.
16 Commanded by Albrecht von Wallenstein, who raised mercenary armies to fight for the Catholic cause against the forces of the Swedish king, Gustav II Adolph.

> And then five German soldiers were hastily hanged from the branches of these oaks. Not because they had done something wrong or committed a crime. The Higher Command, in their wisdom, demanded drastic measures to maintain discipline and the spirit of battle. And these commands were indeed obeyed.
>
> With the customary zeal, young, pale and trembling teenagers were hoisted up to the branches. All the same, one of the sergeants managed to whisper into the ear of his victim: 'Why is your lip trembling? For you, this mess is over. Who knows what will happen to the rest of us?'
>
> And onto the chests of the hanged were fastened pre-written slogans:
>
> 'I hang here, because I did not believe in victory.'
>
> 'He who is too cowardly to fight for his Fatherland dies in the pillory.'
>
> 'I hang here because I did not believe in the Leader.'
>
> 'I am a deserter, therefore I will never experience the change of our fortune in Our War.'
>
> 'All traitors will die like me.'
>
> Then the patrol marched off and darkness and silence fell. In the early morning mist the guards, in their fear, mistakenly shot the manor's blacksmith, who was going to the dairy on his tractor, because it was mistaken for an enemy tank. And then came the Russians.[17]

Janovskis sheltered at the manor house as he made his way west, having lost his unit when he fell asleep in a barn. He befriends a Polish orphan called Tadeusz who is being raised by the manor's gardener, who tells him of the madness and horror when the Soviets arrived here. 'But can one believe a boy?' Janovskis asks his readers.

> In his fear and horror, this mad Russian night might have confused him, jumbling things which were told, heard, read about or just imagined. Maybe the shots into the ceiling of the manor's ballroom had been just for fun; sheer high spirits and the joy of victory, yet in the boy's imagination they were already transformed into corpses?
>
> Maybe the Russians only pinched the thighs of German wenches in a friendly manner, yet to the boy it had seemed unimaginable insolence? Maybe the old Baroness was tired of living and it was sheer coincidence that, on that very night, she drowned herself in the millpond?
>
> And maybe the old Baron was not nailed to the table, but – made drunk by the Russian soldiers – was lying on it with arms outspread. You can never believe a boy. Maybe the Germans had intimidated him and made him tell all kinds of tales.[18]

The horror and revulsion Janovskis felt at the carnage and sadism he witnessed makes his work extremely powerful. When more Red Army soldiers arrived at the manor house, an encounter with a lieutenant revealed a reason for his personal rage.

---

17 Janovskis, pp.86–87.
18 Janovskis, p.89.

Seven men holding machine guns disperse in their appointed directions. In a split second, the courtyard and cluster of buildings is surrounded. As a warning, a volley of shots is sent thundering in all directions.

A moment later, a heavy boot kicks open our door and through it comes a youngish man, a pistol in his hand. Gilded lieutenants' epaulettes shine on his shoulders. Black curly hair falling over his forehead, eyes bloodshot, his round Slavonic face screwed up in an ugly contortion. The open mouth, breathing heavily, fills the room with a reek of vodka.[19]

The Russian lieutenant questions the people there as to who they are and where they are from, then demands food and girls – young ones. Tadeusz, who speaks Russian, acts as translator, and tells the officer there are no girls. Staring down the barrel of the officer's pistol, lips trembling, the boy tells him the soldiers who came before killed all the young girls and took the rest away. He points to the graves behind the church.

The officer relents, puts his pistol away and calls for more vodka and tobacco, which he then offers to the group in front of him. They are too terrified to refuse. He rolls a cigarette from newspaper and tells his sergeant they will eat and move on. At this point he begins to talk.

> Look at these hands. I have killed and murdered with them. There is a stream of blood which I have left behind, beginning at the Masurian Lakes, across Prussia, Pomerania and whatever this province is called. Mecklenburg? Well then, even over Mecklenburg.
>
> There was a time when all I wanted to do was kill and slaughter. Now it is all finished. A few more corpses? A few more shrieking women? Nothing helps. That does not ease it. Sometimes I think: 'I will take revenge. Then there will be peace for my heart.' But there isn't.[20]

As the officer talks it becomes clear why he has such hatred in his heart. What the Germans did in his home town in Belarus has filled him with an overwhelming desire to avenge the death of his mother and sisters, killed in front of him by a unit of partisan-hunting Nazis.

> I was sixteen years old. The Germans held the towns but the countryside was in the hands of the partisans. Nothing great. The odd train derailed, a smaller unit attacked (as they would say at the front) 'disturbing fire'. If the Germans were in the majority, the men retreated into the forests. There, the woods are so dense you can't walk through them. On retreating, mines were placed here and there. As they said, 'Greetings from Stalin.'
>
> And then one day a whole band of 'blues' raided our village. They knew – the bastards – that the partisans had been there, and they were afraid of mines. In

---

19 Janovskis, pp.116–117.
20 Janovskis, p.122.

the collective farm's huge barn they gathered all the women. And teenagers. Me, also.

An arrogant captain stood up front and started to speak. In Russian. But like a German, as if a spoon had got stuck in his gullet. 'We will not harm you,' he says. 'Just show us where the mines are buried.' The women are silent. The captain pulls out his watch. 'You have five minutes to consider.'

Silence. With him are two sergeants, huge and fat. Like bulls. Then you could hear his watch lid snap shut, it was that quiet in the barn. He nods his head. Both sergeants walk out and return after a while. Each had a fat iron chain around his hand.

The two sergeants beat the women with the chains, inflicting terrible injuries on the group. Then one woman dies. They attack the next woman in line, then the next. The silence of the women as they endure this furious battery enrages them even more. The lieutenant's mother is killed in this way, then his older sister. Then it is the turn of his younger, beloved sister Marusya. But she too will say nothing, and is beaten to death.

When the slaughter is over, all the teenagers are forced to cross the thresholds of every house to check for boobytraps. The teenagers know how the mines have been set, so are careful not to step on floorboards which have been mined. The barn is set alight and the Germans occupy the houses, but many are blown up and killed by booby-trapped beds, steps and floorboards which had been mined.

The lieutenant is reaching the story's conclusion.

I fled that night ... and so began my *partizanka*.[21] Then the front closed in, and we stormed Mazuria. And there I avenged Marusya a hundredfold. Every day, every night, I have avenged her death ... Her whole youth, her whole life – and a German smashed it up with a bloody iron chain.[22]

---

21 Time as a partisan.
22 Janovskis, pp.122–124.

3

The Medal Ceremony at Cölpin Manor

The Latvian 15th Division spread out in a series of manor houses in the area around Cölpin in Mecklenburg to regroup and re-form after Pomerania. Relations between the Latvians and both the German military and local population were not entirely harmonious, as 2nd Battalion commander Fricis Mežgrāvis recalled for the 'Green Books' official history of the Legion.

> The squadron was billeted in four manors within a radius of three kilometres. Upon nearing the first building, a large manor house, the senior billeting officer Lieutenant Cīrulis approached me to say that the owner of the manor – the Baron – had refused to let them enter, saying that there was no room there for Latvians, even though Lieutenant Cīrulis had shown him the division commander's order.
>
> I went to the Baron to talk to him myself. I found him standing on the manor steps. Politely, I explained to him our order and, in accordance with the area commander's and division commander's order, I have to billet one of my battalion's companies in his property. Would he be so kind as to show me where the company should go? To this the Baron snapped back that to him these orders are irrelevant … He will not give me any rooms. I politely thanked him for his courtesy and marched on.
>
> I called in at the next manor house, about two kilometres further on, which, strictly speaking, according to the order, wasn't down for billeting. I asked the owner of the manor, a German Army Major's widow, permission for 1st Company and Battalion HQ to stay in her property. Permission was courteously granted. The battalion was shown rooms in the manor. It turned out later that this lady was the aforementioned Baron's sister.
>
> The manor inspector told me later that the Baron had rung his sister and told her not to let the Latvian officers into the manor but to show them a place in the stables. The lady had refused to do so. In the evening, the whole of the Battalion HQ was treated to a robust meal. The lady even sent us a couple of bottles of apple wine.

The medal ceremony at Cölpin Manor. Legion chaplain KazimirsRučs addresses the men before the awards ceremony on 25 March 1945. To his left, Colonel Janums, Adjutant Lieutenant Verners Eše and Major Augusts Alksnītis stand with bare heads. Picture: Leopolds Sipolins, Latvian War Museum. LKM 5-55608 (10)

The next day, 23 March, I turned up at squadron HQ to see [the commander] Hēmel and informed him of yesterday's events. I requested his help so that in future any similar treatment of Latvian soldiers could be avoided. He began to defend his compatriots. We had a sharp exchange of words.[1]

I told him we do not consider ourselves to be of a lower breed than Germans. We are not German employees but voluntary fighters against Communism. I do not wish for my soldiers' morale to be diminished because of humiliation from Germans. I can't be responsible for the attitude of my subordinates to Germans in the future. I also mentioned the propaganda article in the Usedom newspaper, where we were described as 'Pomeranian monsters.'

Hēmel promised to report this to the division commander and, in future, try to prevent something like this happening again. The next times when I called in at squadron HQ Hēmel was politeness itself to me. He hadn't, however, notified the division commander.

---

1 Hauptsturmführer Heinz Hämel, an early volunteer and highly decorated SS man who had fought in Poland, France and Russia, then at Leningrad, Narva and Courland before being sent to Pomerania. Hēmel is the Latvian spelling of Hämel. Source: Traces of War website at <https://www.tracesofwar.com/persons/13430/H%C3%A4mel-Heinz-Waffen-SS.htm>. (accessed 25.12.2023).

The battalion spent a couple of weeks in this location, digging trenches and carrying out drills. We weren't allowed to dig in the fields, only on the boundaries. I gave permission for the company commander to send soldiers to help those manor owners who had been good to us with the planting of their potatoes. In return we received potatoes and other benefits.

The lads were very willing to lend a hand; it meant they all ate well. Our 'friend' the Baron turned up to ask me to send my soldiers to help plant his potatoes. His sister's fields were all finished. I got my own back by using the self-same words as he had to me [and refused]. He went away, head down.[2]

Legionnaire Pēteris Krievs of the 15th Division Fusilier Battalion described that period.

The front had now been pushed back to the Oder. All around, on the walls and trees, we saw flyers announcing *Oder ist die HKL [Hauptkampflinie]* which translates as '*The Oder is the main front.*' Below, they continued: '*There is no further retreat*'.

After the offensive in Pomerania, we were entitled to one month's holiday behind the lines. We received better food and tobacco; ten cigarettes a day (the *Sondermischung* brand). Even so, we didn't have enough to eat, so we looked for more at farmhouses. I found the family of an older farmer who treated me to dinner.

We never saw any younger German men in the countryside; they had all been called up into the army. A young woman from Hamburg was living with this farmer to escape the horrors of war in a quieter place.

During the days, we did training; mostly field training in the surrounding fields. There was nothing new there that stuck in my memory. Easter was in April. In honour of this, we were given spirits, but the amount they gave us was so small that I exchanged mine for a daily bread ration, and I woke up in a barn in the hay on Easter morning to eat a piece of dry bread.

Dry bread then tasted more delicious than the best cake or gateau had tasted at other times. For two days, we heard an accordion and singing coming from the commander's apartment.[3]

The division was brought together for a medal ceremony at Cölpin Manor to recognise and reward the bravery of the men in the retreat across Pomerania. The manor house had been built between 1778 and 1785 by the estate owner, Stephan Werner von Dewitz, on land his family had owned since 1303.

---

2   Mežgrāvis in Freivalds, Caunītis, Bērziņš, Kociņš and Hāzners (eds), *Latviešu Karavīrs Otra Pasaules Kaŗa Laikā (The Latvian Soldier During World War Two vol. 6)* (Ziemeļblāzma: Västerås, Sweden, 1970–1979), p.155.
3   Pēteris Krievs in *Mums Jāpārnāk* by Aivars Pētersons, trans. Māra Walsh-Sinka.

The ceremony was photographed by Leopolds Sīpoliņš, then a 24 year-old covering the war with the Latvian SS war correspondents' *Kriegsberichter* company. He had retreated with the 15th Division along the Baltic coast and into Mecklenburg, taking photographs along the way. In front of huge swastika flags, the medal ceremony took place in the Cölpin Manor courtyard on 25 March 1945.

Following a parade and marchpast led by Colonel Vilis Janums, Adjutant Lieutenant Verners Eše and Major Augusts Alksnītis, commander of the 2nd Battalion, the men were addressed by company chaplain Kazimirs Ručs. Ručs wrote later:

> In April 1945 after the battles in Pomerania many Legionnaires from the 33rd Regiment of the 15th Division were given medals for bravery. Before the heroes' award ceremony, I hold a short service and prayers for the Legionnaires who fell in Pomerania.
>
> Behind us, in the Cölpin Manor House, the Germans, not the Latvians, have hung out swastika flags. The table for the Latvian Legionnaires is laid with a Latvian flag, on which about 30 medals for heroism are laid out. And just there, the commander of the 33rd Regiment, Colonel Vilis Janums, with the officers of the regiment all standing to prayer. The Latvian Legionnaires completely ignored the German National Socialist flags.[4]

Three of the eight men awarded the Iron Cross First Class were in hospital and unable to attend so the photographs feature the men well enough to attend the ceremony.[5] For their bravery and actions leading the men out of Pomerania, Major Jēkabs Lazduzieds, commander of the 1st Battalion, Lieutenant Aloizs Strauts and Cadet Officer Jūlijs Bebris were decorated with the Iron Cross First Class. Lieutenant Eižens Bonoparts, killed in action at Domslaff, was awarded the Iron Cross First Class posthumously. He was considered one of the most courageous and able of the new generation of Latvian officers.

Two corporals, Meikuls Buls and Roberts Lindenbergs, received their Iron Cross First Class for different reasons. Buls was decorated for his actions destroying tanks on 24 January 1945 while Lindenbergs was nominated for the Order of the 32nd Grenadier Regiment on 20 March 1945.[6]

Major Augusts Alksnītis, adjutant of the 15th Division in Pomerania and Germany, was awarded the Iron Cross Second Class by Colonel Janums. Janums had known Alksnītis since he trained at the War School in Rīga and later as a staff officer at Army HQ, and he had served as Janums' right-hand man through combat in Pomerania at

---

[4] Ručs, *Dzīve ar Dievu* p.69. The caption accompanying the photographs in the Latvian War Museum incorrectly names the pastor as Jūlijs Straume, who was killed in February 1945 at Landeck in Pomeria. See Hunt, *The Road of Slaughter* (2023), p.252.
[5] 1st Lieutenant Kruka and Lieutenant Lejins were awarded the Iron Cross 1st Class for their actions at Tiefenort in Pomerania, so these are possibly two of the three missing.
[6] The date of Buls' Iron Cross corresponds with the destruction of Soviet tanks at Immenheim (now Mrocza), an operation in revenge for the killing of 100 Latvians at a school in Neuheim (see *The Road of Slaughter*, pp.106–108).

THE MEDAL CEREMONY AT CÖLPIN MANOR 29

Five of the eight men from the 33rd Regiment awarded the Iron Cross First Class at Cölpin Manor in March 1945. From the left: Major Jēkabs Lazduzieds, commander of the 1st Battalion; Lieutenant Aloizs Strauts; Cadet Officer Jūlijs Bebris; and Corporals Meikuls Buls and Roberts Lindenbergs. Four have the 'Order of the Frozen Flesh', marking their service in Russia. Picture from the Latvian War Museum, Rīga: LKM 5-55608-4008-FN

Relaxing with a drink: Two soldiers of the 33rd Regiment after receiving the Iron Cross Second Class. Picture: Leopolds Sipolins. Latvian War Museum. LKM 5-55610 (74)/4008-FN

Colonel Vilis Janums, commander of the 33rd Regiment presents Major Augusts Alksnītis with the Iron Cross Second Class at a medal ceremony at Cölpin Manor. Picture: Leopolds Sipolins. Latvian War Museum. LKM 5-55608-4008-(20)

Hammerstein, Sparsee, Kamin and Horst. Fifteen years later, Janums gave the eulogy at Alksnītis' funeral in London.

> I have vivid memories of Major Alksnītis from the days of the Kamin siege. We were in enemy territory and pushed back into the small town of Kamin. To break out we needed a man with a clear vision and a brave heart. I had seen that in Major Alksnītis as the 32nd Regiment battalion commander and I trusted him with my battalion to carry out the break-out. I wasn't wrong because this dangerous mission went off without a hitch, and the rest of the regiment could retreat along clear roads to the west.
>
> Again, the battles at Hammerstein, Sparsee and Zierflies Brook [in February 1945]: in all of these places Major Alksnītis served with courage and remained calm under fire – and always found a way out. There were days when the men were tired and hungry, but with his own calm composure he always managed to take care of his men.
>
> And then there were good days where we found abandoned houses and manor houses with food and supplies, including full cellars which served us well as places to stay for short periods.[7]

The ceremony was followed by a Divisional dinner, to which the residents and staff at the house were invited.[8]

The next day the Latvians left Cölpin in three columns, giving the Nazi salute and an eyes-right to the SS HQ staff as they marched towards Neubrandenburg.

Sigrid Meyl (then von Dewitz) was just a baby living with her mother and three brothers at Cölpin Manor at the time the Latvians arrived there, and knew nothing of their brief stay. The war had already affected her family profoundly. Her father was away at the front – she wouldn't see him again until 1951 – and her uncle Friedrich had been killed in the German defence of Mogilev in summer 1944. Then her grandmother died in a typhoid outbreak that November. Even after that, things got worse, about a month after the Latvians left:

---

7   Born in Rīga in 1902, Alksnītis grew up in the Urals as his parents went east as refugees during WWI. In 1923 he studied at the War School, graduating as a lieutenant and eventually chief adjutant for the 15th Division infantry, transferring to the 32nd Regiment as major and battalion commander. After the heavy casualties at Flederborn in February 1945, the 32nd Regiment merged with the 33rd and he served directly under Janums. Major Alksnītis was in charge of the reargard at the crossing of the Oder at Berg-Dievenow in March 1945. From Daugavas Vanagi newspaper reports of Major Alksnītis' funeral, London 1960, online at <http://periodika.lv/periodika2-viewer/view/index-dev.html?lang=fr#panel:pa|issue:/p_000_xdav1960n02|article:DIVL478|query:Kelpinas%20mui%C5%BE%C4%81|issueType:P>. Trans. Aivars Sinka (accessed 12.05.2020). See the author's previous book *The Road of Slaughter* (2023) for detailed accounts of these engagements.

8   Information from captions accompanying the Sīpoliņš photographs in the Latvian War Museum picture archive.

Nazi salutes as 33rd Regiment Latvian Legion commander Colonel Vilis Janums marches his officers and men away from Cölpin in the direction of Neubrandenburg. Picture: Leopolds Sipolins. LKM 5-55610-4008-FN(85)

The war had a horrible effect on our family and ended with the loss of the *Herrenhaus* [manor house and family home] and all of the family's possessions. On 28 April 1945 the order came from the Party leadership to leave Cölpin in great haste at 2300 that evening and flee towards the west. Everything had to be packed up and horses and carts made ready for all the people in the village.

So it was that four wagons were packed for the family, and another cart and driver stood ready for our mother, together with us three children. All the most necessary possessions were got together in a great hurry. While the wagons were being loaded, groups of deserters, soldiers and strangers were already coming to loot the house.

The intended route [six kilometres north-west] from Sponholz to Neubrandenburg was already blocked. It was not long before all the roads were clogged up with people fleeing from the east with horses and carts. The Russians were getting ever closer. In the early morning we stopped for the first time to rest in a wood. The thunderous noise of gunfire was getting ever closer and was coming scarily loud from the direction of Altentreptow. Russian tanks began shooting from the edge of the woods. The horses were immediately hitched up again and driven on at a gallop.

We had to make another stop to rest the horses, during which time we were held up by Russian soldiers with raised weapons. The carts were looted, the horses stolen and back to Cölpin we went by foot with only our rucksacks left, past the burning town of Neubrandenburg and uninterrupted columns of tanks. When we arrived there we were confronted with a house that had been completely plundered. We were then forbidden from setting foot in our own home. At the same time a column of people from the village were working under the supervision of Russians with raised weapons. Everyone from our family was also put to work.[9]

Sigrid's mother managed to find somewhere to stay with her small children until the family was expelled by the Russians, after which they lived in refugee camps in Thüringen for 18 months. Her mother then found accommodation on a small farm by the North Sea and the von Dewitz family settled later in Lübeck. Cölpin Manor was used to house refugees at the end of the war, and a school and a restaurant were subsequently set up there. It's now a stud farm.

Cölpin Manor today, now a stud farm. The house was used as the base for a medals ceremony in March 1945. Picture: public domain.

9 Letter from Sigrid Meyl to author, 1 June 2020, translated.

4

Himmler's Hospital at Hohenlychen

In early April 1945, 2nd Battalion commander Fricis Mežgrāvis received orders to relocate to Fürstenberg am Havel, about 80 km north of Berlin. In his diary, he wrote:

> Before leaving for the new place, three German officers from Berlin arrived to see me in the battalion. They were recruiting volunteers for the parachute regiments as saboteurs behind the Russian lines. One of the officers spoke Latvian – probably a Baltic German. They asked permission to speak to the soldiers.
>
> I insisted that they speak only about volunteers against the Russians and not for fighting on the Western front. This was accepted. Twenty seven men from the regiment, who were fed up with the present life and humiliations, joined up. They went off to a special training camp. As far as I know, out of this number only two men survived. One of them, my ex-sergeant, I met in Belgium in captivity, but by then [he was] a lieutenant. The other, his companion, stayed in Germany, 'captured' by a woman.
>
> At Easter 1945, the battalion was on a long rest at Gross-Teumin forestry, halfway to Fürstenberg. Twenty four battalion soldiers received the Iron Cross for bravery here. Having rested for two days, we moved on to Fürstenberg, where the battalion was billeted in a school, the Battalion HQ in a hotel. The squadron HQ also set up in Fürstenberg. The 1st Battalion was stationed in Himmelpfort, a few kilometres away.
>
> At this point squadron commander Vīksne and 2nd Battalion commander Major Balodis returned to the squadron from hospital. The latter took up command of 1st Battalion. Major Hēmel was transferred to Vienna as battle commander. The squadron was taken over by Lieutenant Vīksne.
>
> In Fürstenberg the battalion's objective was to make tank blocks in the gaps between lakes and to dig trenches on the roads along the Havel as a defence position.
>
> Fürstenberg was under the authority of the town's battle commander, Major Pischer; a real soldier. He was happy that he now had a real army under his command. One battle platoon was formed led by Lieutenant Rugājs. Due to the lack of weapons, it wasn't possible to form anything larger. That, then, was the only assault strength.

HIMMLER'S HOSPITAL AT HOHENLYCHEN 35

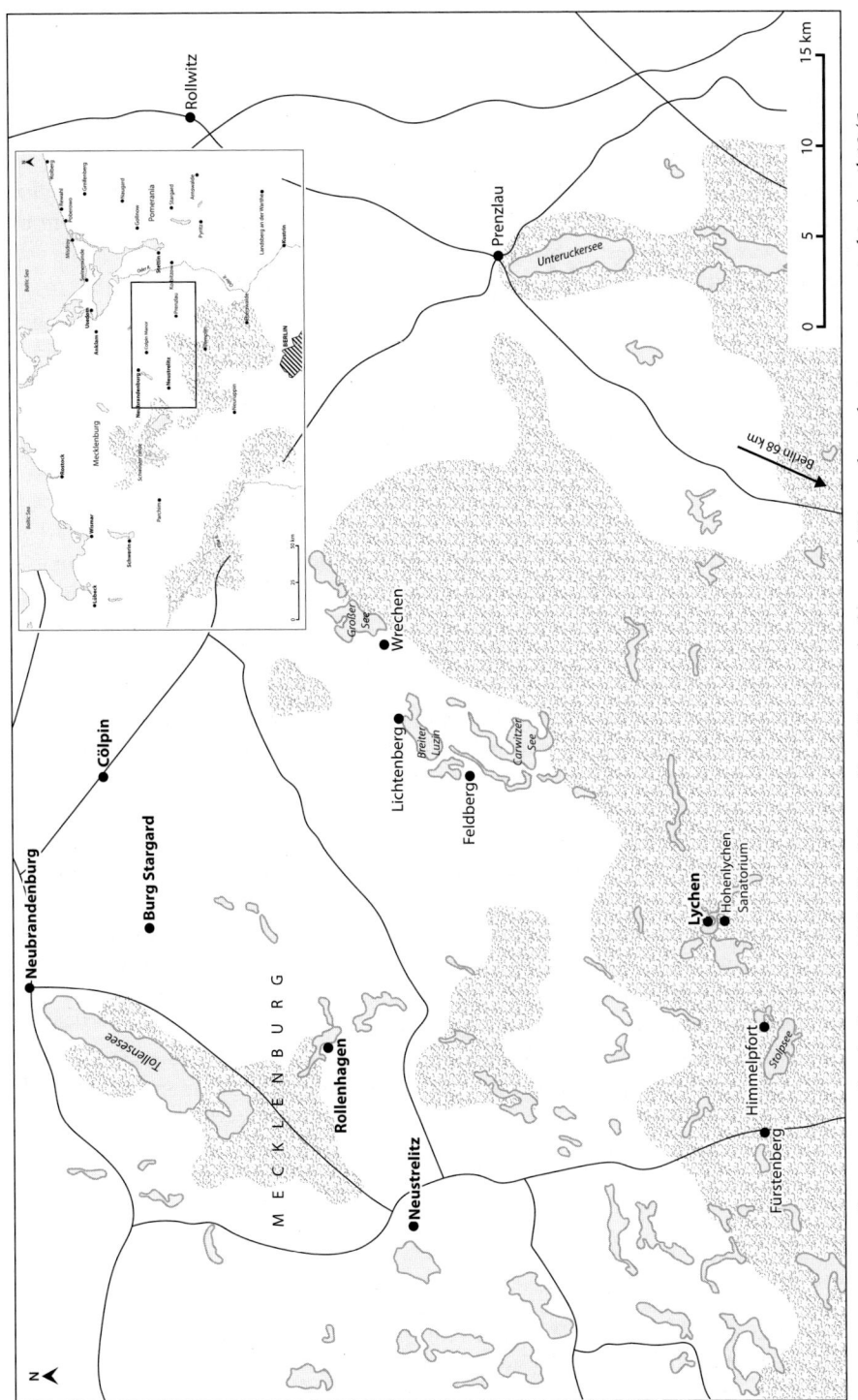

Map 3 Billet positions for the Latvian 15th SS in Neustrelitz, Neubrandenburg and Fürstenberg during a rest period in April 1945.

> The battalion had to guard the crossings at the railway station and the munitions factories in the town, padding out the *Landsturm* guard numbers. In order to carry out this task, we received French-type rifles from WWI with a few bullets for each rifle.[1]

The Latvians rested in Mecklenburg for several weeks, regrouping in Neustrelitz. Medical Corps orderly Harijs Valdmanis had escaped from the siege of Kolberg by boat and was shipped west to Swinemünde unscathed. From there, he made his way to rejoin the Latvian units.

> We didn't have any trucks or ambulance cars or anything as that was all the way back in Kolberg, and we walked to a place between Neubrandenburg and Neustrelitz in Germany. We stayed there for some time, first one place then another, and then the end of the war was coming. There were some ideas to send the 15th Division back to Latvia.
>
> About mid-April myself and another guy from our company were sent as outlookers [scouts] to some other places in the area. For many units I think the idea was that we should go to Kurzeme [the Courland Pocket frontlines in Latvia] but it was too late and we got the order to go back to our company. The top officers were all Germans, but the unit commanders were Latvians and they were not interested in being captured by the Russians: much better to be prisoners of war of the Western Allies.
>
> So one day our company [decided to] move west to the next town. We didn't have any order from the division. The company commander left me with a bicycle in this place where we were all staying, and [told me] I should wait for the order to move west. I can't remember how long I was told to wait, but the company went to Neustrelitz.[2]
>
> I remember I waited till midnight and nobody came, so I just took my bike and went west. It was night, it was dark and I came to some military units which were also moving west, but they were talking Russian. I wondered if I was a bit late with my withdrawal, but they were Vlasov units, the Ukrainians who were fighting with the Nazis.[3]
>
> I found my unit in Neustrelitz and the next day we went on west. The Latvian commander who was organising all this was Major Baumanis, who was in charge of the supply division – the transport company, the ambulance car company and supply units, not fighting units.[4]

---

1 Mežgrāvis in Freivalds, Caunītis, Bērziņš, Kociņš and Hāzners (eds), *Latviešu Karavīrs Otra Pasaules Kaŗa Laikā (The Latvian Soldier During World War Two, vol. 6)* (Ziemeļblāzma, Västerås, Sweden, 1970–1979), p.155.
2 Just south of Neubrandenburg in the Mecklenburg region.
3 The Russian Liberation Army of Andrey Andreyevich Vlasov, a Soviet general key to the defence of Moscow who was captured at Leningrad and fought against Stalin. Captured by the Soviets at the end of the war he was hanged in 1946 as a traitor.
4 Telephone interview with author, 4.10.2018. Valdemārs Kristaps Baumanis (19.04.1905–24.04.1992) was one of two officers with that name in the Legion, both *Sturmbannführers*. The

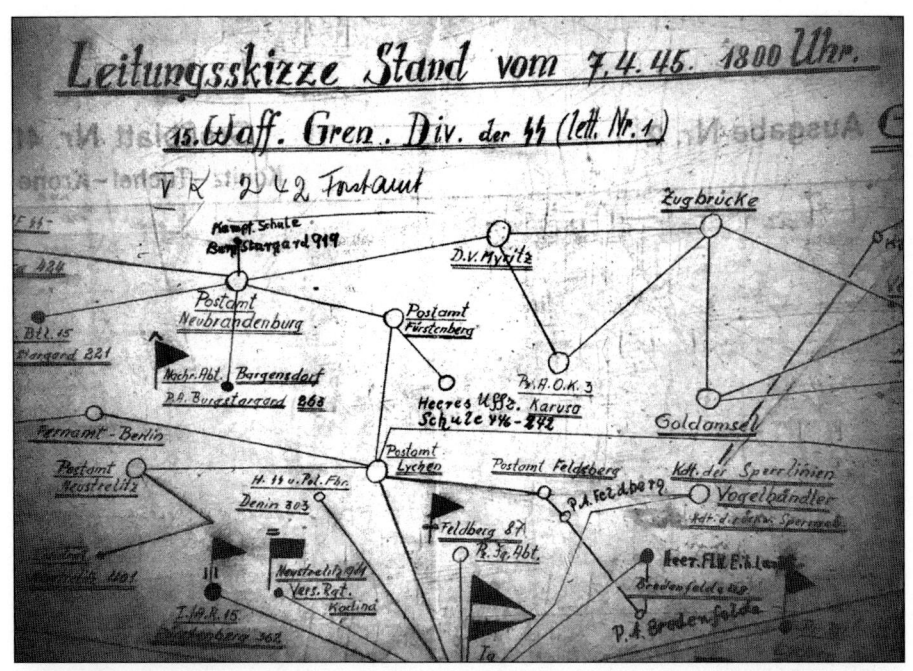

Diagram of the communications network of the Latvian 15th SS at 7 April 1945, when they were billeted around the Hohenlychen medical sanatorium run by Prof. Dr Karl Gebhardt. Himmler had a base here, with the connection 'RF-SS'. Gebhardt was his personal physician. From the 15th Division war diary at the National State Archives in Rīga. Picture: author.

The Latvians were grouped in an area from Neustrelitz to Feldberg, Lychen and Fürstenberg.[5] The 15th Division war diary bought by the Latvian War Museum from Belgium in 2006 includes a line drawing of what appears to be the communications network linking the various elements of the 15th Division stationed there, their positions and telephone numbers where they could be reached, as of 7 April 1945.

At the centre of the map is the Chief of Staff of the 15th Division, linked by the phone exchange to the 32nd Regiment in Lychen, the 34th Regiment in Fürstenberg,

other was Ernests Baumanis (born 26.02.1903). Born in Liepāja, Valdemārs Baumanis played basketball at school, studied economics at university then in 1927 was drafted into the Latvian Army. He graduated from military college as a lieutenant. His basketball career included seven years playing for a Latvian Christian Youth team 1923–1930, winning the national league twice and six caps for Latvia's national team. Injury forced a switch to coaching in 1931 and for nine years he was head coach of the Army team Rīgas ASK, winning the League in 1932, 1939 and 1940. He was head coach of the Latvian team which became European champions in 1935 and refereed the basketball at the Berlin Olympics. During the Nazi occupation of Latvia, he coached Rīgas ASK to the League title in 1942 and 1943 then was drafted into the Legion as a staff officer with the 15th Division, ending the war as a Major commanding all the supply units. After being released from the Putlos camp he lived in Lübeck, then France and finally Chicago, where he died in 1992. A film *Dream Team 1935* celebrates the achievements of the European champions.

5   Silgailis, *Latvian Legion,* map pp.158–159.

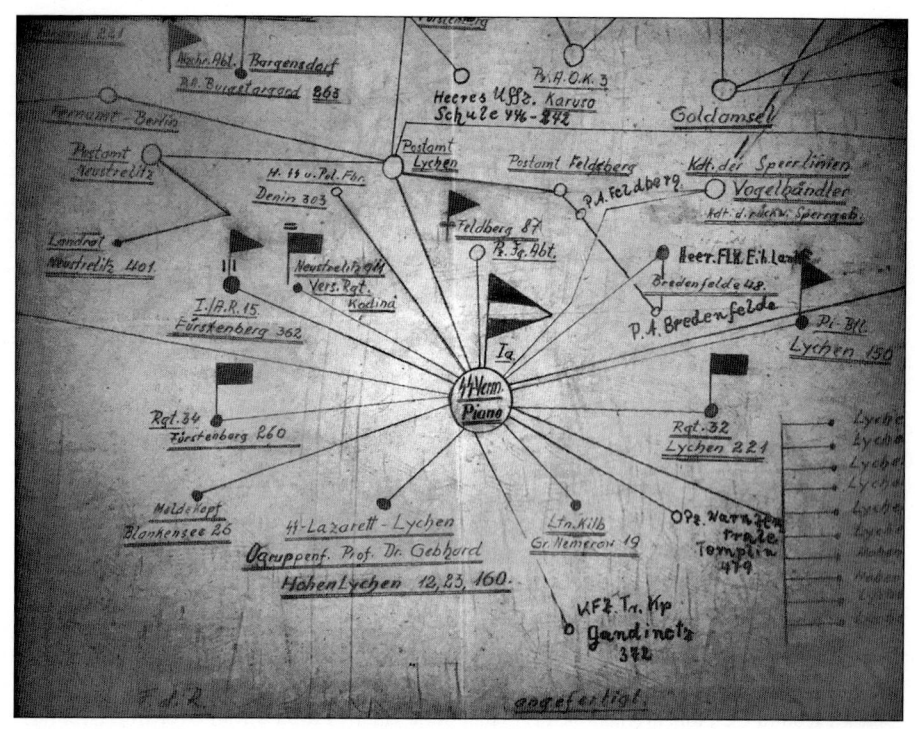

The network of communications at Hohenlychen on 7.4.45. Diagram from the war diary of the Latvian 15th SS Division held at the National Archive in Rīga. Picture: author.

the 1st Battalion of the Artillery Regiment and the 15th Fusiliers – the Recce Battalion – at Burg-Stargard. Other lines connect to a Panzer unit in Feldberg, the officer training school in Fürstenberg, post offices in Neubrandenburg, Lychen, Neustrelitz and Feldberg, and various units in Gandenitz, Blankensee and Groß Nemerow on the shores of the Tollensee south-east of Neubrandenburg.[6]

The map also details the German military and Nazi Party structure in the area. Lychen 168 connected with the local Nazi Party, controlled by the district commander or *Ortsgruppenleiter*, responsible for civil defence and the *Volkssturm* militia of older men and Hitler Youth.[7] Lychen 107 called the *gendarmerie*, Lychen 180 'Information' and Lychen 185, the post office manager. Hohenlychen 99 rang the high school and Hohenlychen 12 the local hospital.[8]

---

6   Map of communications network at Hohenlychen, photographed from microfiche at the Latvian State Archives.
7   *Ortsgruppenleiter* details from <https://www.wehrmacht.es/en/ss-sleeve-insignia/2347-nsdap-ortsgruppenleiter-armband.html> (accessed 15 May 2020).
8   Sketch of telephone network in Lychen area from *Leitungsskizze Stand vom 7.4.4 1800 uhr 15 Waff.Gren.Div der SS (lett Nr.1)* retrieved from 15th Division war diary, National Archives, Skolas iela, Rīga. Author's visit 22.11.2019. The *gendarmerie* are the German military police.

These connections reveal the extent of the Nazi network of evil into which the Latvians had strayed. One telephone link – Neubrandenburg 424 – is a line to the *Sonderstab* RFSS, the SS Special Staff responsible for the running of the concentration camps and the deportation of Jews. There were sub-camps of the Ravensbrück women's concentration camp at Neubrandenburg, Feldberg, Hagenow and – tellingly – at Hohenlychen. In January 1945, the camp had more than 50,000 prisoners, mostly women, from more than 30 countries, with the greatest number from Poland (36 percent) and the Soviet Union (21 percent).[9]

The telephone link to the SS Lazarett-Lychen, the SS medical centre at Hohenlychen, indicates the number of men receiving treatment there in April 1945 as 12 officers, 23 NCOs and 160 men. While it was a place of recovery for these men, the medical centre had a dark history. The commanding officer, Obergruppenführer Prof. Dr Karl Gebhardt, was a specialist in reconstructive surgery and a close friend of SS chief Heinrich Himmler.

Karl Gebhardt became notorious for his experiments at Hohenlychen sanatorium on women prisoners from the nearby Ravensbrück camp. He is seen here on trial at Nuremberg for war crimes and crimes against humanity. He was convicted and sentenced to death in August 1947 and hanged in June 1948. Picture: United States Holocaust Memorial Museum, public domain.

Gebhardt had joined the SS Medical Corps in 1936 and later the Waffen SS and worked his way up to the rank of SS-Gruppenführer. He developed Hohenlychen as a treatment centre for his fellow SS officers and also kept wards for the patients who came to see him as private clients: among them diplomats, politicians, industrialists, athletes, members of European royal families and high-ranking Nazis.

Hohenlychen became well-known for its work with sports injuries. Athletes taking part in the 1936 Olympics had treatment there, including the American sprinter Jesse Owens.[10] Hohenlychen, Gebhardt and his deputy Ludwig Stumpfegger became

---

9 The prisoners fell into various categories: political prisoners, Roma, Gypsies, Jews, Jehovah's Witnesses, criminals, the 'work-shy' and 'race-defilers'. In early 1945 the SS built a gas chamber at the camp and murdered 5,000–6,000 prisoners before the Soviets liberated the camp in April. Details from the Holocaust Encyclopaedia, online at https://encyclopedia.ushmm.org/content/en/article/ravensbrueck (accessed 15.05.2024).

10 J.R. Silver, *Karl Gebhardt (1897–1948) A Lost Man*. Paper for the Journal of the Royal College of Physicians, issue 41:366–7 (2011) at <http://www.rcpe.ac.uk/journal/issue/journal_41_4/silver.pdf>

notorious in Holocaust history for medical experiments on prisoners from the Ravensbrück concentration camp for women – the 'women's hell' – where between 25,000 and 26,000 women died between May 1939 and April 1945.

As well as deliberately injuring prisoners in trials to develop anti-bacterial medicines to treat wounded soldiers, bone, nerve and muscle transplants were carried out on human 'guinea pigs'.[11] In one transplant operation, a prisoner '…had his legs amputated and carried away in a sack by Gebhardt who then attempted to attach them to a soldier whose lower limbs had been amputated at Hohenlychen hospital.'[12]

Ravensbrück was built in 1939 to hold 6,000 inmates, but by January 1945 there were 45,000 female and 5,000 male prisoners there and in its sub-camps. They included large numbers of Polish after the failed Warsaw Uprising as well as Hungarians, Slovakians and women from other camps, including Auschwitz: 40 different nationalities, in total.[13] While the commanders were male, the 150 camp guards were women, who became known for their cruelty and harshness.

Among them was Irma Grese, an SS volunteer who became an *Aufserin* (overseer) at Ravensbrück in 1942 then transferred to Auschwitz in 1943, becoming warden of the women's section at Bergen-Belsen. Witnesses said she beat prisoners until they collapsed, often with a cellophane whip. Known by inmates as 'the Hyena of Auschwitz' and 'the Bitch of Belsen' she was captured by the British at Belsen in April 1945 and sentenced to death for crimes against humanity. She was hanged, aged 22, by executioner Albert Pierrepoint.[14]

Conditions at Ravensbrück were so overcrowded and unsanitary by January 1945 that a typhus epidemic swept through the main camp. Groups of Jehovah's Witnesses held as prisoners were used to clean the streets of Hohenlychen. Camp inmates tended the gardens. Some with specialist technical skills operated X-ray and photographic equipment.

Himmler had retired to Hohenlychen in March after his promotion by Hitler to command Army Group Vistula in Pomerania was exposed as a calamitous error; responsible, as Third Panzer Army commander General Erhard von Raus put it, for the collapse of the Eastern Front. Himmler told his Prenzlau HQ he had 'flu' and left for Gebhardt's clinic. In memoirs written in American captivity, Raus described how he went to see Himmler at the sanatorium in Hohenlychen on the afternoon

---

11 G. Megargee (ed), *US Holocaust Memorial Museum – Encyclopaedia of Camps and Ghettos 1933–1945, Vol I, Part B*, p.1188.
12 J.R. Silver, *Karl Gebhardt (1897–1948) A Lost Man* (2011), p.370. In the doctors' trial at Nuremberg in 1947, Gebhardt showed no remorse for his actions. He was convicted of carrying out inhuman experiments in the concentration camps and executed in June 1948.
13 Megargee, *US Holocaust Memorial Museum – Encyclopaedia of Camps and Ghettos 1933–1945, Vol I, Part B*, p.1188.
14 From L. Willmott, *Irma Grese and Female Concentration Camp Guards,* article for History Today dated 01.06.2015 online at <https://www.historytoday.com/archive/history-matters/irma-grese-and-female-concentration-camp-guards> and D. McGuinness article for BBC Online 18.01.2021 titled *Nazi Ravensbrück Camp: How Ordinary Women Became SS Torturers,* online at <https://www.bbc.co.uk/news/world-europe-55661782> (accessed 15.05.2024).

Irma Grese, the 'Bitch of Belsen' who became known for her brutality as an overseer at Ravensbrück, then transferred to Auschwitz and Bergen-Belsen. She was hanged for her crimes in December 1945. Picture from the United States Holocaust Memorial Museum, courtesy of Hadassah Bimko Rosensaft.

of 7 March, where the Reichsführer was apparently suffering from angina.

While Himmler sat up in bed, Raus described how he had eventually stabilised the frontline on the Oder after the Second Belorussian Front attack had 'sealed the fate of Pomerania'. When Himmler's aide left, Raus laid into him, criticising him for allowing the Pomeranian front first to be weakened then smashed by the Red Army, as Raus had predicted.

Raus told him that not allowing defences to be shortened to well-prepared defences between lakes caused unnecessary losses and wasted reserves that could have strengthened weaker forces elsewhere. Panzer Division Holstein was needlessly exhausted and when needed most east of Stargard, it was not there when Soviet tanks outnumbered German forces twenty to one.

Instead of allowing Corps Group Tettau and X SS Corps to withdraw and avoid encirclement, Himmler had refused and threatened officers with court martial. As a result both Corps were captured and shattered on the fifth day. 'These staggering events led to the tragic loss of Pomerania as far west as the Oder,' Raus wrote. The disaster he had predicted came true. Himmler, Raus noted, '...consistently crippled my conduct of operations with rigidly-binding orders, threats and demands with which we could not possibly comply.'[15]

15 Raus, *Panzer Operations,* p.331.

When Raus gave several examples of the fighting spirit of the German soldiers desperately resisting the Soviet assault as a result of his incompetence, Himmler suggested he report personally to Hitler, who liked stories of such bravery. He promptly picked the phone up to the Führerbunker and made him an appointment for the next day, 8 March. Raus reported to Hitler in his bunker and watched the Führer pick up maps and compare them with trembling hands.

> I found myself facing a physically broken down, embittered and suspicious man that I scarcely recognised. The knowledge that Adolf Hitler – now only a human wreck – held the fate of the German people in his hands alone was a deep shock to me.[16]

Raus told Hitler about an attack by 15 Soviet tanks on Baldenburg (now Biały Bór) when 50 year-old men and recruits in construction battalions used Panzerfausts to fight them off after they rammed the roadblock into town at high speed. Three tanks were knocked out in the process. The tanks re-grouped and attacked again the next day near Bublitz (Bobolice), breaking through weak lines held by the Reserve Division *Pomerania*.

Each time the tanks broke through, the gaps were plugged, slowing the momentum of the tank attack. Then the tank destroyer teams hunted the tanks down in the woods where they had gathered outside the town, destroying 16 in one day on 23 February and a further 12 the next day.[17]

Hitler dismissed Raus without comment and, after he had left, turned to Heinz Guderian, Chief of the General Staff: 'What a miserable speech! The man talked of nothing but details. Judging by the way he speaks he must be a Berliner or an East Prussian. He must be relieved of his appointment at once.'

Guderian insisted that Raus was one of Germany's most capable panzer generals and an Austrian, like the Führer. But Hitler relieved Raus of his command the following day.[18]

By mid-April the 15th Division was grouped around Fürstenberg, close to Berlin. The war was into its final days and the Latvians were aware they must make a move soon to ensure their survival. If they were captured by the Russians, they would be considered traitors and war criminals. Execution or years of hard labour in Siberia were very likely outcomes. Artilleryman Laimonis Ceriņš remembers the men discussing possible options.

> Fürstenberg was the most rest we had and from there we had to 'dash to the West'. That was the idea from the beginning. There was no chance of getting

---

16 Raus, p.334.
17 Raus, p.335.
18 Guderian, *Panzer Leader*, p.420.

Artilleryman Laimonis Ceriņš, one of 10,000 former Latvian Legionnaires who came to the UK after the Second World War. His personal collection of notes and literature from his time as quartermaster of the Zedelghem camp in Belgium where the Latvians were held after their surrender is now an important archive for the Latvian War Museum in Rīga. Picture: author.

back to Latvia so we decided to try and surrender to the Allies. That's what the commanding officers were thinking of: 'Say nothing, but if we get the chance, surrender to the Americans'.

We were very, very close to Berlin and we were worried we might be sent there. Probably the Germans had something on their minds: plans to get rid of us. They told us to take positions against the Russians in a tricky area, and that's what our leaders didn't want to do. That was somewhere around Fürstenberg, I'm not exactly sure [where]. We were short of ammunition, so what can you do? They [the Russians] are using tanks, so what can you do? I think the main aim of the Russians was Berlin. I don't think they were bothered about us much.[19]

---

19 Interview with author, Derby, 2018.

5

'If There is an Order to Move, Try to Break Through to the Allied Front.'

At the end of March 1945, Lieutenant-Colonel Osvalds Meija had been appointed commander of the 32nd Regiment. SS-Hauptsturmführer (Captain) Eldon Walli, an American-born German-speaking Austrian promoted from the Reserve, took command of the 1st Regiment, the 15th Fusiliers, known as the Recce Battalion. His presence would have significant consequences for the men of the 15th Division over the next few weeks as the Latvians were moved closer to the doomed Nazi capital.

Colonel Janums, commander of the newly-formed Janums Battle Group, did not trust Walli and felt his presence was binding his hands to suicidal Nazi orders. He was keen to get rid of him – understandably so, as Walli's background as a member of the Nazi Party from 1931 and his rise to prominence as a reporter detailing significant Nazi operations such as the burning of a synagogue in Vienna on Kristallnacht in 1938 would have given him a high profile as a loyalist. So too would his status as a 'celebrity Nazi' radio presenter, compering 'Strength Through Joy' (KdF) theatre events with some of Austria's highest-profile artists such as the film star Hans Moser.[1]

Born in New York on 28 January 1913, Walli grew up in Austria and his political sympathies were always with Hitler. He joined the Hitler Youth in 1927 and was active first in the development of his local group in Bad Vöslau then the establishment of a network across Austria. In 1931 he joined the Nazi Party and the SA and became involved in violent anti-Semitic operations, coming to the attention of the police for blowing up a Jewish cinema. He fled to Germany to avoid indictments in 1933 and 1934 for high treason and planning an attack on the Baden train. After spending five months in Dachau – then used as a reception camp – he took a private job.

In 1937 he got a job in radio, no doubt helped by his political beliefs, and this led to him being in the Austrian town of Kufstein as a reporter for the Reichs-Rundfunk-Gesellschaft on 12 March 1938 – the day of the Nazi annexation of Austria – making Walli one of the first broadcasters to bring news of the Anschluss.

---

1 The actor Hans Moser was married to Blanca Herschler, a Jew, and would not divorce her to suit the Nazi line on mixed marriages.

That same month he joined the evening programme at 'Zeitfunk' broadcasting 'ideological educational work' every night from 1930 hours – presumably Nazi propaganda. In November that year, Walli reported excitedly from the Leopoldstadt synagogue in Vienna as it burned to the ground on Kristallnacht. The recording is still available as part of the archives held by the broadcasting network SVR.de. Of the recording, it says, 'In this report from 10 November 1938, Eldon Walli, a native American, reported on site about the destruction of the Leopoldstadt Temple for the National Socialist station *Reichssender Wien*.'

> The tone of voice is remarkable. At the beginning you could almost hear a certain sympathy, but then he becomes more and more cynical and it becomes clear how the reporter sympathises with the destruction of the synagogue. A firefighter explains that the fire could not be extinguished, so the firefighters could only warm their hands.[2]

After this report, Eldon Walli switched to the morning slot, presenting a breakfast show called 'We want to start the day happily' every day from 0700.[3]

Records begin for Walli's SS military career in June 1941 as an SS-Untersturmführer (Lieutenant) in the 2nd Battalion of the 9th SS Regiment *Germania*. He may have come to this unit through the 4th SS-Regiment *Der Führer*, which was formed in Vienna in 1938 from local recruits and fought throughout the war as part of the *Das Reich* Division.[4] After seeing action in France and the Low Countries, it was merged into the 5th SS *Wiking* Division, which took part in the invasion of the Soviet Union and fought as far east as Rostov, until being halted and pushed back by Red Army offensives in winter 1941.[5]

In June 1942, Walli was promoted to Obersturmführer (First Lieutenant) in the war correspondent platoon of the 4th SS *Polizei* Division, which at that time was in positions in the marshy area outside Leningrad. After battles around Lake Ladoga and Kolpino the unit was sent to northern Greece, where it was involved in anti-partisan war crimes and atrocities, including at Kleisoura, where the death of two German soldiers prompted the killing of 215 civilians, and the Distomo massacre, revenge for a partisan attack in which 218 men, women and children were killed on 10 June 1944.[6]

However, by May 1943 Eldon Walli was in Norway working for an Nazi ideological training unit called Department VI, and – as on 15 September 1943 - having

---

2   Webpage of SWR.de, a broadcasting network in Baden-Württemberg and Rhineland-Palatinate, online at <https://www.swr.de/swr2/wissen/archivradio/reportage-aus-der-zerstoerten-synagoge-in-wien-1938-102.html>.
3   Forum pages at Forum der Wehrmacht, online at https://www.forum-der-wehrmacht.de/index.php?thread/38104-ss-standarte-52/ (accessed 7 April 2024).
4   Walli is listed as a member at <https://forum.balsi.de/index.php?topic=7174.15> and unit history at <https://www.panzergrenadier.net/df/history.php> (accessed 7 April 2024).
5   Details from Feldgrau.com online at <https://www.feldgrau.com/ww2-german-5th-ss-panzer-division-wiking/>.
6   Axis History website online at <https://axishistory.com/4-ss-polizei-pz-grenadier-division/> (accessed 17.04.2024).

meetings with powerfully-placed Nazi figures such as Werner Best, who, as the first head of the Gestapo established a registry of Jews across Germany and, as Reinhardt Heydrich's deputy, set up the Einsatzgruppen death squads.

At the end of 1944, the fight to hold back the Red Army centred on the Vistula river and having taken heavy casualties in the Soviet Budapest Offensive the remnants of the 4th *SS Polizei* division were sent to Pomerania. Here too, at Immenheim, Nakel, Jastrow, Flederborn and Landeck, were the Latvian 15th Division. The casualties under the leadership of divisional commander Adolph Ax were immense (the author's previous book *The Road of Slaughter* estimates 5,000 Latvian casualties in a 15km stretch of encircled road between Jastrow and Landeck) and he was replaced by SS-Brigadeführer Karl Burk. In February 1945, possibly in the widespread replacement of Latvian commanders with German officers, the now-Hauptsturmführer (Captain) Walli became the commander of the Latvian 15th SS Fusilier Battalion.

German war correspondents were expected to fight if necessary and also received decorations. The Latvian officer Valters Krūmiņš, who served with him in the centre of Berlin, believed Walli was awarded an Iron Cross.

With a track record like his, Janums would be under no illusions that Walli had worked for and served alongside of the most brutal and hardline Nazis – and had now been given the chance to command the men he had vowed to protect.

During the battle for Pomerania, Lieutenant Atis Neilands had been the 15th Division Reconnaissance Battalion adjutant. He was one of the 300 men sent into the centre of Berlin and one of very few – possibly 20 – to survive. Here, he describes how a plan to remove the dangerous Captain Walli was thwarted.

> Battalion commanders changed frequently – sometimes there were none. After leaving Pomerania, German SS Captain Walli was appointed as battalion commander. Foreseeing the end of the war, the most active of the division's commanders took care to isolate the German officers and planned for the surrender to the Western Allies.
>
> At the beginning of April, an officer was sent by Squadron Leader Janums who announced that if necessary we have to take Captain Walli into custody and for me to take over. Somehow Walli got to hear about this and removed me from my position.[7]

Legionnaire Brunis Rubess, who had been so awed when first in the presence of Colonel Janums, noticed the mood was changing among the men. They were now starting to think about the future, after the end of the war.

> In the middle of April we were in the Lichtenberg region in Mecklenburg. It almost seemed like we had won the war ... Several officers had been found by their families. We listen to *Soldatensender Calais* – British broadcasts in German.

---

7 Atis Neilands, in Leititis, p.96.

One day, Colonel Janums called the officers together and gave them the opportunity to choose: 'The end of the war is so close, I can understand those who want to go their own way. I won't hunt anyone. But those who stay with the regiment must promise not to leave – until the end – and they also have to free themselves from their families.'

I was sent to escort one of these families by train, about 90 kilometres. I was back after two days but the regiment wasn't there any more. The colonel and the regiment's 1st Battalion had been sent to Berlin. Again, I was alone, just like at Dievenow seaside. I stood in the courtyard of an abandoned manor house and now I really didn't know what to do. Such individual, separated soldiers had, generally, a short predicted life span…

Miraculously, a voice called out from a first-floor window: 'What do you want?' It was the division's dentist, Leopolds Rumba, who was left in situ with his surgery when Janums left the manor house. So, for the remaining days, until Major Baumanis collected us all together for the last long march westwards, I helped mix amalgam for fillings. Who would have predicted that?!

Soon we start a two-week movement in a westerly direction. We marched for four hours, sat down for an hour, etc. We ate what we could steal on the spot. We slept – in late April – under the blue sky. Just away, just away![8]

One of the most important accounts of this time from a Latvian perspective comes from the adjutant with Colonel Janums' regiment, 36-year-old First Lieutenant Edvīns Bušmanis. His diary is a beautifully-written, detailed and gripping account, published here in English for the first time.

It's April 1945. WWII has entered its last stage. Of course, that's not written anywhere but everyone feels it. Everyone with a head on their shoulders can see the collapse of the army, the nation, on whose side fate has had us fight.

At the present time, the 33rd Company [Regiment], in reality all the 15th Latvian Division of which it is part of, finds itself away from the battle, shoring up positions and tank defences in the Mecklenburg area. The soldiers have almost no weapons. Since being surrounded in the Pomeranian battles, they were taken off the squadron as being more necessary for other units. We, however, think the reason is completely different.

The squadron's two battalions and their companies are scattered in a 10 km radius in the local villages. The squadron has set up its HQ in Lichtenberg, in a small Mecklenburg village manor house. It's a manor house in name only … transformed into an army barracks. Everything is neglected, ravaged and

---

8   B. Rubess and N. Ikstena, *Brīnumainā kārtā: stāsti par Bruņa Rubesa trim mūžiem* (*The autobiography of Brunis Rubess*), (Nordik, 1999), p.83. At Dievenow Mr Rubess had been sent to deliver his unit's positional information to the HQ only to find it had 'scarpered'. Leopolds Rumba later became head of Daugavas Vanagi in London and a mainstay of the UK capital's Latvian community.

squandered away. On the first floor is the HQ office and the Squadron Leader himself, sq. leader J.[9] The remaining officers and soldiers become part of the HQ staff, as the 1st Company have quartered themselves on the upper floors.

I have also based myself in a small room on the upper floor, along with squadron adjutant Lieutenant E. Our room is very small; there is barely enough room for two beds, a cupboard and a few chairs. But we're satisfied because it also contains an important item – the stove. The weather is still cold and when lit, the stove gives us warmth and cosiness in our free evenings and other spare moments.

In addition, our room houses the radio, the only means of contact with the outside world. A pity though that it's only a mains radio as the electricity often disappears. We can't help being angry when the electricity cuts out exactly when we need to listen the most.

We listen to both ours and the enemy radio stations – the latter under pain of death – but at the end of the day how else can we learn what is happening in this wide, topsy-turvy world? Our own – that is, the German news service – has long since lost any credibility. If, to begin with, listening to enemy radio stations was considered to be a forbidden activity, it has now become a necessity.

The Squadron Leader is increasingly seen in his office contemplating a map on which the frontline situation has been carefully drawn according to enemy information. We have been through Russia and Pomerania together and therefore trust each other.

In reality we are in an unenviable situation. We are faced with the enemy – the Bolsheviks against whom we are fighting, but also the Germans themselves. They've never really trusted us and now, when betrayal is seen to be everywhere and behind the frontlines is full of their own deserters, they watch us especially carefully. They know that we have sworn everlasting revenge on our most hated enemy – the Bolsheviks – but also realise that our sympathies lie with the Americans and the English a lot more than they do with themselves.

A German is also in our HQ amongst the Latvian officers. The German High Command has proclaimed that every Latvian unit – squadron, battalion, HQ – has to include a German and always precisely from 1st Special Assignment Group.

We know he is amongst us for a specific reason; to listen to what we are saying, discussing, doing … and to report to his superiors. We have got used to it. In his presence we are careful not to say our real thoughts or an unguarded word, because even though he might not pass it on, he wouldn't understand fully.

We have known this man, Leutnant Matten, for nearly half a year. I don't think he's malicious, but at the end of the day, he's a German. Even now, when the result of the war is clear to everyone, he unbendingly believes in his Führer

---

9 Colonel Janums. Bušmanis is very respectful to Janums throughout. What the English call the ground floor is considered the first floor by Latvians.

and victory. His presence doesn't allow us to listen to forbidden enemy radio stations and therefore the Squadron Leader often takes him along when visiting other units.

In the evenings, when we are free from our duties, we all gather together, most often in our little room. We are a fairly large number of officers: Adjutant Lieutenant E, myself (II Special Assignment officer), weapons expert Oberleutnant B, infantry company commander Lieutenant A, communications section commander 1st Lieutenant J. Usually the small room is full of people with everyone sitting and philosophising, enveloped in blue tobacco smoke. Sometimes the Squadron Leader comes up too.

The main topics of conversation are: *what will we do when the Bolsheviks turn up? Why are the Americans and British so slow at moving forward?* No-one believes in the possibility that we will have to fight again. We know that the Germans want to get rid of us and send us to Kurzeme to help the 19th Division, but consider that this idea is too difficult to implement. After the fall of Königsberg, Danzig and Gotenhafen, the sea route is under such threat that it is impossible to use.[10]

So, in the evenings we sit and we speculate. During the day we automatically fulfill our duties and silently reconcile ourselves to losing the fight. Whatever we might do, it's not in our power to change the outcome of the war. As well as which, we're no longer soldiers but workers. In place of rifles, of which each unit has only a few, we work with spades and chisels.

Day after day … half of April has gone, the weather is getting warmer and spring is increasingly making itself felt. The soldiers are still working on digging trenches and building tank barriers, which, according to orders, should have been ready long ago. In their free time soldiers sunbathe, fish in the local lakes or hunt in the local forests (the latter of course is expressly forbidden) and in so doing add to their extremely meagre rations.

Every now and then someone comes from the division to inspect our work but that happens very rarely. First there is not much faith in anything there: secondly the division is a good 30 km from us and transport is hard to come by. Of course, by car this distance wouldn't be a problem but due to a lack of petrol, cars are only to be used in special and urgent cases.

There's hardly any telephone contact. The days when the communication section battalion had enough cable to bring a line to the units have long since gone. Communications resources were last abandoned when we were surrounded in Pomerania. Now everything is organised using the local telephone network exchange. But that is so overloaded that there is a wait of hours.[11]

---

10 Shortages of coal were another factor in this idea being abandoned: sending Latvians back to Latvia was not a priority when they could be used to defend Berlin.

11 The diary of First Lieutenant Edvīns Bušmanis, April to May 1945. Unpublished, from the archive of the Rīga War Museum. Used with permission. Trans. Daina Vītola.

Oswalds Meija commanded the 32nd Regiment from the end of March 1945 onwards. His ID card is among his personal effects in the archive of the Latvian War Museum in Rīga. Picture: author.

Osvalds Meija was overseeing the rebuilding of the 32nd Battalion at this time.

> In the second half of February 1945, I was transferred from the Rīga Police Regiment to the 15th Division of the Latvian Legion near Neubrandenburg, where I was ordered to reform the 32nd Regiment from scratch and take command of it from 27 March. As a core group, I received Captain Alksnītis' battalion from the 33rd Regiment.
> On 30 March, the 15th Division was moved from the Neubrandenburg region to the Fürstenberg, Feldberg and Lychen regions, with the 32nd Regiment moving to the Lychen region. There, the regiment's units were involved in fortification work on the Fürstenberg-Lychen-Feldberg-Fürstenwerder line, digging anti-tank ditches, setting up road blocks, and installing positions for German units for potential defence activities.
> At the start of April, the regiment was reinforced by a battalion formed from police units, led by Captain Kronis, which was soon also involved in the fortification works. The days passed at work, but nobody was really sure whether the trenches and blocks would ever be used, because everyone could feel the war coming to an end.
> On 11 April, all regiment commanders were called to the division headquarters, where the division commander [SS-Brigadeführer Karl Burk] passed on passed on the secret information that the 15th Division's regiments would be moved to Kurzeme. This information worried the regiment commanders, because it seemed to reflect a wish by the German commanders to get rid of

Soldiers of the 32nd Regiment digging anti-tank ditches near Lychen, April 1945. Picture: Latvian War Museum LKM 5-13770-1452-FT.

the Latvian soldiers before surrendering, despite the fact that this would be giving them up to die. You could see the insincerity in the division commander's flattery.

After leaving the division headquarters, the regiment commanders, after discussing amongst themselves, agree: if there is an order to move, the regiments will try to independently break through to the West, to the Allied front.

On 13 April, General Bangerskis visited the regiment to talk to the commanders and calm them down, as there were worries that the soldiers may start dispersing independently and die as they wandered. Although General Bangerskis was successful in persuading the Germans to abandon the transfer of the 15th Division regiments to Kurzeme, the unknown continued to weigh on the regiment's soldiers like a heavy burden.[12]

The crossing of the Oder by the Red Army in April 1945 was a vast military undertaking. Two and a half million men massed on the eastern banks of the river from the Baltic to Czechoslovakia ready for the final push to Berlin.

Although Soviet forces had reached the city of Küstrin (now Kostrzyn nad Odrą) on the Oder to the south-east of Berlin at the end of January, the island fortress withstood heavy bombardment and repeated attacks until 22 March, when it was

---

12 Osvalds Meija's memoir: *We Didn't Follow Our Final Order* in the journal Lāčplēsis No. 24, published in the USA, 1987.

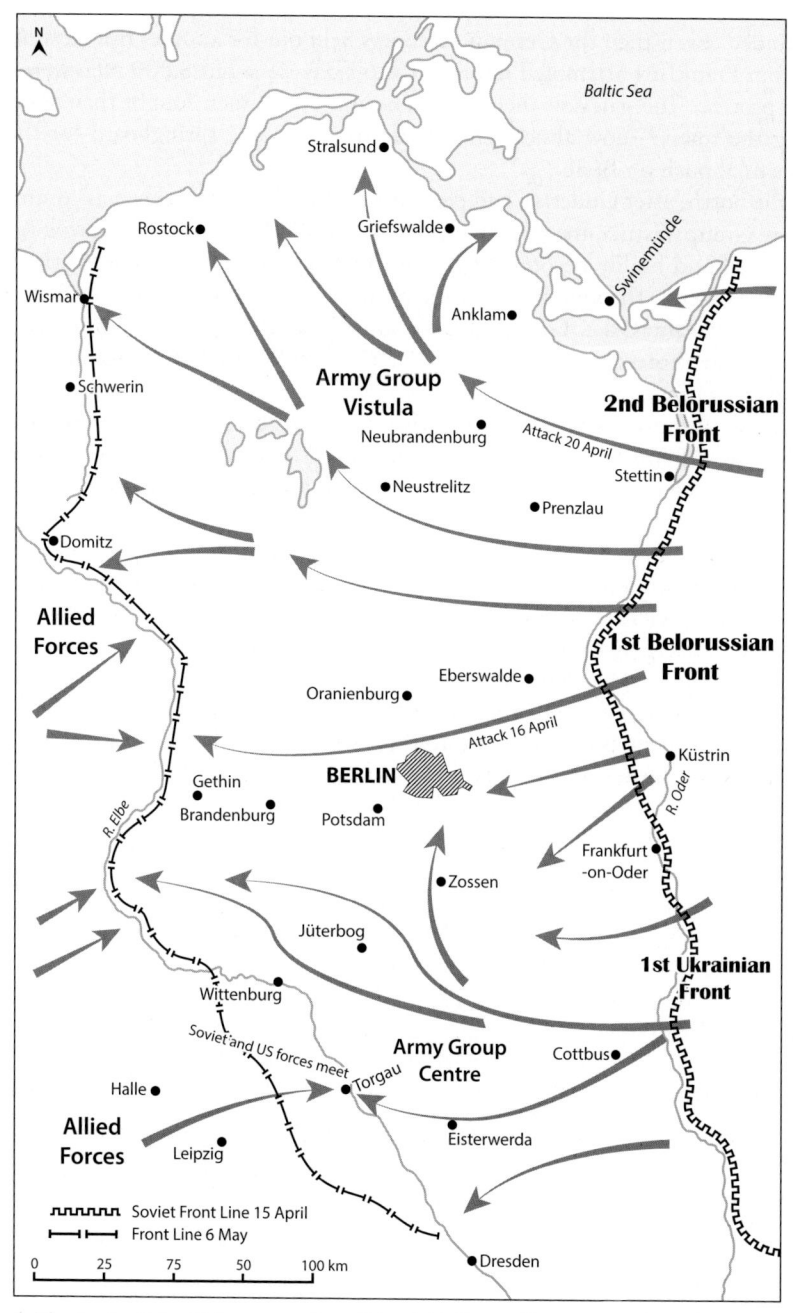

Map 4 The Soviet Oder-Neisse operation of April 1945, an offensive stretching from the Baltic Sea to the Sudeten Mountains. Initially positioned to the south-east of Berlin, Colonel Janums' Battle Group would have been directly in the path of Marshal Zhukov's First Belorussian Front. When the Latvians abandoned those positions and headed west, they were in danger of being intercepted by Marshal Ivan Konev's 1st Ukrainian Front.

surrounded. Even then the German defenders held out for another five days. A force sent from Frankfurt attempted to break the 60-day siege but 8,000 men were killed in the process. The garrison then broke out and 1,000 men fought their way west, leaving the town – now almost entirely destroyed – as a springboard for the Red Army's final push on Berlin.

To the north, after Guderian had persuaded Himmler to step down as commander of Army Group Vistula, the veteran General Gotthard Heinrici took control. A vastly experienced and highly decorated defensive war expert, Heinrici ordered the Ninth Army of General Theodor Busse to dig in on three defensive lines on the Seelow Heights above the Oder. General Hasso von Manteuffel's Third Panzer Army was positioned to protect against a flanking strike by Marshal Rokossovsky's Second Belorussian Front to the north.

Henrici's defensive strategy during the three-day battle at the Seelow Heights between 16–19 April extracted a heavy price in Russian lives: 30,000 men killed, while on the German side, 12,000 men died resisting the 1st Belorussian Front's offensive.

To the south of the Küstrin bridgehead, General Chuikhov's Eighth Guards Army met well-organised and stubborn resistance on the most direct route to Berlin. This was directed by General Helmuth Weidling, bolstered by the arrival of the 11th SS Nordland Panzergrenadiers – Danes, Norwegians, Swedes, Estonians and Finns commanded by SS-Brigadeführer Joachim Ziegler.[13]

The Soviet pressure on and around the main combat points became overwhelming and the Ninth Army began to split into three smaller groups. The order was given to withdraw from the Seelow Heights on 19–20 April.

---

13 Beevor, pp.219–235, 245. From the start of 1945 the 11th SS Nordland lost 4,500 men killed and missing and a further 10,000 wounded in fighting around Stettin. The Latvian 15th SS had fought alongside Ziegler at Nakel in Pomerania – where he withdrew without notifying them – and the men of the 15th Recce Battalion would meet him again in Berlin centre.

6

19 April 1945

19 April 1945 is a key date in the history of the 15th Latvian SS in Germany. On that day the German commanders broke the force up into units defending the various approaches to Berlin. When a call did come through for the Latvians at Fürstenberg on the overloaded telephone network, it brought unwelcome news, as First Lieutenant Bušmanis wrote in his diary:

> It is 19 April. About 1000 we receive a telephone telegram from the division for the Squadron Leader to use a car and present himself at HQ. The Squadron Leader leaves. Because he has been ordered to use a car, his trip to HQ seems very important. We haven't got time to discuss it. Those of us left behind have our duties. Me, too.
>
> After considerable hesitation, yesterday the Squadron Leader granted leave to Adjutant Lieutenant E to sort out family problems. Of course, leave is not allowed these days, therefore E has gone on official military business. He left early this morning and I am in his place. I've got enough to do; not only my own duties but his too. I have to finish the report about our company battle exploits in Pomerania. One of the HQ clerks is copying it now. Because my handwriting leaves a lot to be desired, I have to be around at all times.[1]
>
> Lunchtime comes but the Squadron Leader has not returned. At last, about 1400 his eagerly-awaited car drives into the yard. The Squadron Leader comes in looking serious. We who know him realise that something important has happened. The messenger hurries to lay the table for a late lunch but the Squadron Leader waves a hand. 'Later!'
>
> Indeed, something serious has happened. According to High Command, the 15th Latvian Division has been ordered to form a combat group of three battalions for immediate inclusion in the campaign. The division commander orders the 32nd and 33rd Squadrons to provide two battalions and the Division Reconnaissance Battalion to be the third. In addition, 33rd Squadron has to provide the battle group HQ and the units belonging to it: communication, infantry and tank destroyer.

---

1 Adjutant Lieutenant E is Verners Eše.

> To arm themselves, all available weapons must be collected. Transport does not need to be included: it will be provided. Everything must be ready by 2000 when transport will arrive to take us to the appointed place. Even though our commander has been given leadership of the battle group, he doesn't know where we will be going. It seems the division commander is afraid that if we learn where we are being sent, we might try to refuse to go.
>
> The Squadron Leader has become very curt. He reads his orders again and then dictates his own. He has never been one for thinking things over and now time is extremely short. Following his orders the 1st Battalion is included in the 33rd Squadron. The Regiment's HQ men are going almost to a body, except for Lieutenant B and some NCOs who have to stay behind with equipment. Due to lack of space on the transport, we are only allowed to take the most necessary items.
>
> The squadron supply store has just received the longed-for and necessary clothing and other accessories for the soldiers. Therefore, the Squadron Leader orders 1st Leutnant Martin, the squadron administration officer (also a German) to distribute them to the departing 1st Battalion by 1600 and for the 2nd Battalion to hand over all their weapons. I pass the orders on.

Legionnaire Jānis Urpens, a corporal, had been assigned to kitchen duties and digging anti-tank defences. Now he was told to take a group of men to the stores to gather fresh kit for the mission.

> The war is nearly over and it is a job to find anything new. Of course I cannot lose because the bottom parts of my trousers have rotted off. After the clothing, we go the weapons store. *Pick your rifle.* I see a Russian machine pistol and grab it, for the simple reason that ammunition is in short supply and, in the next action, if I lose my way and find myself behind Russian lines there will be a chance to find ammunition.
>
> By now it's early evening and the lorries arrive. The order comes to board them. Our colonel [Janums] turns up and he cannot accept that we don't have any kitchen stoves in the lorry. So out we come and lift one in but then we find the room [for ourselves] has shrunk: we feel like sardines in a tin! It has turned dark but the sky is clear and while we do not know where we are heading the northern star is showing us our direction.[2]

Captain Vilis Akermanis writes that because the Latvians had handed over their weapons to German units, they thought their war was over. So when the order was given to create a new battle group commanded by Colonel Janums, they were surprised.[3]

---

2   Memories of Jānis Urpens, private notes given to author.
3   Akermanis, who later emigrated to Australia, dates the order to the Division on 15 April.

The newly-formed battle group was subdivided into the 33rd Infantry Regiment's 1st Battalion, the 32nd Infantry Regiment's 1st Battalion, and the Division Reconnaissance Battalion. The trip to the operations centre was to be made by motor vehicles. These units were then ordered to leave their vehicles and were told that they would be returned to them when they showed up at the correct battle station.

If those in charge of the Division chose Colonel Janums as the commander of this battle group, it was probably because he particularly stood out in the Pomeranian battlefields with his leadership skills.[4]

Janums had fought in the First World War, the Latvian War of Independence, graduated from the best military school in Czechoslovakia and lectured in the tactics of retreat at military school in Latvia, Akermanis writes.

> He had already put his theoretical retreat knowledge into practice on the Eastern Front. As the only commander of his regiment since it was founded, he had gained the confidence and trust of his soldiers. The division soldiers usually called the regiment 'the Janums Regiment' amongst themselves.
>
> The promotion of Colonel Janums to commander of the battle group strengthened the morale of the group, who figured that the 'old guy' probably knew what to do.[5]

First Lieutenant Bušmanis describes the activity as his unit prepared to move.

> The next hours pass in a hurry. I tell the HQ clerks what is to be taken and what is to be left behind in between trying to sort out my own personal property. Even though everything was lost in the Pomeranian battles, I have begun to accumulate bits and pieces. I also ring the Division HQ war correspondent section, where my brother works.
>
> Even though I don't know where we are going and what our fate will be, I would like to invite him along so he remains near me. Unfortunately, it's not to be. When I finally get a connection, it turns out that there are no war corrrespondents around. I immediately place another call.
>
> Preparations for the departure on the whole are coming along nicely, the only exception being the squadron's directorate. There, the men – who are mostly Germans – are working so slowly that by 1800 equipment is only just being sent to the units. The hour of departure approaches. We are trying to guess our destination while waiting for our promised transport, although we don't believe it will arrive on time.

---

4   Akermanis' memoir *To the Americans* in Daugavas Vanagu Mēnešraksts, Nr.5 (01.09.1988) online at <https://periodika.lv/periodika2-viewer/?lang=fr#panel:pa|issue:159534|article:DIVL117|query:Zerbstas%20> trans. Māra Walsh-Sinka.
5   V. Akermanis, *To the Americans* (1988). Janums' men were known by the affectionate diminuitive *Janumieši*, which translates as 'Janums' lads' or 'Janums' men'.

58　ESCAPE FROM BERLIN

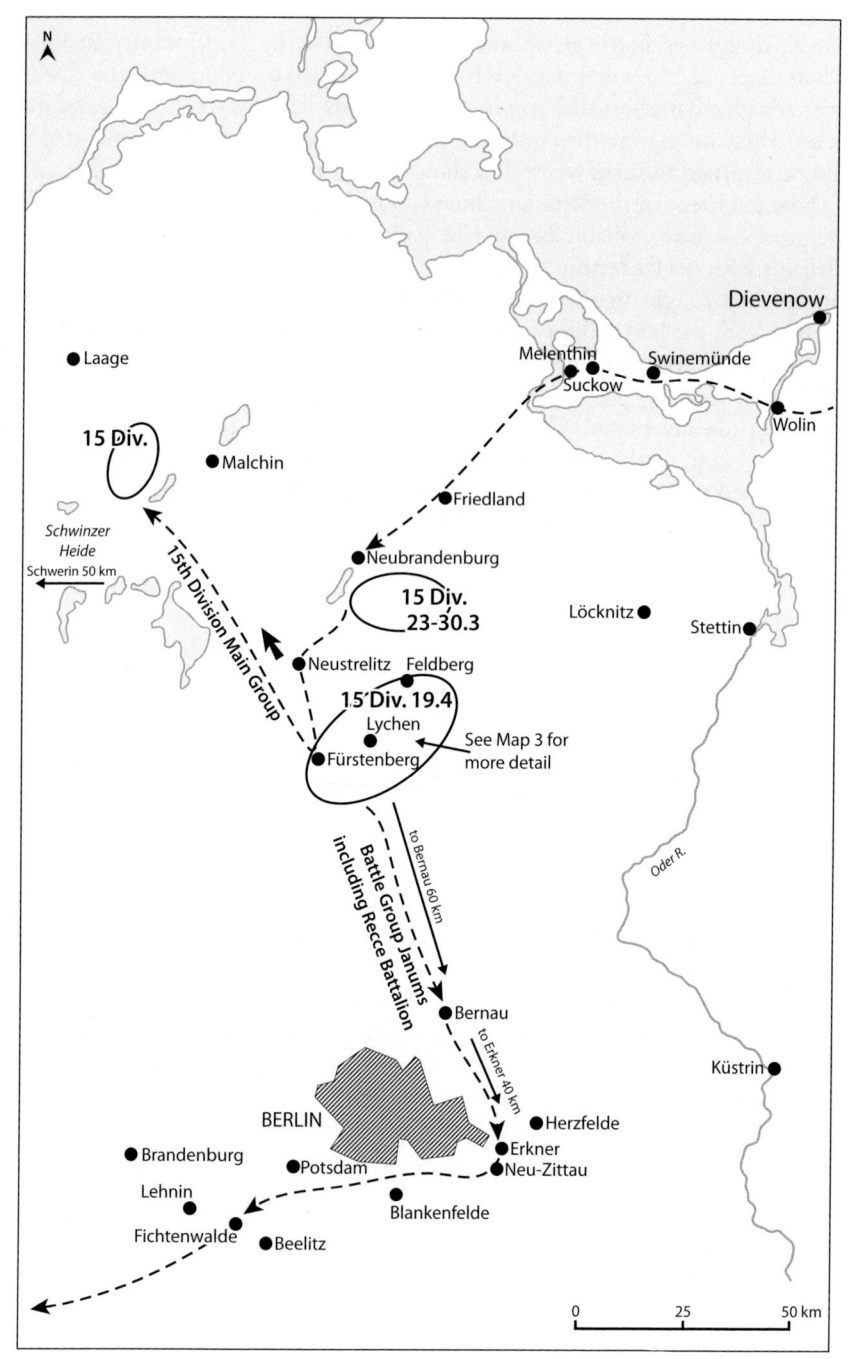

Map 5　The position of the Latvians on 19 April 1945, when they were broken up into three separate groups. Colonel Janums took two battalions drawn from the 32nd and 33rd Regiment to the south-east of Berlin; SS-Hauptsturmführer Eldon Walli took the Recce Battalion into the centre of Berlin and Fricis Mežgrāvis took the 32nd Regiment and the remainder of the division to Mecklenburg.

But the unbelievable actually happens. At about 1930, which is half an hour before the appointed time, five military lorries with trailers roll into the yard. With them is also the military messenger with our destination. It falls to me to receive it.

Nervously I tear open the envelope and read that our destination is Herzfelde, which is 15 km east of Berlin. So, we are condemned to defend Berlin. The Squadron Leader's face becomes inscrutable. We keep two of the lorries, sending the remaining three to the 1st Battalion units.

The soldiers begin loading immediately. When the kitchen, some provisions, the HQ equipment, all the 1st Company, the squadron HQ communications and infantry soldiers are all aboard, the two huge lorries and their trailers are so full there isn't room for a needle to fall. The directorate men, who according to orders have to accompany us, are late and the transport leaves the yard without them.

While the transport is being loaded, I ask the division dentist to finish putting fillings in two teeth. Even though the dentist – First Lieutenant K – works at incredible speed, the Squadron Leader is waiting impatiently for me. I don't have time to wait for the second phone call [placed to his brother].

The moment I jump into the car, it hurries after the departing transport. In a while we are at 1st Battalion HQ. Here, there's total chaos. The lorry we sent is standing half-empty in the middle of the yard because the 2nd Company, billeted in the neighbouring village, has not arrived. It's a few minutes past 2000 when they finally do. The men get into the lorry and trailer and it moves out onto the road. Still missing are the 3rd and 4th Company lorries sent to Warbende, as too are the squadron ambulance and doctor, Lieutenant P. We wait.

In conversation, the reason for the delay becomes clear. It turns out that at lunchtime today the unit received its canteen supplies, which also included alcohol. That has already been partly distributed.

Waiting on the road half an hour goes by, an hour … Apparently our waiting patiently is to no avail as the lorries sent to pick up 3 and 4 Companies are nowhere to be seen. We can't hear the carts bringing medical supplies and the doctor from Wrechen either. The Squadron Leader decides to go to find the overdue men and invites me along.

We find both the lorries and companies still in the village. Thanks to the alcohol, it's impossible to instill any order. The company commanders are helpless. As soon as one group of soldiers is pushed into the lorries, another group tumbles out of the other side.

Friendship has played a part. On our arrival in the village, the soldiers were greeted coldly and with reserve. Now however, they're not being let go. The village girls, tears in their eyes, want to hold on to their friends. Hugs and kisses are never-ending.

The Squadron Leader's authority finally has an effect. Everyone gets into the lorries and accompanied by lively singing, they make their way back to the main road to join up with the others.

But – the squadron ambulance still hasn't arrived. A messenger is despatched to Wrechen on a bicycle to find it. After a while he returns to confirm that the ambulance car is on its way. About 2200 the long-awaited ones arrive, shouting and yelling. Lieutenant P gets out and goes to report their arrival to the Squadron Leader. He is swaying like water weed. The following conversation ensues:

Lieutenant P: 'Squadron Leader, sir, Lieutenant P has arrived with the ambulance.'

Squadron Leader: 'You're drunk!'

Lieutenant P: 'You're right, Squadron Leader, sir. Completely drunk.'

Lieutenant P takes a step back and falls backwards on his head into the ditch. We rush to help him but see that nothing untoward has happened. Lieutenant P has managed to fall asleep on the spot. We leave him there so that we won't be bothered by him and busy ourselves transferring the ambulance supplies into the lorries.

The remaining medical personnel aren't in a much better state. Boxes slide from clumsy hands, medicines smash and break, ampoules crunch under men's feet. The chief culprit, 1st Battalion directorate officer Lieutenant L, who ordered the canteen supply to be distributed – not consulting with squadron HQ – hasn't arrived. He is at home, asleep. We can't wait any longer for him.

I check once again that everyone is in the lorries. After a few unsuccessful tries I help 'Doctor' P out of the ditch and make sure he's not left on the road. Finally everything is in order. I squeeze in with the others in the car and the journey to an unknown future begins.[6]

The memoirs of a second soldier, Arvīds Kalupnieks, outline the fears of the Latvians at this time. Kalupnieks writes:

After heavy retreat battles in Pomerania, Colonel Janums and his men are having a rest, if you can call it that, in Mecklenburg, in the Neubrandenburg region. Colonel Janums has installed his command point in Lichtenberg and his units are stationed in the surrounding villages.[7] Here, the plan is to bolster our numbers, train and equip us, to later be sent to the Kurzeme Front (that's what the Germans say).

Suddenly, news of the start of an Allied offensive on the Western Front spreads around the world. With great interest, we listen to messages on the swift progress made by the Allied forces. Coarse wrinkles appear on the Colonel's otherwise calm face. In the mornings, you can see that the Colonel has slept little. Those who know him realise what these sleepless nights and wrinkles mean. Entering his office, you see the Colonel bent over maps. He works quietly. His orders and answers are short but clear.

---

6 Diary of First Lieutenant Edvīns Bušmanis.
7 A suburb of north-eastern Berlin, about six kilometres from the centre of the city.

He is occupied by one thought: how to get his soldiers through the final obstacles. Threatening clouds gather over the Colonel's plan, as the Russians are also preparing to attack in the east. It seems like the Allies' push has slowed to a halt.

The Colonel senses that the Germans are preparing a betrayal against his men, the Latvians. Every day it gets more clear that we will be pushed into a place which, the Germans believe, means our certain death. There are rumours of our being sent to Kurzeme. Some already know the date and even the port from which we will supposedly be sent.

But the following events impact even our – the young men's – course. The Russian attack at Küstrin begins. The German forces have been weakened, so there are warranted doubts about them enduring this pressure.

The morning of 19 April 1945 arrives. We are still receiving telephone messages and instructions: 'Hurry up with building the defence line!' Thoughts and assumptions trouble our minds; only the Colonel is strangely calm – the same calmness and confidence he had in both the Russian and Pomeranian battles. In the afternoon, the division messenger arrives in a hurry, bringing an order: the Colonel and his men must be on the move within a few hours. Trucks with trailers arrive a few hours later to take us to the front east of Berlin.

The units organise themselves and climb into the cars. Everything is ready to start the journey. The unit commanders tell the Colonel that their units are ready to leave. We are promised more weapons along the way. Still the Colonel delays. He has a short discussion with Major Ķīlītis, who is staying here with the 34th Regiment's 11th Battalion in our current location. What the Colonel and Major Ķīlītis are discussing remains, for now, a secret from us.

Colonel Janums comes out of his quarters. His serious face shows a strong determination to overcome all difficulties. His gaze slides over the men's faces as if wanting to read their hidden thoughts. The *Janumieši* know their Colonel and trust their war leader completely. This calms the grey-haired Colonel, as he knows that his men are one strong unit.

Car engines roar, goodbyes are said. Sincere messages are exchanged between those leaving and those staying: 'See you soon.' The Colonel exchanges a few more words with the commanders of the units which are to remain. 'Sons, we're off,' are the Colonel's final words, as he says goodbye to those staying. The cars start moving.

When we leave Lichtenberg, it is already deep dusk. We are packed tightly into the cars, meaning we have to stand. On the way, the 1st Battalion and Reconnaissance Battalion of the 33rd Regiment join us at Lychen. We discover that the remaining units will follow in the next few days. We also receive additional weapons, around 90 guns. Most of the soldiers, however, are unarmed; they are given Panzerfausts.[8]

---

8 Kalupnieks, *Colonel Janums and his Men,* in J. Leititis, *Pulkvedis Vilis Janums,* trans. Mara Walsh-Sinka (1986).

But transport problems broke the Latvian group up, as Captain Vilis Akermanis writes:

> The hurriedly-formed battle group – with the exception of the 15th Reconnaissance Battalion, due to their lack of transport – left its positions on the 19th April at 2130. This action was the reason why, despite all efforts, all contact was lost with the 15th Reconnaissance Battalion, and the group continued as just two battalions. As was later discovered, the 15th Reconnaissance Battalion ended up in Berlin, where, upon being unable to make contact with the battle group, they were ordered to help with defending the city. In the hopeless and heavy fighting, the Battalion's members perished.[9]

Arvīds Kalupnieks continues:

> We drive all night. The men are tired and try to sleep somehow. As the morning approaches, with the light just breaking, we reach the Berlin suburbs. In the suburb of Rüdersdorf our column stops and we have to disembark.[10]
>
> We are handed over to a tank army (of course, they had no tanks). All the bridges are blocked with anti-tank obstacles guarded by members of the German *Volkssturm*. I pitied the old men and the children literally taken from their mothers' breasts who are entrenched and standing guard by the obstacles. They are armed with guns and Panzerfausts.
>
> Somewhere in the distance, we hear the roar of battle. There are streams of refugees. The Colonel has left to find out the situation. The unit's task is, for the moment, to stay put. During this time, the local battle commander finds out that we have arrived and hurriedly orders us to take our positions, noting that there are five more defence lines ahead of us.

Captain Akermanis writes:

> Near Herzfelde, on their way to Berlin, Janums received orders that his battle group was thereafter under the command of the XI Tank Corps of the German Army, tasked with participating in the defence of Berlin. After contacting the headquarters of the XI Tank Corps, Janums was told that the Corps commanders did not want to take on a group without its own transport, as they themselves had no spare vehicles.
>
> During these discussions, the Corps headquarters received a message that the enemy's tanks were approaching the location of the headquarters. The news caused panic, and the headquarters left their location in a great hurry, leaving the group to their own fate. This situation gave the battle group the chance to be rid of all outside command, which Janums successfully took advantage of.

---

9   Akermanis, *To the Americans*.
10 Rüdersdorf is 25 km east of Lichtenberg, two km from Herzfelde and 11 km from Erkner.

His plan since forming the battle group had been to use their approach to the front as an opportunity to surrender to the Allied armies, saving his soldiers not just from capture by the Bolsheviks, but also from death in the ruins of Berlin.

According to the news they heard on the radio, the American Army west of Berlin had already reached the River Elbe and had taken up bridge positions on the eastern bank of the river near Zerbst. With these unexpected conditions and promising radio news in mind, Janums and the senior officers of the battle group decided to avoid getting pulled into defending Berlin.

To achieve this, Janums decided to skirt the south of Berlin and begin the march to the Americans at their bridge position near Zerbst.[11]

The Latvians knew defending Herzfelde and the south-eastern approaches to Berlin was a suicide mission. Everyone knew it. The war had been lost for a long time. The Soviets were advancing on the German Army's communications centre at Zossen by the hour and tightening their net around the capital in the north, from the south and from the south-east. Soviet bombers were in the skies above the capital and the wounded were being treated in beds in the streets as many hospitals were now too badly damaged.[12]

Fricis Mežgrāvis, the commander of the 2nd Battalion, became suspicious of visitors wanting to talk to his men – even fellow Latvians.

In the second half of April, I had to hand over to the newly-formed Janums fighting group all the soldier-NCO Iron Cross recipients in the battalion, excluding officers, who could volunteer. The battalion numbers fell considerably. Only two officers volunteered to defend Berlin. We carried on digging trenches.

In the town centre, next to the railway crossing was a pile of about 400 Panzerfausts, beside which was a sign saying: 'These are the last ones – only to be used with the permission of Fieldmarshall Göring.' One day at the station, written on wagons with chalk, were the words: 'And we old monkeys (silly fools) are the new weapons.'

At this point, the owner of the hotel my HQ was in returned from Berlin. In conversation he told my HQ men that we could thank God that we escaped from the siege. This man was a high-ranking official in Berlin, in the German forestry administration.

One day a corporal – a Latvian – arrived from Division HQ. He had been sent to gauge the mood and attitude of the soldiers as to the Western Allies. The corporal bypassed the section commanders but gathered together the cultural department heads in my HQ and began questioning them, completely ignoring my presence. Having listened to this questioning for a while, I called a halt.

I told the corporal to tell the divisional commander that there isn't anyone in my battalion who will voluntarily fight the Westerners. But if some could be

---

11 Akermanis, *To the Americans*.
12 E.F. Ziemke, *Battle for Berlin*, pp.85–88.

found who loved new adventures, then [that would be] no more than one per cent. I am convinced that among my officers there is no-one. So he should stop wasting his time questioning people who have less to do with the mood of the soldiers than the battalion commander.

The next day the divisional commander Karl Burk called a meeting of all the division officers in the squadron HQ. The Latvian officers were reprimanded and told 'they were no use'. However, the soldiers were good, and so were the NCOs [non-commissioned officers].

Therefore the German authorities have decided to replace the Latvian officers with German ones. There was uproar. The division commander was told that the Latvian officers have trained both the soldiers and NCOs. If they are good fighters, it would be thanks to the Latvian officers, not the German ones. If the German officers now take over, then the result would be catastrophic. The Latvian soldiers would not fight.

In the end, the divisional commander asked all the officers agreeable to fighting the West to stand up. No-one did. Then those willing to continue to fight against the Communists were told to stand. As one man, everyone stood.

Burk just said: 'Well, I'll hold you to that. But to those of you who are quietly flirting with the English and Americans, I can tell you it won't work.' With that the meeting was over.[13]

Lieutenant Atis Neilands was the commander of the Latvian units in the Battle of Berlin and one of very few men who survived. He escaped from Soviet captivity and later emigrated to Australia, and wrote of that time:

On 19 April Colonel Janums' squadron and the Reconnaissance Battalion received orders to make their way to Berlin and take part in its defence. The Reconnaissance Battalion was at the time under the leadership of Colonel Janums but received a direct order to go to Berlin centre and be under the orders of Hitler Leibstandarte commander General-Major Moncke. Janums' squadron left first and because of transport problems, we were left waiting. It's possible that Janums didn't know anything about this change in orders.

On arriving in Berlin, we were unable to make contact with the squadron and eventually Captain Walli disappeared. He did reappear a few times: one day he said he was going to look for Janums' squadron. Naturally, we thought that Walli knew all along where Janums was. I was again elected to the post of adjutant, which Walli as Battalion commander accepted, giving me the general order to go to the centre of Berlin.[14]

---

13 Mežgrāvis in Freivalds, Caunītis, Bērziņš, Kociņš and Hāzners (eds), *Latviešu Karavīrs Otra Pasaules Kaŗa Laikā (The Latvian Soldier During World War Two, vol. 6)* (Ziemeļblāzma, Västerås, Sweden, 1970–1979), vol. 6, p.158.
14 Atis Neilands, in Leititis, p.96. Wilhelm Moncke was the commander of the Berlin government *Zitadelle* sector, including the Reichstag, Reich Chancellery and Führerbunker.

The Latvians began their journey towards Berlin and First Lieutenant Bušmanis – 'B' – kept a detailed record as they left their base with Colonel Janums – the 'Squadron Leader' – in charge. The first stop was at Divisional HQ at Lychen to get maps and weapons.

> B looking for maps, which are very hard to find. Squadron Leader wants to meet up with commander. Returns to car accompanied by 2nd Battalion commander, a German, Captain Walli, who has his own car. Back into the cars. Soldiers receiving weapons at Lychen station. Not many rifles and over the three battalions only a couple of hundred Panzerfausts.
>
> There is more ammunition but as we're already overloaded, we can't take it. Squadron Leader arranges for ammunition to be picked up the following day. I'm approached by Lieutenant Kipert from Division HQ, asking our battalion's strength. I'm not sure exactly but I waffle through.
>
> On our way again. Don't know where 2 and 3 Battalions are; they're travelling separately. Very squashed on journey. B sitting between Ltns Martin and Metten.
>
> Wake up in the early morning. The lorries have stopped at the side of the road. Coming toward and past us is a never-ending stream of vehicles and carts, both military personnel and civilians. The carts are pulled by tractors and horses. Where have they come from, where [are they] going? It's 0530.
>
> For a while we headed east and the lads start to say we're heading to Latvia, where Kurzeme is still free of Russians. But no, the lorries turn south and we know where we are going: we are going to defend Berlin. After several hours of standing and shaking the morning is here. We stop and disembark. The kitchen stove is lifted out, and there it remains when we move on.
>
> Our Colonel arrives. He has now got his own car. The fighting group under his command consists of three battalions, but we have lost the Fusilier Battalion. The commander arrives but has no idea where his battalion is. The Colonel is fuming, and the Major gets a good telling-off. He is the only German officer in our Latvian unit.
>
> The Colonel has no intention of fighting the Russians: the war is ending and all he is planning is to get his unit over to the Americans and surrender to them. So he has to get rid of the Major. After a lot of telling off and shouting he orders the German to take his car and not come back until he has found the Fusilier battalion.[15]

Legionnaire Arvīds Kalupnieks writes on 20 April.

> The sun rises, and soon the roar of battle gets louder and comes closer. The whole horizon boils as if in hell. The Colonel has not yet returned. We start to worry that the Russians have cut off his route back to us. We all know that only

---

15 The diary of Edvīns Bušmanis, pages 1–5, from the archive of the Latvian War Museum, courtesy of Jānis Tomaševskis. Translated by Daina Vītola, March 2020.

he knows what to do. Russian aviation becomes increasingly intense. Bombs fall. We worry about the Colonel.

We send messengers out to various crossroads so they can notify the Colonel of our position if he drives past. An out-of-breath messenger arrives: 'The Colonel's car is coming this way!' A few minutes later, the Colonel arrives. Everyone knows what his downcast face means. But even now, the Colonel's characteristic calm has not left him. Succinctly, the Colonel tells his commanders the situation. We find out that the Germans have taken the Reconnaissance Battalion down a different path.[16]

It is clear that the Germans want to lead us to destruction. It seems like there is no escape from the hell that is approaching us. But our Colonel has a plan. He wants to defy the draconian powers. He knows that everyone who he has led, some from out of nine encirclements already [in Pomerania], will follow him again. The biggest problem now is how to get the battalions out of their battle positions. Soon, the situation is appraised and action is decided on. The roar edges ever closer. We can't delay, because our success requires every minute.

The typewriter hurriedly clatters, writing orders for the battalions on where to go. The next orders will await them there. This is all required for us to move forward as the German military police are waiting at every point to block our way. Everyone is clear: if we want to escape this hell, not a step different from what the Colonel orders. Hurrying, the men go along the sides of the road. A Russian plane flies over and throws down its greetings: leaflets.

Our plan: to go around Berlin and reach its western edge. We have been left without transport. In the afternoon, we reach the south-east edge of Berlin and stop to rest in a forest. We have managed to get rid of a few Germans seconded to our regiment. They were sent to Berlin, to the main battle commander, to await orders. We are able to get through all the German checkpoints. In this forest, we also restock our ammunition.

We are near Erkner and staying in some wooden barracks. In the evening, the big Russian attack on Berlin begins. Berlin is bombarded all night. Our barracks sway and squeak from the closest explosions. It feels like the air pressure will knock them over but we still sleep soundly, as we are tired from the journey and the fast march. Towards the morning the bombardment quietens, but the activity along the front begins. This situation has become completely unclear; the battalions take up their positions along the canal edge so that the enemy cannot surprise us.

We still have to get rid of the last few Germans in our regiment's command. The commander of the Reconnaissance Battalion, a German Hauptsturmführer [Walli], comes to speak to the Colonel, accompanied by a senior SS-Sturmbannführer.[17]

---

16 They have been sent to the centre of Berlin.
17 Colonel Janums did not trust Captain Walli, a longstanding Nazi, and did everything he could to get him out of the way. Walli ended up in the centre of Berlin with the Recce Battalion, and

It seems like everything is ruined – the Germans are back and won't allow the Colonel to lead his men out of Berlin. We have to be cunning, and the Colonel already has a plan. He tells the Sturmbannführer to go to Berlin to make contact and receive new orders, while he himself visits the battalions and checks that they have taken up their positions. The Sturmbannführer accompanies him, and on seeing that they are in position, he calms down and goes to Berlin. The Colonel stays with the battalions.

The previous night, the Colonel had a brush with death, as a bomb landed 50 metres from him. The back of his car looks like a sieve, but luckily the Colonel was unharmed. A German Untersturmführer was injured. In other words, fate helped us get rid of our last German.[18]

The commander of the reconstituted 32nd Regiment, Osvalds Meija, recalls:

On 19 April, the regiment received an unexpected order to surrender Captain Alksnītis' battalion and all the weapons in the regiment to Colonel Janums for the creation of a battle group.

Once Alksnītis' battalion departed, the regiment once again shrank to the size of an expanded battalion and continued its digging works, but morale continued to worsen. Both the commanders and the other soldiers became apathetic towards this work, and things were made even worse by the negligible rations.

On 20 April, General Bangerskis once again entered the region the division was stationed in to visit units from the 32nd Regiment in Lychen. There, in a talk with the commanders, he attempted to raise morale by explaining that nobody could blame the regiment for trying to be captured by the Allies, once the fight against the Red Army is over, if there was a chance of being captured by the Reds – but it was important to choose the right moment to leave the division's German commanders to avoid dangerous encounters with German units.[19]

---

survived the war.
18 Memoirs of Arvīds Kalupnieks: *Colonel Janums and his Men* in Leititis, *Pulkvedis Vilis Janums*, trans. Mara Walsh-Sinka (1986).
19 Osvalds Meija, Memoir: *We Didn't Follow Our Final Order* in the journal Lāčplēsis No. 24 (1987).

7

The Janums Battle Group Abandons its Positions

The journey south to Berlin was interrupted constantly for checks on the ever-approaching enemy, as First Lieutenant Bušmanis records.

Column leader approaches to explain to Squadron Leader. We're about five kilometres NW of Bernau, a small town NE of Berlin. There's enemy nearby. There are tank defences on the road, and the road to Herzfelde is closed. Only the autobahn is left. He isn't allowed to use it. Squadron Leader wants to see for himself. Everyone is to remain on this spot. We get in the car to go to look.

The road is overflowing, and we move in stops and starts. Squadron Leader orders that we park in a field to wait for a clearer road. There are sounds of battle all around, planes flying overhead. After a few hours the road clears somewhat. Turns out the tank defence points are still open. We're nearing Berlin.

At 0930 we reach Herzfelde, where we should get new orders. In front of a hospital in the distance we notice a group of soldiers. Turns out to be 1st and 2nd Battalions. Major A and Captain R, both battalion commanding officers, explain that [the] column leader, ignoring an order to wait for the Squadron Leader, received permission to use the highway. When everything had been unloaded, the transport left.

Meanwhile a *Volkssturm* 1st Lieutenant, a German, butts in and tells the Squadron Leader to give orders for his soldiers to take up position nearby. Mockingly, the Squadron Leader asks the 1st Lieutenant who he is, where is he from and why should we take up position right here.

The 1st Lieutenant is a bit put out by the Squadron Leader's tone of voice. He explains that he is acting on the orders of the local battle commander. He has to engage every soldier in his territory. The Squadron Leader in turn explains it's not so simple – he has his own orders. His soldiers are only resting here, so he can't obey. To break the stalemate, the Squadron Leader decides to go to see the battle commander. The 1st Lieutenant leads the way on a motorbike.

We find the command HQ. We are received by a weirdly-dressed, fairly old person. Try as we may, we can't make out his military rank. At a guess we bestow

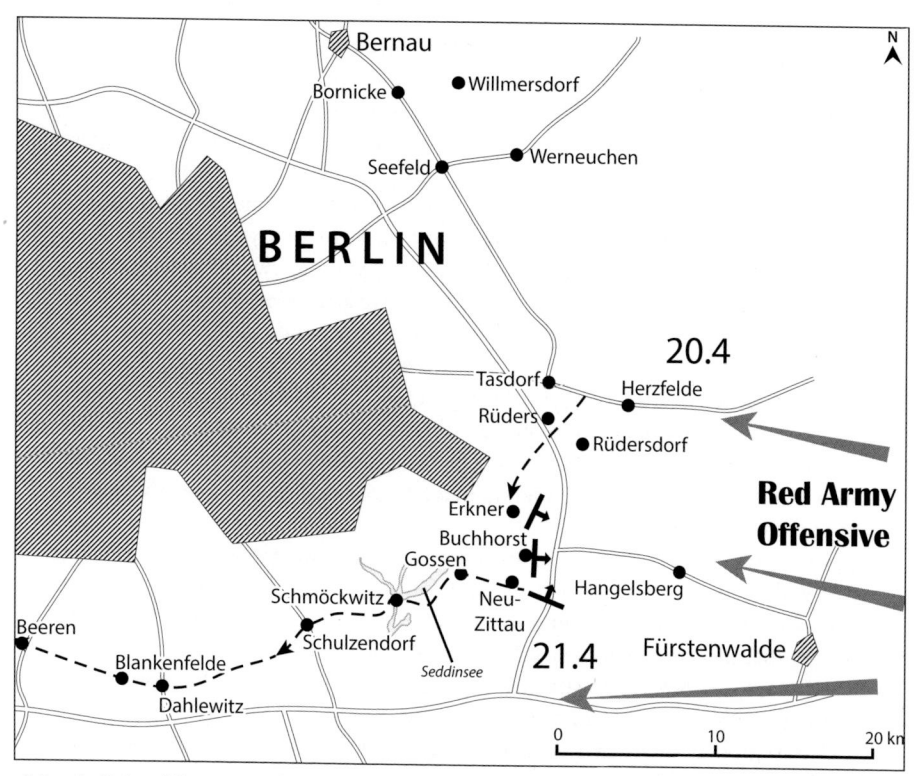

Map 6 Colonel Janums and his battle group were deployed to positions around Herzfeldee and Rüdersdorf on 20 April 1945. Having sent SS Hauptsturmführer Walli to Berlin for fresh orders, Colonel Janums marched two battalions of men west, around the south of Berlin. The men of the Reconnaissance Battalion who remained, fell back into the centre of Berlin.

the rank of Major on him. The 1st Lieutenant jumps in to explain our arrival and refusal to obey his command. So the Squadron Leader in turn explains he has special orders and can't be under commandant orders. The German won't give up. It's clear to see he wants our men in position in his district.

To calm things down, the Squadron Leader agrees that until his orders are received, he will put his men into position but as soon as those orders come through, they will be off. The 'Major' has to accept that. On our return, the soldiers are sent to various positions.

B and Leutnant Metten are sent to Herzfelde to fetch the orders. The orders say our battle group has to go to Hangelsberg, where the 2nd Tank Corps is already. We will be under their command and will receive further orders there. Hangelsberg is about 25 km SE from Herzfelde.[1]

---

1 Hangelsberg is a heavily-forested area to the south east of the city, outside the road ring and about 20 km from Erkner. It's now a nature reserve, the Naturschutzgebiet Löcknitztal.

We want to go back but the driver says we are out of fuel. The commandant at Herzfelde hasn't got any so we are directed to the nearest petrol station, which is also empty. A German soldier happens by and tells us that not far away is a factory yard, where, a few hours ago, there was a barrel full of petrol. He offers to show us.

To begin with we don't find anything but finally we come across a row of barrels full of something resembling petrol. The driver says it will do. Then factory watchmen turn up. At first they are angry but a few cigarettes mellows them. Add a few cigars and they are ready to give away everything going. Why not? Anything that's left behind will fall into enemy hands today or tomorrow.

We go back to the Squadron Leader and the two battalion commanders. The former is especially pleased about the fuel. 'Good,' he says. 'Now we're off to see our friend the Commandant, to give him the good news that we're leaving.' The Major tries to raise objections but no-one takes any notice. On the way back we stop at our HQ which has been set up in a refugee-filled small room. We squash in too and have a bite to eat.

I have time to take a look at my suitcase, broken on the way, not realising this will be the last time I will see it. In it are almost all my reports on our battles in Pomerania. Returning to the battalions, the Squadron Leader orders the commanders to recall their soldiers from their positions.

1 Battalion is ordered to advance to a crossroads about four kilometres south of Herzfelde and wait for further instructions.

2 Battalion is to reach the road and autobahn crossroads two kilometres south of Erkner and wait for him.

Some men will be left with our equipment as transport will be sent for it. There is no news about 3 Battalion. We don't even know if they have left.

We get back into the car, very squashed, off to find the Corps HQ. To get there faster the Squadron Leader chooses a shorter route through the forest. The road turns out to be bad, very sandy, furrowed. Suddenly we hear explosions nearby, similar to anti-tank shots.

We stop the car. I take my sub-machine gun and we steal into the forest because we have seen movement there. It turns out to be some German soldiers. They're scared. They say the enemy has to be very near: the explosions were enemy anti-tank guns. We don't believe their story but decide to turn back as the driver says it's impossible to carry on.

On the way back to the road we try to gain information at a German unit command point. They don't know anything but hearing that the enemy is so close they get ready to leave. We drive back to Hangelsberg on the main road. All around we see devastation left by air bombardment: collapsed and burnt-out houses, shattered windows, holes in the road, etc. Further on the forest is burning on both sides of the road and thick smoke makes it difficult to see for a number of kilometres.

There's so little movement on the road we begin to think we're on the wrong one. When we meet a car we stop it to ask the person inside if Corps HQ is in

Hangelsberg. Our doubts turn out to be correct, since this morning Corps HQ transferred to Spreenhagen, 15 km further on to the south-west. We turn round and go to find the new place. From a distance we can see this is the right road. There are military vehicles going in both directions.

We arrive half an hour later. Corps HQ is in the forest in a barracks. It takes a lot of questioning to find the Ia department [the command centre]. The corps commander is not at HQ. All news and answers are given by the Corps Ia, who is very happy to see us.[2]

The Squadron Leader gives information about his battle group. It is in the forest about 27 km away, without transport, food, medicines or ammunition. In other words, it is at present incapable of movement and fighting. He asks for at least two lorries.

Hearing this, Corps Ia is not at all happy. Having listened to all the requests, the commander says he has little to give. They ring around but no-one wants a battle group as poor as we are. Whilst the Squadron Leader is with the Ia, I try to get maps. This time it's relatively easy: I'm given a whole pile. Only when I examine them do I find that large areas are already occupied by the enemy. I'm told they don't have any others.

Corps HQ is by a canal. There are lots of barges full of refugees. Working near HQ under the watchful eye of guards are three Russian prisoners. They are very pale and weak. On their backs they have a small bag, apparently with all their possessions. As far as I can see that means a cup. I don't realise that in a week's time I'll be like them, supervised by guards.

Out comes an angry Squadron Leader. I ask him the outcome. The HQ commander's last words were: 'If you can't move, then stay where you are and put yourself under the Berlin commandant's command.' The only good thing we have learned is information about the enemy.

---

2 The Ia was the second-in-command at the command centre.

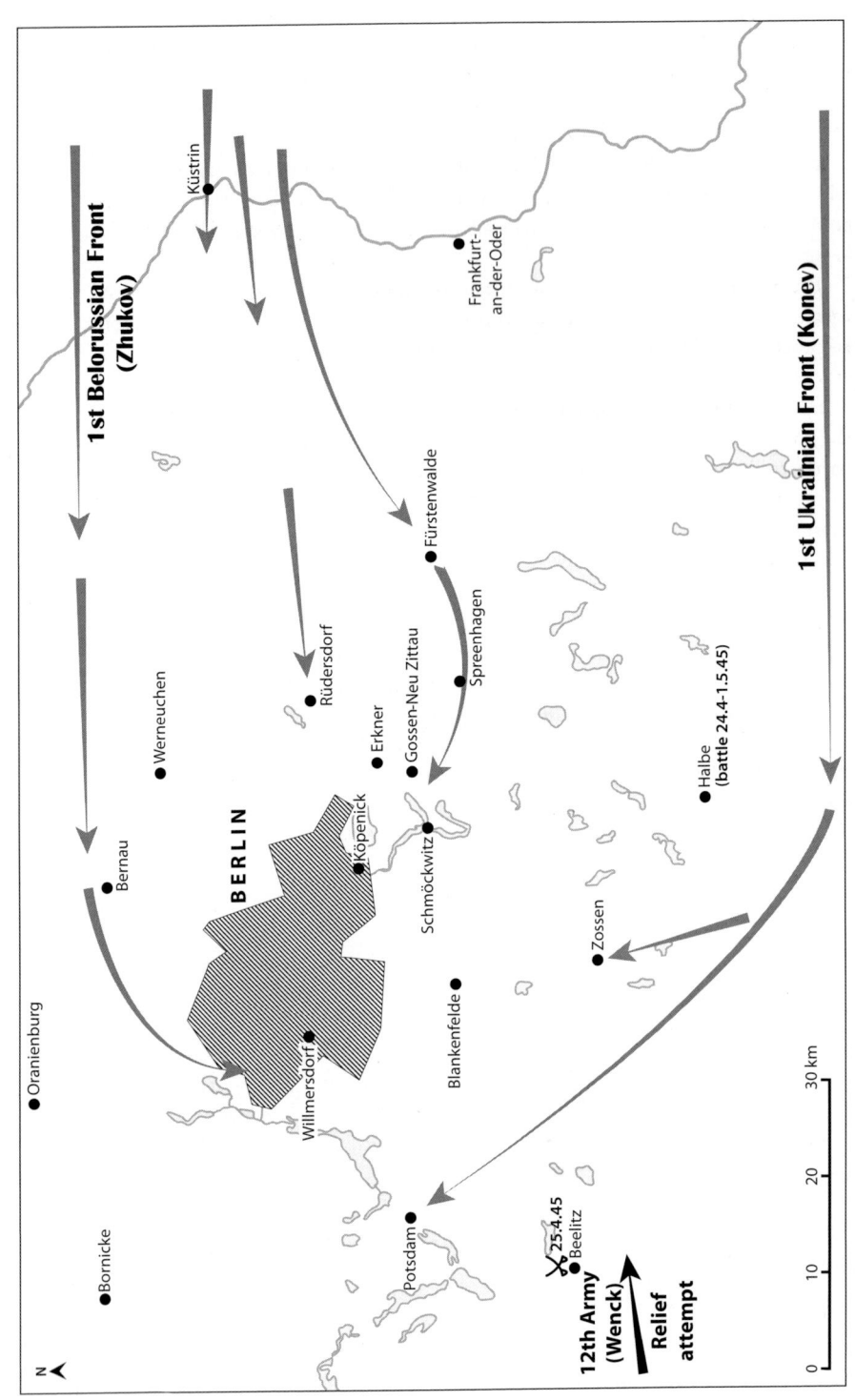

Map 7 In April 1945 the Red Army had crossed the Oder at Küstrin (now Kostrzyn nad Odrą) and Frankfurt and broken German resistance at the Seelow Heights. The Latvian 15th Division was positioned at Rüdersdorf to the south-east of Berlin to stop the Russians advance west. Colonel Janums took his men west, to the south of Berlin, turning into the forests around Beelitz.

Part Two

The Incredible Journey

8

The Decision to Desert

Despite the high price paid in human lives, the Red Army breakthrough at the Seelow Heights struck a devastating blow to Hitler's ability to continue the war. On 20 April, his 56th and last birthday, Soviet troops from the 3rd and 4th Guards Tank Armies were pushing towards the German Army's largest ammunition depot at Juterbog and the communications centre at Zossen. The 2nd Belorussian Front reached Bernau, 16 km north of the capital on the Berlin–Stettin autobahn.

To the south-west, the 1st Belorussian Front was moving through Muncheberg to Fürstenwalde, pursuing the retreating Ninth Army which now had orders to join up with Walter Wenck's 12th Army, approaching Berlin from the west.[1] Berlin was on the verge of being encircled, and for Colonel Janums and his 800 Latvians, that meant a move had to be made now – or they were doomed. In his diary, First Lieutenant Bušmanis recorded this bleak assessment of the situation in the south-east of the city.[2]

> The enemy is attacking Berlin from the east and in a wide sweep attempting to fight their way into the city from the north and south. The sky is full of enemy planes. It's hard to see if they are Bolshevik, American or English. I can't make it out.
>
> They attack moving vehicles and other targets both singly and in groups. On the way here we had to hide in the ditch on a number of occasions. Now, too, driving through one of numerous suburbs, we hear the roar of a plane above us. The driver drives on about 10 metres and parks under a tree.

---

1 Ziemke, p.84.
2 The retreat of the Ninth Army from the Seelow Heights, with orders to head west and join forces with the Twelfth Army of Walter Wenck, led to the encirclement of 88,000 troops in the Spree Forest near Halbe. Vastly outnumbered by 280,000 Soviet troops with 280 tanks and 1,500 aircraft, the Ninth Army made three attempts to break out over the final week of April 1945, losing 30,000 men killed. Units from the Ninth Army did meet up with the Twelfth Army and then retreated westwards to the Elbe where they crossed the river using the partially destroyed bridge at Tangermunde and surrendered to the Americans between 4–7 May 1945. Soviet casualties at Halbe were also extremely high, with around 20,000 men killed, along with an estimated 10,000 civilian dead.

We hear the familiar sound of a falling bomb. Leutnant Metten, sitting on the left, tears open his door and jumps out. I want to do the same but don't have time. The others don't either. There's a shattering explosion behind us. The car is thrown forward three to four metres, followed by a wave of falling stones, sand, broken branches, shattered glass. A moment later it is all past.

On the road, not far from the car, lies Leutnant Metten, moaning. I jump out and go to him. At the same moment, I hear a new roar. I press myself to the ground. Again the same: stones, sand, branches, glass. This time the bomb is further away. I hurry to the injured man.

I can see a big wound in his back, and blood is squirting out. I press with my hand to stop the bleeding. Leutnant Martin, seeing his compatriot injured, goes for help. Metten pleads not to be allowed to bleed to death. Two stretcher bearers arrive and he is carried away. I just manage to squeeze his hand in farewell.

We're all fine but the car is in bad shape. The first bomb made a sieve of the back. All the tyres are in shreds, the fuel container is leaking in two places. The driver opens the boot. It's a complete disaster. Everything is ruined, including both bottles of cognac, our prized possession.

But it looks like the boot has saved us. No bomb fragments have managed to penetrate the tightly-packed contents and reach us. The driver, ignoring all the flat tyres (the engine is fine) drives the car about 20 metres further on to a square to try to fix everything.

The Squadron Leader and I use our maps to ascertain where we are; about two kilometres from the place where 1 Battalion have been ordered to be. We decide to walk there. As we go, we see that the car couldn't have made it through to the battalion as the road is blocked. About 20 minutes later we reach them. Soldiers waiting for orders are resting, not at all concerned that the enemy may be nearby.

The Squadron Leader informs Captain R about the situation and orders him to meet up with the other battalion. We walk back. The driver is still trying to fix the car. I hurry to help. The priority is the fuel tank, so as not to lose its precious contents. We try everything to close the holes, to no avail. In the end we succeed by sticking postage stamps over them. The tyres have so many holes that it's impossible to find enough material to mend each one. I go off to search for something suitable.

I search all over town and go into a burnt-out yard. In the corner is a pile of burnt tyres and inner tubes. I find one inner tube for a car intact. Waving it like a trophy, I hurry back. The driver wastes no time in using it to fix the tyre. Leutnant Martin returns, saying he has managed to get Leutnant Metten to a *lazarett* [field hospital].

There is a new air raid. We hide in the nearest shelter, leaving the car to its fate. As soon as the raid is over, back to work. When the car is ready we drive to 2 Battalion [and] 15 minutes later 1 Battalion arrives. The Squadron Leader gathers together all the officers and relates the conversation in Corps HQ and our present situation.

Everyone understands that without transport we're battle-incapacitated. All the squadron property, left in the ditch in Herzfelde about 12 km from us, is basically written off, as there is no chance of getting it here. We are surprised – what kind of corps is it that doesn't have two heavy vehicles to give us to use?

What do we have? Food: as much as each soldier has in his bread bag. Ammunition: as much as a soldier has in his pocket or bag; six to nine rounds for mortars. No other medicines other than those in the orderly bags. The worst thing is there is no news about 3 Battalion. Some soldiers say that on the way here they saw some soldiers at the side of the road with the Latvian emblem. The two units were actually agonisingly close. The 3rd (Recce) Battalion had been unable to continue down the road to Fürstenwalde and took up positions in the forest by Erkner, between the autobahn and the town, while Janums' men were by the motorway junction near Erkner.

The Squadron Leader questions these men carefully; he's decided to go and have a look. In an effort to recover property, squadron commanders will send out some men to try to find any vehicles or carts. I try to persuade passing drivers to go and get the property. Everyone refuses, and I bid a silent goodbye to my things for the fourth time in this war.

After the events at Corps HQ, seeing the chaos in the German army, an idea is hatching in the Squadron Leader's mind not to get involved in any more battles but to try to take the whole squadron out of the Berlin arc by using the present lack of specific orders.

He has decided to do it soon, as [if he doesn't] Berlin will be completely surrounded from all sides. If not today, then in the next few days. He wants to make the squadron pull out to the west, to reach the Americans or English. The only problem is that it's not clear exactly where they are.

He shares his idea with the officers with the proviso not to tell the soldiers. With his next order, so as to hide the retreat and not allow the enemy to surprise us, the Squadron Leader orders both battalions to take up positions: 1 Battalion east of Erkner and Woltersdorf and 2 Battalion east of Neu Zittau, with HQ in the village of Gosen, about four kilometres west of Erkner.

The Squadron Leader invites Oberleutnant Martin and myself to accompany him in looking for 3 Battalion. We drive around, it's very dark, we can't see much. Now and then we get out of [the] car to have a closer look. Nothing. Hours pass. We have a problem: one of the mended tyres is letting out air.

The driver stops to change the wheel. Planes fly over and drop a series of bombs where we would have been had we not stopped to change the tyre. We thank God. Eventually the Squadron Leader says, 'We won't find anything in the dark. Let's go to Gosen. We'll carry on looking tomorrow.'[3]

After a number of near-misses involving planes dropping bombs where their car had been moments previously, Bušmanis and commander Colonel Vilis Janums realised

---

3 The diary of Edvīns Bušmanis, pp.5–10.

that when the Squadron Leader used his torch to read the map in the car, the light from it could be seen from the sky much better than he had thought. From then on, Janums covered his head completely when reading the map.

Sent to defend the land gap between the canals at Erkner and the Seddiner See north of Gosen, Colonel Janums had decided that now was the moment to take advantage of the chaos and confusion to withdraw the 850 men with him and abandon his positions in the south-east. It was a high-risk strategy if the group was apprehended – he would almost certainly have been shot on the spot for desertion. First he needed to get rid of the two SS officers who were attached to his unit. He told the story in his autobiography *Mana Pulka Kauja Gautas* (*My Regiment in Battle*):

> On 21 April Hauptsturmführer Walli made himself known at the Army unit HQ early in the morning. He didn't know where his battalion – the Recce Battalion – was. I said to him sharply, 'You personally don't matter but I want to know where the Recce Battalion is, as it's assigned to me.'
>
> Walli tried to defend himself, saying that the men were not where they should have been when he went there. I said to him, 'Use every available method to find them.' But Walli showed an unmistakeable wish to remain in my command post.
>
> As well as Hauptsturmführer Walli there was also an SS-Obersturmführer Martins with him. It's possible that both SS men suspected something, because they followed me like shadows everywhere, and I was afraid they could mess up our plans. I had a sudden thought as to how to get rid of them. I was convinced these men would be unwilling to follow me into intensive enemy fire, so I took them with me to check the situation at the front.
>
> When we arrived at the area of Neu Zittau the enemy opened fire, as if I'd given an order. I went straight to the end of the bridge which at that moment was under intense fire. When we found ourselves in the line of fire, both SS men were obviously nervous. I was sure that at this moment they would be happy if there were an excuse for them to be somewhere else.
>
> I pulled them behind the corner of a house and showed them where the battle was going on at the present moment at the front. 'Obviously I can't leave the area,' I said. 'But very soon we are going to run out of ammunition, and apart from that the men are fighting completely separately and it's now the second day that there have been no direct orders from above.'
>
> I asked Hauptsturmführer Walli to go the general HQ to inform the commanding general of the regiment's situation and to get orders for further activity. I ordered SS-Obersturmführer Martin to go with him and secure ammunition, food and transport. Both men happily departed, having been given the excuse to leave that they were looking for.
>
> I too could breathe more easily, because wasn't anybody now in the regiment who could interfere with me putting my ideas into practice. Without wasting time I returned to HQ and wrote an order for the 32nd Regiment to move to Blankenfelde when darkness fell, where they would receive new orders.

> I told Lieutenant Stanovskis, who had arrived to receive these orders, that the battalion was not to engage with the enemy in serious fighting. I added that this written order was given so that the battalion could go past gendarme checkpoints without hindrance.
>
> On the map I saw that on the eastern side of Schmöckwitz was a bridge. I was afraid that guards might be on this bridge and that they might not allow us across to the western bank of the canal. I wanted to tread carefully. So I order 2nd Company commander Lieutenant Vaivads to go with his company to Schmöckwitz, to take this bridge and ensure that the regiment can cross over it..[4]

At the southern end of the Seddiner See where Berlin meets Brandenburg, the bridge at Schmöckwitz was a strategically important obstacle for Colonel Janums and his escape attempt. If they could get across it, then they could stay off the main roads and avoid German patrols and military movements as the Wenck Army advanced east to Berlin. Once far enough west, they could divert south into the forests once across the Oder-Spree Canal – which they did.

This was a risky calculation for Colonel Janums as he prepared his men to march west at 1800 hours on 21 April 1945. If they hit a checkpoint manned by gendarmes, they risked being accused of desertion by the Germans and the alarm being raised. If they stayed, they would be right in the path of the advancing Red Army. Although some Latvian historians – and even Colonel Vilis Hāzners – took the view that 'Janums lost a battalion', in effect he rolled the dice and won, saving the lives of 850 men. But taking advantage of this short window when he had sent the SS men away meant that he had to leave the Recce Battalion behind.

Among the Recce Battalion men left behind was Oļģerts Bunga. His group moved south without any problems.

> On 20 April 1945 we were seated in trucks, issued cartridges for our guns and Panzerfausts, then driven through Neubrandenburg and Neustrelitz to the Berlin suburbs. I don't remember where we were dropped off. We walked through several suburban regions without any serious contact with the enemy; nobody was killed or injured.
>
> We were stationed in a forest on the outskirts, near Erkner. I didn't notice any arrangements for fighting. It seemed like everything was happening chaotically. I didn't notice any strict, specific, planned order; the trenches had been dug previously, but there was nothing else here.
>
> We saw Colonel Janums' unit when our company was sitting at the side of the road. That might have been on the second day after arriving in the Berlin suburbs, so around 22 April.[5]
>
> Janums was marching at the front of his unit. Soldiers from his unit told us that he was Colonel Janums. Those who knew people in the unit went and

---

4 Janums, *Mana Pulka Kauja Gaitas*.
5 Probably the day before this, either 20th or 21st April.

80 ESCAPE FROM BERLIN

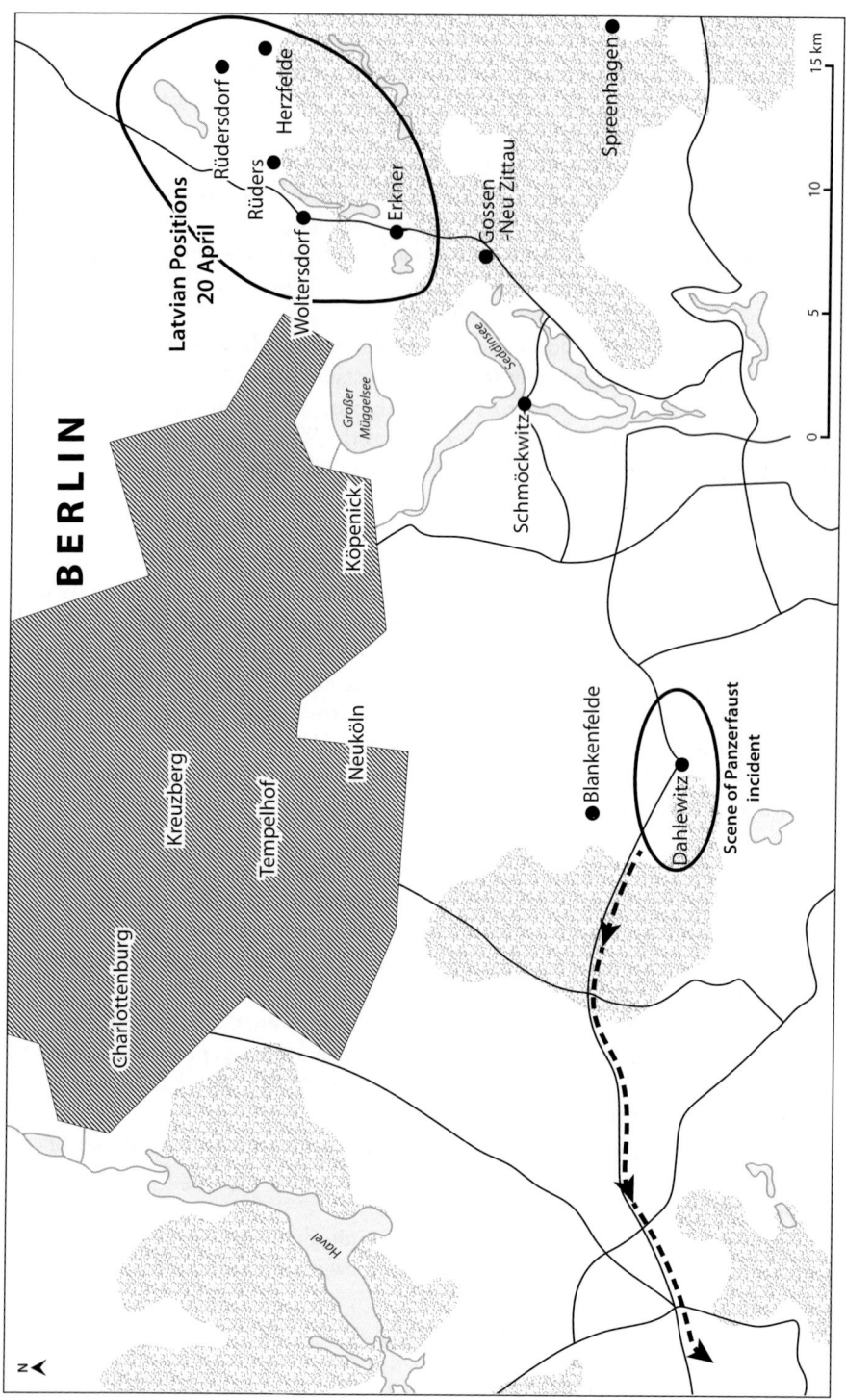

Map 8 The bridge at Schmöckwitz.

joined them. The unit wasn't big, I think it was no bigger than 100, 200 or 300 soldiers. I didn't know anyone there, so I stayed in the Reconnaissance Battalion. Janums' unit didn't stop and didn't make contact with us. This meeting was before we reached our Erkner positions.[6]

Uldis Dukurs had commanded a machine gun section through the battles in Pomerania; at Immenheim, Jastrow and the battle of Landeck Bridge. He arrived in Berlin freshly promoted to sergeant, with an Iron Cross First Class from Jastrow. In video interviews recorded by the Museum of the Occupation of Latvia in 2003 and 2005, he described the journey to Berlin.

> From the Mecklenburg area where the 15th Division was, we travelled through the Berlin suburb of Bernau. All the roads were blocked with anti-tank mines and the remains after a heavy bombardment. At that moment Allied bombers appeared who, for some reason, didn't drop a single bomb. This was the last air raid on Berlin by the Americans and English. We were travelling in the direction of Frankfurt until battalion commander Walli had a wheel shot off his vehicle – the Russians were so near. We instantly made a U-turn back to Berlin.
>
> At that time Janums' squadron was retreating, as he had taken up position before us. Some say they met up with Janums' men and were invited to go with them. Janums, in his memoirs, states that he didn't find the Recce Battalion. That's not true. We retreated together. Janums didn't want to meet the Recce Battalion because it contained some Germans and he couldn't afford to begin his retreat with Germans present. The Recce Battalion knew he had left them behind [...]
>
> In one place we came across about 16 gendarmes on motorbikes, with MG-42 Bonesaws fitted to them. They stopped us. I tell them we have to go in the direction that Janums went. They say: 'Janums had 800 men. We couldn't stop him. But you – we'll send you where we need to.'
>
> We find a horse and a mortar. We get the horse, mortar and ammunition and so from now on we'll be a mortar brigade fighting from the rear. We spread out and enter Berlin, given the password 'Latvian 15th' and told to move to the centre of Berlin. We come to a canal with the Deutsche Reichsbank on the other side. We set up base there.[7]

---

6 Bunga's account confirms contact between the Recce Battalion and the Janums group, but as Colonel Janums was driving around at this time, it's unlikely it was him that Bunga saw. It's more likely to be the 1st Battalion led by other officers moving down from Herzfelde to link up with the 2nd Battalion at the autobahn junction at Erkner.
7 Uldis Dukurs (25.12.1924–16.09.2009), interview with Andrejs Edvīns Feldmanis from the Museum of the Occupation of Latvia 18.12.2003 and 19.01.2005. With thanks to Evita Feldentale and Daina Vītola. Dukurs is speaking with many years of hindsight, and – amid the 'fog of war' – Janums had to make a quick and fateful decision under pressure while Walli was away. It's clear there was contact between the two groups, but no-one with any seniority seems to have connected the two, and with ongoing air strikes and tanks approaching, finding cover and surviving was probably the priority. Janums did look for the Recce Battalion, could not find the men in the dark and then had to make a decision.

9

Edvīns Bušmanis, 21 April 1945

Colonel Janums and First Lieutenant Bušmanis reached Gosen after midnight and woke up the local Bürgermeister to demand a bed for the night. No soldiers from HQ had arrived by then. The next day, Bušmanis continued keeping his detailed diary:

> Next morning, 21 April, we're up for 0700. We find a piece of salted pork in the boot of the car and exchange part of it for bread. While we're having breakfast, a car drives up. To our amazement, out gets 3 Battalion commander Captain Walli and two other officers, both Germans.
>
> The Squadron Leader is furious. Curtly, he questions the Captain: where is his battalion and why has the commander only just arrived? Captain Walli is forced to admit he doesn't know where his battalion is as they aren't where they were ordered to be. He's been looking for them all this time, as well as us.
>
> We aren't happy about this. We had hoped the commander would bring the battalion to us. The Squadron Leader brings Captain Walli up to date with the present situation and says he has planned to go to Berlin to see the Chief Battle Commander for orders. Captain Walli will have to come with him. Then our soldiers arrive, led by Captain A.
>
> The Squadron Leader decides to go to Berlin, afraid the Germans will get a whiff of his plan to leave Berlin. Before leaving he gives Captain A. an order to find new premises for the HQ.
>
> Our driver has found out there is fuel to be had at the nearest petrol station. I sign the required requisition form. For a time we have fuel again. The Squadron Leader and Captain Walli go off in the car. Leutnant Martin very slowly gets ready to go to search for food in the Captain's car.
>
> About half an hour later the Squadron Leader's car appears again but only Captain Walli is in it. He says they haven't got to Berlin as the enemy began an offensive at Erkner and traffic to the centre stopped. The Squadron Leader has therefore stayed with 2 Battalion and ordered him and Leutnant Martin to go to Berlin. The latter likes this job much better than his original one and both proudly set off for Berlin.

> After a short while Captain A's messenger arrives to announce that a new HQ has been found not far away, about a kilometre away at the other end of village. I tell the men to collect everything and move to the new place.[1]

After more confusion, the HQ was finally set up in the village of Schmöckwitz. Janums spread the word among his officers that they are going to try and leave the Berlin arc and reach the Americans. Bušmanis keeps track of events.

> Captain Walli and Leutnant Martin have not yet returned. Loitering with us is a 3 Battalion Oberleutnant: a German who arrived at HQ together with Captain Walli and has stayed put. When the German goes out, the Squadron Leader announces that he has already begun to instigate his plan to leave the Berlin arc. He's given written orders to the commander of 2 Battalion to pull out to the south-west, make his way to Blankenfelde, about 30 km from Schmöckwitz, and wait for us there. 1 Battalion is already amassing in the woods behind the village.[2]
>
> The biggest problem is going to be with food. As the soldiers haven't eaten since yesterday, the Squadron Leader sends Captain A to the town commandant to clarify if anything can be obtained. He goes and soon returns. It's possible to get something to eat but first the town battle commander wants to meet the commander.
>
> The Squadron Leader is agreeable but while he is still getting ready, the town commander – some German, with the rank of Squadron Lieutenant – comes to us. We stay on the verandah and listen to the conversation. The commander requests information about the battalion personnel and, as expected, wants to ensure that the soldiers take up defence positions south of Schmöckwitz.
>
> Our commander's attitude this time is overwhelmingly cool. He explains that he anticipates a special assignment. Two of his officers have already gone to Berlin to receive it. If they haven't returned by 1800, then in the interests of safety, he will give the order to take up position. Otherwise, he will act according to the order. On his part, he asks the commander about feeding the troops.
>
> The Squadron Lieutenant promises to do it. We can feel that the German does not trust us because, suddenly, he asks the Squadron Leader to show his documents, which of course he does. On leaving, the commandant promises to return at 1800. Left alone, we discuss our situation.
>
> The Squadron Leader has already said that he doesn't intend to wait for the commandant. Shortly before 1800 the battalion will leave the town and go to

---

1 The diary of Edvīns Bušmanis, pp.10–16.
2 Both *Latvian Legion* by Arturs Silgailis and the official history of the Legion *Latviešu Karavīrs Otra Pasaules Kara Laikā* (*The Latvian Soldier During World War Two*) refer to Blankenfelde, which is nearby, but in his diary First Lieutenant Bušmanis repeatedly refers to Blumenfelde. I have amended Bušmanis' version, quoted from direct orders to him from Colonel Janums, but for location, this area is south-west of Schönefeld airport.

Blankenfelde, irrespective of whether the food is ready or not. Of course, the stranger German is not present. His presence we feel the most keenly, because he is the only German, and he interferes with our plans the most. We can't decide how to get rid of him.

When the German returns, the Squadron Leader begins to question him about 3 Battalion: where is it, why wasn't it at the arranged place, etc. The 1st Leutnant of course can't answer. Then the Squadron Leader wants to know what is he going to do to find the battalion, what is he waiting for and why isn't he doing something?

The 1st Leutnant is so confused that he is ready to do anything. He asks the Squadron Leader for a car. The request is refused: the Squadron Leader hasn't got a car to give him. If Mister Oberleutnant wants to ride, he suggests using a 'tram'. The conversation ends with the German going to the local Post Central to ring the Berlin chief commandant to find out where Captain Walli and 1st Leutnant Martin have got to.

The stipulated hour approaches. At the moment there are no Germans among us who could hinder the start of our march. The ones sent to Berlin still haven't returned and the third one, sitting by the phone, hasn't shown himself.

Captain A. has been to check on how the food preparation is progressing and concludes that it won't be ready before 1800. The Germans aren't hurrying with it; they obviously want to see us in position first. But that makes no difference to the Squadron Leader.

At 1745, he orders 2 Company to leave their positions by the bridge and all the battalion to be ready to leave. Fifteen minutes later we leave our verandah and, undisturbed by anyone, leave town. We have decided to use only the small roads, avoiding main roads and highways. We're happy to get rid of all the German officers.

Amongst the soldiers there is a German – Obersergeant Ortner – but he, not suspecting anything, marches along with the others. The Squadron Leader's car with another officer inside bounces along at the head of the march. Shortly after leaving the town, our chosen route takes us past an aerodrome for a good distance. We can see planes taking off and landing.

We think to ourselves that if the Schmöckwitz commandant had notified our departure, here would be a good place to stop us. But nobody does.[3]

After the Janums Battle Group had been marching west for about 10 km, they were joined, to their disgust, by the German Oberleutnant they had left at Schmöckwitz. The two German officers had not returned from Berlin, and the phone call from Central Command never came. Finding out that his unit had gone he jumped on a bicycle and chased after them. When he caught them up, he tried to find out where the battalion was heading, but the soldiers couldn't tell him as they didn't know – and

---

3   Diary of Edvīns Bušmanis, pp.16–19.

he didn't dare ask the Squadron Leader or any of the officers. Bušmanis continues the story.

> Marching on, near a village, we are stopped by gendarmes [military police], who ask for the commander. We're not surprised by the question, as we've been waiting for the Germans to try to delay us. We explain that the Squadron Leader is in his car far ahead and can we help instead?
>
> The gendarmes explain that they want the battalion to turn back to the previous village to pick up some automatic rifles and other weapons. The squadron weapons officer, 1st Lieutenant B, at first wants to refuse, but having thought about it, he takes a horse and cart from the village and goes to pick up the weapons. The battalion, contrary to the military police expectations, continues to march on.
>
> Arriving at the designated place, 1st Lieutenant B doesn't find any weapons after all. By now the soldiers have been on the move all day and are hungry, but they march robustly. At a crossroads, where for a moment there is a traffic jam, our last remaining German officer disappears. The soldiers say he was seen getting into a truck driving off in the direction of Berlin.
>
> There are tank defences on the road, which are already closed off. Soldiers on foot have no problem getting round them. The Squadron Leader's car is not so fortunate. He is following a group of young people in uniform but with no recognition marks who are pulling a huge cart. They obviously have to open the defences by hand; not an easy task. When they do so, the Squadron Leader's car sneaks through and disappears into the night.
>
> The youth group have caught on to this 'trick' and I am approached by one of the column leaders, who suggests our soldiers could help with the opening and closing of the defences. 'Why?' I cheekily reply. 'We don't have any vehicles. As far as we're concerned, the defences can stay shut!'

In his memoir, Legionnaire Arvīds Kalupnieks looks back on how the Latvians slipped away in groups from their positions at Erkner, Rüdersdorf and Gosen as the Soviets closed in:

> The Colonel and his battalion commanders discuss and decide their next plans. The Russians, not meeting with any resistance, are advancing quickly. We just worry that they'll cut off our path. The German assault troops are, literally, useful only for scaring birds. The military police, who still yesterday were a key factor in the city, have suddenly disappeared. Over the canal, the *Janumieši* can already see the first Russian assault troops, flowing towards Berlin in an uninterrupted stream. It would be foolish to start shooting at them now, and some of us have to control our hate and get it together so as not to get us all killed.
>
> A delicate plan for going forward has been worked out. Every man knows that every obstacle, if there is no other way around it, has to be destroyed with the

gun in his hands. The battalion leaves its positions and goes to Schmöckwitz, as ordered, around 20 km away. The regiment's officers, communications and field engineer platoons and the anti-tank group have already reached there.

The battalions camp in a small forest on the west of the town. It seems like the battle has died down. Further away, we hear the clatter of tank chains and the noise of motors. We have not yet had any fighting with the Russians.

The Colonel is very tired, but he doesn't want to rest. No time; he has to look over the initial plans, because the latest news is that the Russians are also driving a wedge from the south, towards Potsdam. We have to get past them first. Plus our rations ran out today.

A German *Volkssturm* commander, having discovered that a regiment two battalions in size has arrived, hurries to give the order that we have to come under his command and take up positions over a 15–20 km wide zone. The Colonel explains that we have a different job, and that we are awaiting our communications commander's arrival from Berlin at any moment with fresh orders.

This doesn't seem to placate this 'gentleman' because he returns in 10 or 15 minutes accompanied by a Lieutenant-Colonel from the German Army, who announces himself as the battle commander for this suburb, and explains that all units within his area, even those who arrive later, must be instantly re-routed to defending Berlin. Based on this, he as the battle commander orders us to take our positions according to his instructions.

The Colonel once again states that our communications commander has been sent to Berlin for further orders. But it seems like this doesn't interest the German Lieutenant-Colonel, who is more concerned with his high rank and wish to command something – anything. That's why he feels like he has a delicious morsel in his hands and he can't put it down. The argument gets to the point where the Colonel is teaching this man battle tactics. The most interesting is when he states his intention to take up front positions in an area already defended by natural barriers – canals and rivers, forests and bogs – leaving an undefended area to its right easy to capture. Plus, the frontlines, canal and hill passages are already guarded by German assault troops.

The Colonel sees how difficult it will be to get rid of this man, because he is back again 20 minutes later. That means we can't delay any longer. The final argument between the Colonel and the Lieutenant-Colonel is particularly sharp.

The Colonel gives the battalion commanders the final orders to march, and gives further details on what to do and how to act. To avoid being noticed, each battalion will go a different way. Our meeting point is at 2200 in a village around 15 km from Schmöckwitz.

The Colonel will go with the first battalion, communications and field engineer platoons and the anti-tank group. The Russian attack on [the Berlin suburb of] Köpenick has begun. The second Russian arm is going further south from Fürstenwalde towards Potsdam and Brandenburg. The units organise themselves and we start the march. The Colonel says, 'Sons, we'll have to march all night tonight. I don't see any other option if we want to break out of this encirclement.'

So our big march begins on 21 April at around 1500. Basically, it's a race against the Russians. Who will be first? It seems like that is what is on all of our minds. The Colonel, despite his 51 years, walks at the front, and some young men lack the stamina to keep up. He is everywhere in his fatherly care. He is caring but strict. It seems like the Colonel and his men have grown together into one flesh.

The column heads along small roads past an aerodrome. German planes still roar. Some lift off and head east. On the sides of the roads are trenches, but there is nobody to fill them. We have marched for an hour when we have our first break of five minutes. Our pace is fast. Two hours later we reach a crossroads, where we receive the order to rest. We have a small meal. German columns heading towards Berlin approach from our left.

A car drives along the road we have been marching down. Through the twilight, stuck on at the front next to the vents, we see the word *Feldgendarmerie* [Military police]. The car stops at the crossroads and an officer steps out. He asks for our Colonel. We start to worry about the Colonel's fate: we wish he was with us so we could defend him if something bad were to threaten him. We tell the officer that he is further forward. We answer, 'We don't know' when he asks where we're going. His car speeds forward, because he is confused by the movement of the German soldiers. Most of the Germans have no weapons.

We soon receive orders to keep marching. Everyone has serious faces. Quietly, the men start marching; everyone understands that this isn't the time for talking. A secretive, leery silence is all around. Through this silence, we hear the clattering of weapons and the steady sound of marching. We pass the Colonel's car, our only vehicle. His watchful eye passes over every soldier, as if wanting to know their hidden thoughts. Once the final man has passed, he goes to the head of the column. He is satisfied, because he knows that all the men will follow him, and all of our survival or death depends on this.

The roadside trees hide our march well. In the distance, we see the reflections of the Berlin fires. The air is shaken by the roar of individual plane engines and the edge of Berlin drones under the heavy Russian artillery. We have walked a long way when our column suddenly stops. Ahead, our way is blocked by an anti-tank obstacle. We don't want to leave our only vehicle, the Colonel's car, behind. We start dismantling the blockade.

A fleet of cars approaches from behind. It also stops and waits for the dismantling. It turns out that these cars belong to the German Nordland SS division. The men reply to the Germans' questions grudgingly and reservedly. Of course, this doesn't satisfy the Germans' characteristic curiosity. The blockade is dismantled and we continue. It is now very late, approaching midnight.[4]

---

4 Arvīds Kalupnieks, *Colonel Janums and his Men* in Leitītis, trans. Mara Walsh-Sinka (1986).

First Lieutenant Bušmanis picks up the story.

> About five kilometres before Blankenfelde, the Squadron Leader sends Captain A and Ltn V to find out if 2 Battalion has arrived. Left without transport, the Squadron Leader joins in the column and marches with it. I keep near him. For a time we march between 1 Company and the tank destroyer platoon. We are forced to stop at yet another obstruction. When everyone has squeezed through, so do we, but not in the same place as we were.
>
> We are now at the head of the column. Unknowingly, we have saved our lives. A few hundred metres past the blockade, going through the village of Dahlewitz, there is a sudden, powerful explosion behind us. Rockets and shards fly through the air. Even though I'm about 20 metres from the explosion, I feel something sting my left hip.
>
> For a moment I don't understand what happened. Has a bomb been dropped on the road from a plane, an enemy cannon shot? As the noise dies down, I hear moans and calls for help. I hurry there. I see about ten soldiers lying on the road. Others, seemingly less injured, are limping towards me. A moment later it's clear there has been a serious accident.
>
> One of the tank destroyer platoon soldiers had a Panzerfaust hanging round his neck. That has fallen and exploded in the middle of the formation. Three have died on the spot but eleven are seriously injured. Lieutenant P, our doctor, is so far ahead it's impossible to call him back but the orderlies know their job without him and immediately start to give assistance.
>
> The Squadron Leader hurries up. I report what has happened. He is horrified but decisive as always. A moment later he halts a vehicle going in the direction of Berlin and forces them to take the badly-wounded. The dead have to remain where they are.
>
> When half an hour later the column sets off again, the lightly-wounded march alongside. When passing the scene of the accident, the soldiers silently bid farewell to their dead. Only now do I remember the pain in my hip.
>
> I feel that there is moisture collecting in my left boot and my hip is beginning to hurt. I feel around the spot and realise the moisture is blood. I pull out my only dressing and put a dressing on myself there at the side of the road. Late, I hurry after those who have gone on.
>
> In the accident we have lost 14 men altogether because those who have been taken to Berlin to the *lazarett* have to be counted as lost. Later it turns out that of those who fell into Russian hands only one managed to survive – Private Z.[5]

Arvīds Kalupnieks writes of this moment:

> We enter the village of Dahlewitz; our column turns right onto the Dresden-Berlin motorway. Suddenly, close by, a powerful explosion takes place at a

---

5 Bušmanis' diary, pp.16–19.

EDVĪNS BUŠMANIS, 21 APRIL 1945   89

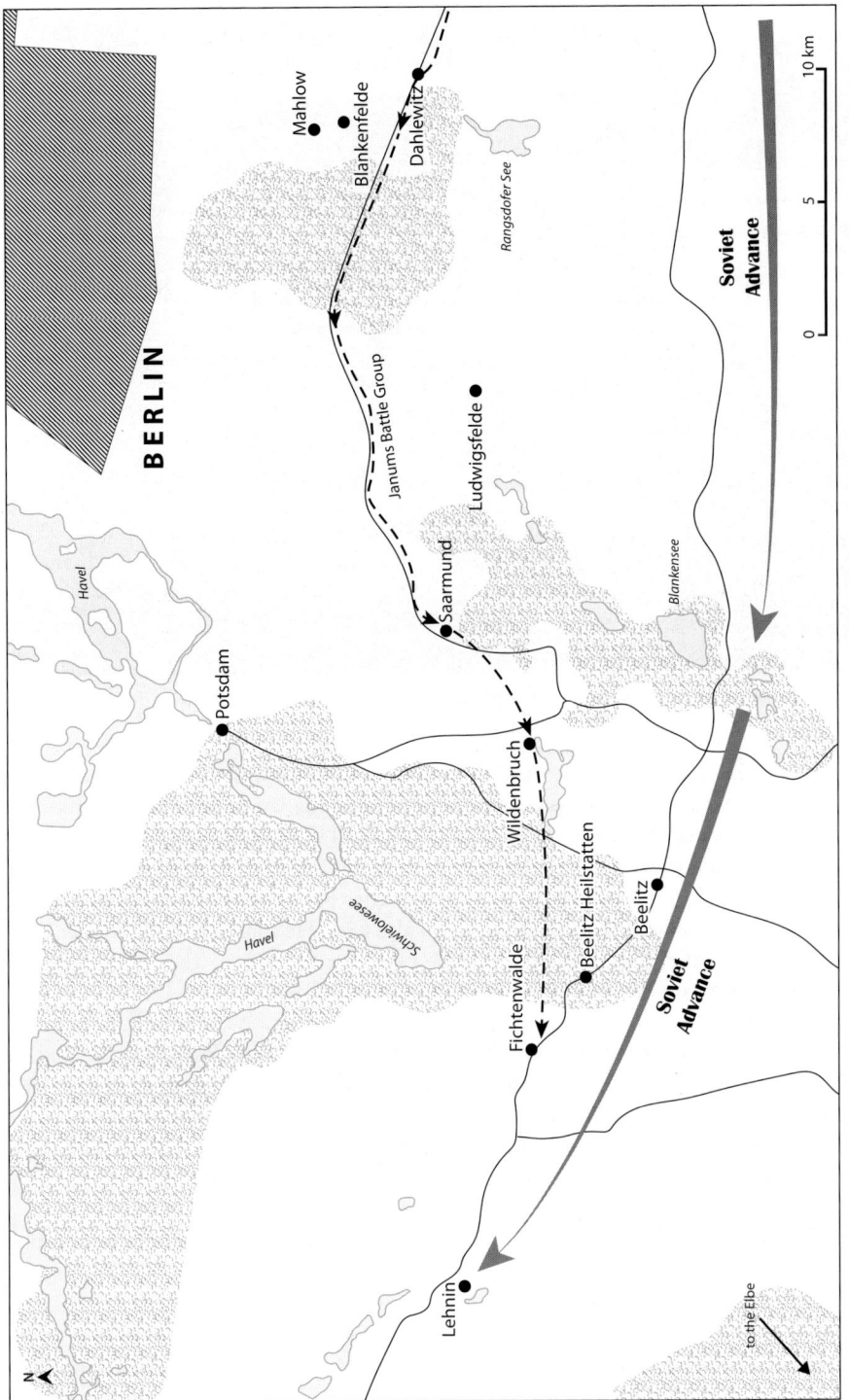

Map 9   The route of the Janums Battle Group south of Berlin in April 1945, marching from Rüdersdorf, Woltersdorf and Erkner west to Dahlewitz.

Jānis Urpens, who was wounded in the explosion of the Panzerfaust at Dahlewitz. Picture: author.

crossroads. Soldier instinct makes the soldiers lie down. It turns out that a Panzerschreck shell exploded. The man was carrying it around his neck, the string broke suddenly, and the explosion happened when it hit the ground.

The shout goes up: 'Medics!' Three die of serious injuries, 12 men are injured. The medics do what they can. German cars drive by, but they don't stop at the scene of the accident. The Colonel is soon also here. He stands in front of a car, stops it, and the wounded are put in the car under his orders. The corpses are cleared, and we can continue.[6]

Seven decades later, I am sitting in a house in Cambridgeshire describing the diaries of First Lieutenant Bušmanis to Jānis Urpens, a soldier who was on that march with Colonel Janums and who is now in his nineties. I'm picking out stories to see if he knows any of them, and I read him the Bušmanis account of the Panzerfaust incident. Jānis suddenly puts down his cup of tea.

'That was me! I was there when that happened – I was one of the wounded!'

I'm staggered. This is the kind of moment documentary-makers dream of, but better. He's obviously a little stunned too.

---

6 Memoirs of Arvīds Kalupnieks. Trans. Māra Sinka-Walsh. Panzerschrecks and Panzerfausts were different types of tank-killing bazookas.

'It changed the course of my life ... possibly saved it.'

He explains. Jānis and his friend Alberts Balodis were each heading a line in a three-line column behind the group commander. Suddenly there were urgent calls from up ahead: 'Tank destroyers! Tank destroyers!' Jānis described what happened next.

'On my left overtaking me came two chaps running. The second one had two tank-destroying rockets [Panzerfausts] tied on his back, swinging about badly. I just had enough time to think, *that's not very safe*, when there was a huge explosion and bright lights and sparks in the distant fir trees. *Just like Christmas*, I thought.'

'What happened to the soldier?' I ask. 'Was he killed?'

'Oh yes,' he says. 'He wouldn't have stood a chance. The rocket would have fallen right behind him – and those things could blow up a tank!'

Jānis wrote down his memories for his family and turned up the papers for my visit. The ink from his old daisywheel printer has faded more than a little, but I can make out the story:

> Then my right eye started to shut and something wet was running down my face, but I didn't feel any pain. There was a lot of running about and I realise that I am not the only one with a bandage. The platoon commander, the first group commander and another older corporal all have leg wounds and scratches further up. Alberts and I both have head wounds.
>
> *Sanitari* [medics] are working fast and soon we are all bandaged. Our platoon has lost all its commanding staff. The company commander is trying to persuade us to stay with the unit so we don't get lost.
>
> But the Colonel [Janums, the Squadron Leader] has different ideas. 'On no account can you boys stay with us,' he says. 'We will probably be marching all night and you won't be able to keep up. Just around the corner there is a Luftwaffe lorry and the driver can take you on.' There was no further argument.
>
> There was plenty of space in the lorry and just enough seats. Hardly anyone talks and the ones who still have cigarettes light them. I try to get one between my teeth and find that my jaw is seized up. The lorry starts up and we drive on, everyone silent with their own thoughts.

Jānis and Alberts were taken to a Luftwaffe hospital at Spandau West, disarmed and given treatment. Jānis lay on a stretcher in an overcrowded corridor and tried to get some rest. The next morning he was woken by Alberts.

> Alberts is shouting in a loud voice: "Get up! Get up! The hospital is being evacuated, but only the walking cases." I struggled to my feet and outside we could see a crowd of wounded, moving slowly, heading to the railway station. The Berlin S-bahn is still working! So we followed them.
>
> We arrive at West Kreuz [Western Cross] near the city centre, find a building that is undamaged and lie down and sleep. Some hours later the commanding officer announces: "Anyone living in Berlin and able to return home will be

given a Certificate of Leave. There is still one road open out of the city through Nauen to the west. Anyone wishing to go west, I will issue a Certificate Richtung West [Direction west]."

We were issued with the certificates and told to go by S-bahn to Potsdam, 16 miles [25 km] away. Our group of five Latvians went straight to the nearest railway station and headed to Potsdam. The station was completely destroyed by bombing but the street outside leading to the palace was quite presentable, still lots of standing houses.

In the distance we could see a gendarme post controlling papers, but by the time we arrived there they had disappeared. We proceed slowly as three of our chaps had shrapnel wounds in their legs. The road to Nauen is empty – just a lorry now and then. Later it starts to fill with pedestrians but they are facing us and going to Berlin. They are agitated and try and persuade us to turn round because 'the Russians are in front of us.' We have been all through Pomerania and experience showed us that there is always a way round. We decide to carry on 'Richtung West'.

Walking along we see a nice villa on the road and coming closer we notice a lorry loaded with several SS soldiers along the side. I have an idea that we should try them for a lift. The Sergeant is very kind and explains that he would save us if he could but he has to load up the general's furniture.

Suddenly he takes out his pistol and goes onto the road to stop an oncoming lorry, loaded with fuel drums. The driver stares at the pistol while the Sergeant explains to him that he has to take the wounded to Nauen. The pistol stays in his hand while we get on top of the drums. He wishes us good luck and we continue 'Richtung West'.

The drive is slow and monotonous and as we get further west there are more aircraft in the sky. Eventually the lorry pulls up in Nauen at a first aid centre, which is very quiet this time of night, and there are plenty of empty beds. What a relief...[7]

Janums' men marched on, shocked and depressed, and reached Blankenfelde village half an hour later, around midnight.[8] They discovered 2 Battalion had arrived an hour before and the battalion commander, Major A, was waiting for them impatiently. Edvīns Bušmanis writes:

With great difficulty, in the dark, in a strange village, we find a small room where we can fix our route onwards away from the keen eyesight of the pilots.

---

[7] Interview with Jānis Urpens and his private notes made available to author, Fenstanton, March 2019. From Nauen they hitched a lift on a lorry to Schwerin, where they found a Latvian hospital, then surrendered to the Americans on 2 May. Both Jānis and Alberts came to the UK for work and never returned to Latvia.

[8] Bušmanis calls it Blumenfelde, and says it was the 2nd Battalion. Kalupnieks has it as the 1st Battalion. It is possible both are right, and they were with separate units.

According to news gained from passers-by, local police and soldiers, we find out that the enemy is also coming our way. An hour ago the Russians took a village five kilometres south-east of Blankenfelde and are now approaching us. The Squadron Leader and battalion commanders have a meeting and decide to move on immediately.

Hearing the decision to move on, the soldiers lose heart. They are all exhausted. Most haven't eaten for two days and now, instead of the expected rest, they have to march on. There's no alternative. You don't argue with an order. Only now do Captain A and Lieutenant V drive up. They've been round and about looking for Blankenfelde. On the way they've found some alcohol and are now in high spirits. With the Squadron Leader's permission I squeeze into the car too, as the two occupants flatly refuse to get out.

Now our column moves along one of the main roads: refugees and other retreating army units walk with us. We haven't been walking long when news reaches us that enemy tanks have reached a village three kilometres to the south of us. So that they can't cut us off, the Squadron Leader orders a change in route and takes a larger detour around the place. Whether the precaution was necessary or not, it's difficult to tell. No-one bothers us on our new route.

It's with considerable difficulty that the soldiers are keeping in formation. Everyone is downcast and quiet after the recent accident [with the Panzerfaust]. No-one tries to leave the formation, lag behind or throw down their weapon. Everyone knows very well that the enemy is following us, who will show no mercy, who can only be greeted with weapons in our hands. With the Squadron Leader's permission our mortars are dumped in a roadside ditch, as there is almost no ammunition for them.

In the dark we pass through the villages of Gudow and Güterfelde.[9] As a new day dawns, we are still on the march. For every fifty minutes marching, we have ten minutes rest. So it was yesterday, so it is all night and without fail continues now. Only the speed at which we are marching, in comparison to yesterday, is considerably slower. We have left behind Kol-Saarmund.[10] If during the night it was possible to move without hiding, then now in the daylight, as soon as any enemy plane appears, we have to find shelter.

All the time, at every opportunity, we collect information about the situation, about the enemy. We are no longer part of an organic unit, whose communication network, reconnaissance, etc., would give regular updates. Now we have to find out for ourselves – and that's not easy.

Questioning the locals isn't very difficult but they don't know much. More can be gained from the local army units, but to do that is much harder. They in turn want to know who we are, where we are going and what our assignment is. On these occasions we have to use all our guile to say as little as possible about

---

9 Around 17 km west of Blankenfelde.
10 Now heading further south but still west.

ourselves and, not raising suspicion, find out all that we can. Up to now it has worked well.

According to information collected, the Russians are moving to the west and north-west, giving credibility to the thought that they will try to encircle Berlin. In our estimation, they are now trying to reach Potsdam or even Brandenburg, in this way closing the circle around the forces in the Berlin area.

We scrutinise the map. It's not only an old edition and therefore doesn't really match reality, but is also large scale, having been removed from a classroom wall. We try to imagine ourselves as Russians in order to second-guess their plans.

To the south of us is the Berlin ring road; in front, to the west, the road to Dresden, more railway lines and larger roads that all lead to Potsdam. Beyond, more wooded areas begin, where the road network is sparser. We consult together to cross the roads today.

At about 1000 we catch up with a small English and French prisoner-of-war group. Like us they are going to the west and without any supervision. From somewhere they have got some carts and piled in all their poverty. (To be honest, it can't be called 'poverty'. They have more than all our squadron soldiers put together. We notice, too, that all their suitcases are exactly the same – and new.)

The prisoners of war pull and push the carts themselves. We don't have either carts or suitcases. It's a bonus if someone has a rucksack on their back – but even though we've been walking for over 16 hours, we move faster than them.

About 1100 near Wildenbruch, we allow ourselves a longer rest. The Squadron Leader again calls both battalion commanders and other officers to discuss the present situation. He has decided to march on, cross two railway lines and roads and reach Fichtenwalde, a small village in the woods, which according to the map is beyond all the roads leading to Potsdam. Even though the officers are as tired as the men, there is no dissent.[11]

---

11 Bušmanis' diary, pages 16–19. Their position is to the south-west of Berlin and south of Potsdam, near where the A10 ring road meets the A2 north to Potsdam. They then leave the roads in the area just after the present junction of the A10 with the A9 Munich to Berlin road, and head further south-west into woodland and swamps towards Güterglück and the Elbe, a distance of around 75 km as the crow flies.

10

On the Trail of the Janums Battle Group

I pick up a dark blue Fiat 500 rental car from Berlin's new Brandenburg Airport and steer it onto the autobahn heading west. Janums and his men marched past this area on their way towards the Elbe, and I am going to follow their route as closely as I can. The Fiat does not have sat nav and my phone cannot find a wifi signal, so I will have to navigate from a road map. Janums had a compass and a map torn from a school classroom wall, as I remember.

The first stop comes after a few minutes at Dahlewitz, where the unfortunate accident with the Panzerfausts happened, killing several men and injuring Jānis Urpens and Alberts Balodis. Dahlewitz seems like a very pleasant and ordinary suburb linked by rail to Berlin with a small shopping centre, easy parking and an excellent kebab shop. I resume my journey west half-looking for places where a Panzerfaust might have gone off but soon I'm clear of Dahlewitz and through Blankenfelde heading for Grossbeeren.

At Guterfelde I turn left and head south to Saarmund, another village built along the main road and notable for its church with its tall thin spire and a schoolhouse dating back 100 years. The school was used until the early 1980s but local children are now taught in a more modern building. A sign nearby goes into the detail of which bits of the building were changed to relocate the road in the mid-1980s, but there's no doubt that this church with its distinctive spire would have been a landmark when Janums and his men went through here.

Leaving Saarmund for Tremsdorf and Fresdorf and heading for Beelitz, the landscape becomes fields of closely-planted sunflowers, their golden faces turned towards the sky, vying with each other for the light. I pull over to take a photograph and hear the sound of crickets coming from all around: one lands near the back of the Fiat.

Passing under Autobhan 10, I stay on the minor roads until Wildenbruch, a picturesque town on the banks of the Seddiner See and clearly very popular judging by the number of eating places I can see. I stop to look at the town's ancient church, which dates back to 1250 and the creation of the Beelitz-Saarmund-Berlin trade route. A bronze bell from the Middle Ages still rings everyday. In the churchyard there is a

The suburb of Dahlewitz today, to the south of Berlin. The village was the scene of a Panzerfaust accident which killed three men and injured twelve. Picture: author.

ON THE TRAIL OF THE JANUMS BATTLE GROUP 97

The church on the main street through Saarmund. Picture: author.

Wildenbruch's church, which dates from 1250. Picture: author.

discreet monument to those who died in the 1939–45 war: the church survived, and was extensively repaired after the fall of the GDR.[1]

There's a great deal of concern locally now about the future of the Seddiner See: climate change and poor water management means that its levels have fallen several metres in the last ten years alone. The lake is a fraction of the size it would have been in 1945, and a town whose coat of arms bears the emblems of a rowing boat and a fish appears on the verge of losing both.[2]

At Wildenbruch the Latvians rested and planned their next move. Colonel Janums sent First Lieutenant Bušmanis and Major A. to Fichtenwalde to scout the position ahead. Janums stayed with the men. Bušmanis writes:

> In 20 minutes we are in Fichtenwalde. On our map it is marked as a small village in a thickly-wooded area. In reality we find a fairly large health resort

---

1 Wildenbruch Church webpage online at <https://www.kirche-michendorf-wildenbruch.de/unsere-gemeinde/kirche-wildenbruch> (accessed 21.12.2023).
2 *Germany's water dilemma – a swimming lake just outside Berlin is dying* – article online at <https://www-focus-de.translate.goog/earth/report/in-brandenburg-der-seddiner-see-stirbt-und-zeigt-deutschlands-wasser-problem_id_203136111.html?_x_tr_sl=de&_x_tr_tl=en&_x_tr_hl=en&_x_tr_pto=sc> (accessed 21.12.2023).

The men of Kampfgruppe Janums at rest in the forest south-west of Berlin, having abandoned their positions in the south-east of Berlin. Photographer possibly Leopolds Sipolins. Picture: Latvian War Museum LKM 5-13974-1495-FT(1-2)

and spa. We stop at a hotel, the only one still open, and begin to collect information about local conditions and the possibility of putting up the soldiers. The answer is not very optimistic. Firstly, the spa is full of refugees. Secondly there are no farms; there are only summer cottages and gardens for spa visitors. The possibility of getting food for the soldiers is nil.

Ignoring such pessimistic prospects, we start searching for ourselves and manage to find room for at least the squadron and battalion HQs. The rest, unfortunately, will have to stay outside. Having done all we can, we return to the hotel and wait for the troops to arrive. We rest, listening to the refugee conversations.

With tremendous effort Lieutenant Z has managed to coax a bowl of watery vegetable soup for each of us. When the first squadron units arrive at 1500, we hurry to greet them. The soldiers are completely exhausted. In their words, the hardest part was the final ten kilometres. No surprise there. Since yesterday we have walked about 85 kilometres.

It turns out the village is also short of water. It's only possible to get it from one house and even then only when the officers interfered after the soldiers complained. Otherwise the owner was refusing to let the soldiers into his yard to the pump. The soldiers are ordered to hunker down in the undergrowth near

Beelitz-Heilstatten Sanatorium, pictured around 1924. The Latvians stationed themselves here overnight on 22–23 April 1945 before crossing the Beelitz-Lehnin road at Fichtenwalde. Picture: public domain.

the houses. They are so tired they fall asleep as soon as they've sat down. Even food takes second place.

Safeguarding against an enemy surprise attack, the Squadron Leader orders a guard to be posted at both ends of the spa. The eastern end is guarded by 8 Company, the south by 3 Company. The last German in our squadron, Obersergeant Ostner, who is part of the squadron kitchen and who has all this time marched with us, is ordered to find food. Because the kitchen men's bellies are as empty as everyone else's, they get ready to go.

In a few hours they return and report that there is no food to be had. There is some to be got in Potsdam, 20 km away, but that needs transport. The Squadron Leader doesn't let the German speak much. He is told: 'Food must be found even if you have to carry it on your backs.'

The men go off again, returning only in the evening to report that transport has been found. Early in the morning [of 23 April] at 0400, they will go to Potsdam to collect the food. They think they will be back by lunchtime.

11

Fiat 500 in Beelitz

Beelitz today is a bustling and charming market town dating back to medieval times, a garrison town since 1731 and now best known for its cultivation of white asparagus – *spargel* – which has inspired a range of local speciality dishes. There is a plentiful supply on the tables of the market traders and the restaurant signs welcome asparagus fans to try their wares.

In the centre of the town is a large wooden model of a stork's nest, with two parent storks and a baby bird inside – another nod to the variety and richness of the Brandenburg countryside. I finish my coffee and drive on, as my destination is the Beelitz-Heilstatten health spa that the Latvians stayed at overnight. This is about five kilometres outside the town and is a sprawling mass of around 60 hospital buildings of various descriptions.

Originally intended at the turn of the 20th century as a workers' sanatorium to treat tuberculosis, it became a military hospital during the First World War. Adolf Hitler was treated here after being wounded in the leg at the Battle of the Somme in 1916. After the Second World War, the Soviet Union had its main hospital outside Russia here: GDR leader Erich Honecker stayed here in the last days of Communism.[1] What were, in 1930, the most advanced lung surgeries in Germany were then abandoned and Beelitz-Heilstatten has become known as a 'lost place' – with photographers and film directors capturing its decaying period grandness while nature reclaims the ground it is built on.

Now however it's a protected landmark and the number of coaches in the car park shows it's a popular tourist attraction, with treetop pathways winding past the ruins of some of the now-overgrown buildings, and Easter egg hunts and flashlight tours attracting new generations to its lush grounds. Some of the buildings have been well-maintained and are still in use as medical facilities.

---

1   *Beelitz-Heilstätten: Adolf Hitler and Erich Honecker were also in Beelitz*, article dated 16 January 2018. Online at <https://www-berliner--zeitung-de.translate.goog/mensch-metropole/beelitz-heilstaetten-auch-adolf-hitler-und-erich-honecker-lagen-in-beelitz-li.51574?_x_tr_sl=de&_x_tr_tl=en&_x_tr_hl=en&_x_tr_pto=sc&_x_tr_hist=true> (accessed 21.12.2023).

The derelict Pavilion B at the Beelitz-Heilstatten TB sanatorium. Picture: Doris Antony, CC-BY-SA-3.0.

Although the main sanatorium has fallen into disrepair, there are still medical facilities at Beelitz operating today. Picture: author.

12

Alarm!

The Janums Battle Group paused at the Beelitz-Heilstätten spa but were short of food and also information. The unit's adjutant, First Lieutenant Edvīns Bušmanis, kept a detailed diary of that time.

> The afternoon passes sorting out accommodation and resting. The squadron HQ is near the road, in a small house with a telephone. At night we sleep where we can. It's cold and there's not much to cover ourselves with, but the night passes uneventfully.
>
> We're up at 0800 but I'm stiff and my wound hurts more. The bad news is that the kitchen group has only just left as the transport was late in arriving. The lateness means if we want food, we have to wait here till evening. According to news coming in, it looks like that won't be possible.
>
> Enemy tanks have been seen three kilometres south-east of us. The Squadron Leader warns both guards and battalions to leave the eastern side of the spa and go into the forest west of the road to Lehnin. Only the HQ and 8 Company remain in the spa.
>
> Learning about the enemy closing in, our landlord starts planning to leave. He puts his prized possessions in a cart and harnesses up a grey donkey. We don't try to hinder him, quite the opposite. Some have noticed his full larder and hope he can't take it all with him.
>
> His cart has only just left the yard when he suddenly returns to announce that the tanks have been destroyed. 'So for the moment I'm staying put,' he announces. Sadly we watch the unharnessing and the unreachable larder.
>
> Suddenly there are two loud booms nearby. Explosions – a tank firing, and grenades. I hurry outside. Two more explosions and the sound of tank treads – very close.
>
> *Tanks!* Therefore the tanks that were 'destroyed' are here. As I go into the cottage to report what I've heard, I meet our landlord. He is ready to harness his cart again.

The Squadron Leader doesn't lose his cool for a moment. Finding out that the tanks have entered the village from the direction guarded by 3 Company, he mutters something about 'cabbages' and orders me to find out more.[1]

I race out towards the place where the tank treads were heard. A few hundred feet further on I hear the sounds of a real battle: heavy machine gun fire, the explosions of anti-tank weapons, tank cannons firing and shell bursts. Black smoke starts to rise. Something is burning.

I can see fighting going on by the Fichtenwalde-Lehnin road, on which we were planning to continue our march, and at about the spot where both battalions had been ordered to be. I go on a bit and can see an armoured car on the road firing in the direction of Lehnin.

Some soldiers [coming back] report to us that they were taken by surprise by enemy tanks. There are a number of tanks, together with motorised infantry. The first two tanks have been destroyed and are burning. Our soldiers have begun to move out westwards.

The Squadron Leader realises we're cut off from the rest of our men. In order to catch up, we have to cross the road before the enemy gets there. According to the map, the nearest place where there is a bridge over the river is Lehnin.

Orders: *messenger to call 8 Company men back from guard duty at the side of the highway, the car to drive to Lehnin and await us beyond there. Leave in 15 mins.*[2]

Contact with the Russians was unwelcome, and would draw attention to the Latvians as well as the danger of men being killed or wounded. Military historian Aivars Petersons writes:

> On the morning of 23 April at around 1000, the mobile units of the Russian 4th Guards Tank Army, who were trying to encircle Berlin from the south by attacking in the direction of Brandenburg, broke into the wooded area where Janums had placed his battalions. They were the shock units of the 1st Ukrainian front commanded by Marshall Konev.
>
> At the beginning of the battle Janums's men had shot up two tanks with Panzerfausts, but the tanks continued to attack and the motorised units with them, spread out for battle. That wasn't in Janums's plan, so he ordered the battalions to pull back.[3]

With a large and heavily armed Russian force no more than a few kilometres away, cover was needed quickly. Bušmanis writes:

---

1 Colonel Janums would regularly use the word 'cabbages' where other officers might use a swear word.
2 Bušmanis' diary, pp.19–23.
3 Petersons, *Mums Japarnak,* p.52.

To begin with we are ten officers: the Squadron Leader, myself, 1st Lieutenant N. Among the personnel present is Major A's son, who suddenly fell ill before the attack and can't walk. I tell him to go in the car and give him my only possession – my little briefcase.

After the specified 15 minutes only one soldier from 8 Company has joined us. We set off along the highway. It's quiet and empty. Far from us, westward, where our men went, infrequent rifle fire can be heard. We march quickly. The road is barricaded with anti-tank defences but that's no problem.

By chance, in a field on the right, I see our car with figures bending down around it, trying to get it out of some boggy ground. I ask the Squadron Leader's permission and take ten men to help. We're taken for the enemy [at first], but with an almighty effort, we push the car free and drive off. I only wanted my case.

We set off to catch the others up but meet them coming back. From the direction of Lehnin about two kilometres away in the distance – where there is a highway, main road and river crossing – the sounds of battle can be heard. Apparently the enemy has already reached the bridge, so there's no point us going there. We have a quick heads-together in the wood and decide the river and road need to be crossed somewhere else.

We'll go back to a stretch where the river is narrower and, having crossed, look for a place where we can approach the Fichtenwalde-Lehnin road from the forest. We have found a place like this on the map but we have doubts it actually exists.

About 1400, having rested, we begin our break-out. We use only a map and compass. Everything is quiet in the forest. Having reached the river, we go along the bank until we find a place where it is easy to cross.

On the other side, we come upon a house whose occupants have not left (of course, the house doesn't show up on our map). Going past, to our great delight, the owners bring out a box of crackers. We take as many as we can, remembering our fellow soldiers.

At the edge of the forest, I go out on my own with binoculars to survey the Lehnin road. I can see a never-ending flow of enemy military transport: tanks, heavy trucks, evidently for ammunition and soldiers. The forest here isn't very thick so we move along very carefully.

Suddenly we realise we're not alone. We freeze, and get ready for battle. It turns out we've been joined by our missing 8 Company soldiers under the leadership of 1st Lieutenant C. He reports that they've tried to cross the road but at the moment it's not possible. He wants to wait for nightfall.

The Squadron Leader disagrees, knowing that to be surrounded isn't good. He is determined to cross during the day, even if we have to fight our way across. We are now about 80 men, and a sudden attack can achieve a lot.

We all move into the undergrowth at the side of the road and wait for further orders. 1st Lieutenants C and N stay with the men and the Squadron Leader and I carefully inch forward nearer to the road.

The traffic is still heavy, without a pause. A tank drives past and takes up position 100 metres further on at a crossing of firebreak and road. We don't like that at all. We wait for the traffic to die down in the hope of getting across the road without a fight.

Half an hour or more passes. The traffic is quietening. For a moment it stops completely but then patrol scouts appear on the road. One stops near us and has no intention of moving on. The Squadron Leader and I whisper that he needs to be got rid of.

I've already pulled out my pistol and stick grenade and estimated how far to throw it when another patrol scout approaches. The two settle down for a friendly chat. The Squadron Leader and I decide to wait after all, bearing in mind the tank further on. Our patience is rewarded. The two patrolmen go off. Time to go. The two are about 100 metres away on the bend of the road, which is empty apart from three German women pushing prams, coming our way. *Move!*

I run across first, into the bushes on the other side. I manage to see the patrol about 500 metres away and the German women going past the stationary tank. No-one has seen us. But as soon as the second group has run across, one of the German women starts screaming. Not sure if the scream was meant as a warning to us or because we suddenly appeared. She screams again when the next group crosses.

I curse her but we are lucky. By the time the tank commander realises what is happening, we are all over and safe. We hear the treads of the tank but know it can't get us. You'd have to be extremely foolhardy to come into a thick forest after us.

Not wasting any time, we make a quick getaway. Using our compass, we travel on. It's not ideal as the thick forest hinders us going in the direction we want. About 1600 we come out to a forest settlement, which again is not on our map.

We take a careful look, then go to collect information: *where are we, where is the forest we've been looking for, have our soldiers been seen?* The inhabitants, for the time being, have stayed put and say the enemy hasn't been seen, nor our soldiers. The forest is 700 metres further on.

On reaching it, we find that our soldiers have passed by. We rest awhile and march on to X…[4] We have gone on a bit when a man and a woman on bicycles catch us up. They complain to the Squadron Leader that they have been robbed. Seven loaves and a bag of flour are missing.

The Squadron Leader is angry at the soldiers for being light-fingered but also at the couple for not understanding that the food had been taken for eating. The couple want it back but the soldiers say it has already gone. The couple insist that the soldiers are searched. I do it very carelessly and find nothing. The couple leave very dissatisfied.

---

4   In the original manuscript, this is a dotted line with no place name.

Moving on using the compass, we find a place where there are many recent footprints. Also a soldier's greatcoat, which no-one wants to carry, so we leave it behind, cutting off the emblem first. As the sun begins to set, we hear, 'Who's there?' and we catch up with the others. It's still not clear where the squadron HQ, 1 Company and 2 Battalion officers are, with Major A in charge.

Talking over events, it becomes clear that two tanks were destroyed in Fichtenwalde. We also have losses: one soldier fallen, run over by a tank. Two were wounded; one badly, the other lightly. Both have been brought along.

It becomes clear why 3 Company didn't warn the others. Lieutenant B rushed to a telephone, but it was out of order. He then tried to get past the tanks on a bicycle down a side street to warn the battalions. The street was so sandy that he was only halfway along before the battle started.

We establish that our thoughts on the Russian movement are, on the whole, correct – only they moved faster than we expected. That means we need to move faster, too. Looking at the map we see that we have a number of larger roads in front of us, which the enemy are likely to use. Going westwards, there is a fairly wide river to cross, the Plane, a tributary of the Elbe. All these obstacles come before the next heavily-wooded area in a 10 km-wide open zone. We need to cross it by night – tonight.

Having considered all this, we decide to set out at 2200. Our target is the small village of Verlorenwasser, in the next large tract of forest.[5]

Legionnaire Arvīds Kalupnieks writes in his memoir:

Soon after Dahlewitz, we turn left towards Blankenfelde. Here, we meet the 3rd Regiment's 1st Battalion, who have already arrived. We have a longer rest here. The Colonel is reunited with his unit commanders and is bent over a map, looking up a route. There is still a long road ahead of us; we can't rest for long. We are here for around an hour, then we get the order to keep marching. It is very difficult for some to get going, as many men have blisters, but nobody complains.

We begin our march. We walk along small country roads, avoiding bigger roads as much as possible. We cross another motorway running south-west. The moon is shining. In the distance, tank alarms are ringing. On the way, we receive information that the Russian wedge is driving towards the north and north-west, with the aim of surrounding and cutting off Berlin from the west. We have to change course. Our breaks are short. The Colonel walks at the front; a moment later he is in amongst the boys. He encourages anyone who he sees is already tired. The day of 22 April is reddening in the east when we receive the order to rest for 50 minutes.

The men are so tired that they fall into a deep sleep. Some light cigarettes, but they remain unsmoked as tiredness overcomes the smoker. It is difficult to

---

5 Bušmanis' diary, pp.23–27. The Plane flows south from Golzow near the B102.

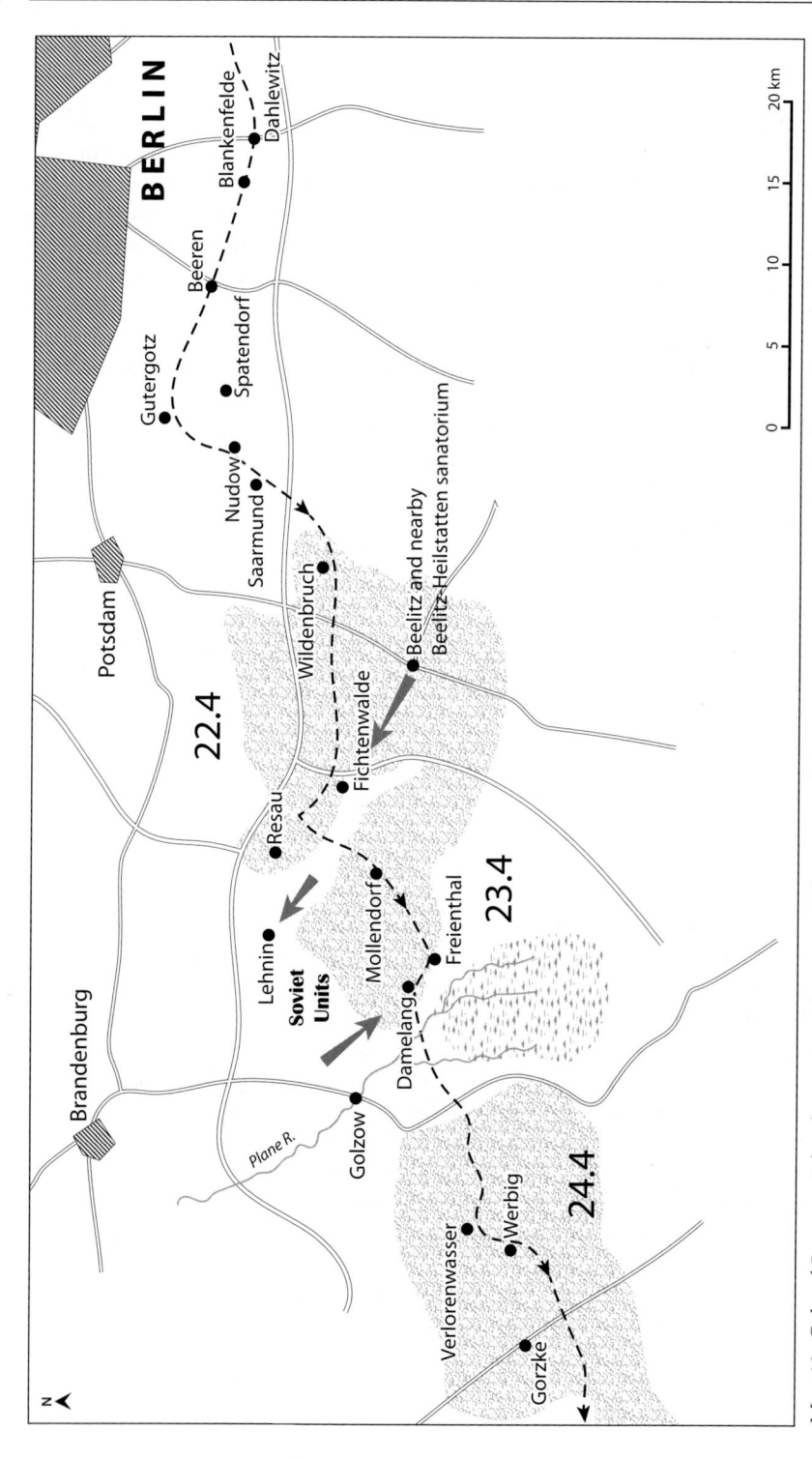

Map 10 Colonel Janums took a detour to get his men off the A10 autobahn, crossing at Saarmund then through Wildenbruch to Beelitz and eventually stopping at the sanatorium at Beelitz-Heilstatten. There, they re-orientated towards Fichtenwalde and headed through forest and across marshland towards the Elbe.

get the men to their feet. But once they are on their feet, we can get going. Our target is still quite far.

Civilians don't understand our march; they look at us inquisitively. Now and then, German assault troops ride past us on bicycles. They don't interest us. Our pace has slowed to 3–3.5 km/h. We cross the Wittenberg-Berlin motorway. The column sticks mainly to the forests. In the afternoon, completely exhausted, we reach our destination and settle in to the forest around 10 km south-west of Potsdam, near Kanin.

Nobody is interested in anything except resting for an hour or so. Food has also run out. Job one: sort our legs out. Significant blisters crowd our feet – we cut and rebandage them. Our requirements after 80 km of marching are very small: just to rest.

The next morning, we receive news that the Russians are advancing towards Beelitz. Around lunchtime, completely unexpectedly, a few Russian tanks appear on their way from Beelitz to Lehnin. One or two of the more hot-headed boys can't control themselves, and in the next few minutes two T-34 tanks are disabled. But this means that we can't stay here any longer, because there are too few of us to get involved in any fighting.

We continue our march towards the west. We go past the village of Rädel. The Russian army goes on towards Lehnin. The soldiers are suffering from hunger; all the food is long gone and hasn't been replaced. But luck is on our side, as we find a secret German food store in the forest. The men's faces grow happier; we take more so that we can share with others later.

In the distance, we can hear individual cannon shots. We reach the edge of the forest. Ahead of us is an approximately 10 km wide plain, and the river Plane, a tributary of the Elbe. We still have to get over those today. We start marching over the plain. The units march one behind the other with large gaps. By 1500 we have crossed the plain and the Plane, and now we have reached the forest to the west of the river. Here, we have a longer rest. The Colonel and the other units leave by a different route. Remaining are the 4th Regiment staff; the communications, engineer and anti-tank groups, and the 1st Company. After our rest, we continue our march and reach a village in the forest, where we stay the night.

We were a 'pleasant surprise' for a group of German airmen who called themselves a tank destroyer team. They were drunk, and young German ladies were lying next to some of them in the straw. They had a rude awakening when one of their commanders woke up, heard a foreign language, and raised an alarm. We had to use all of our eloquence to satisfy these men.[6]

An account of this period by Colonel Janums in his memoir *Mana Pulka Kauju Gaitas* (*My Regiment in Battle*) gives a very personal take on this episode, from Wildenbruch through forests and swamps to Verlorenwasser.

---

6   Arvīds Kalupnieks, *Colonel Janums and his Men* in Leitītis (1986).

110 ESCAPE FROM BERLIN

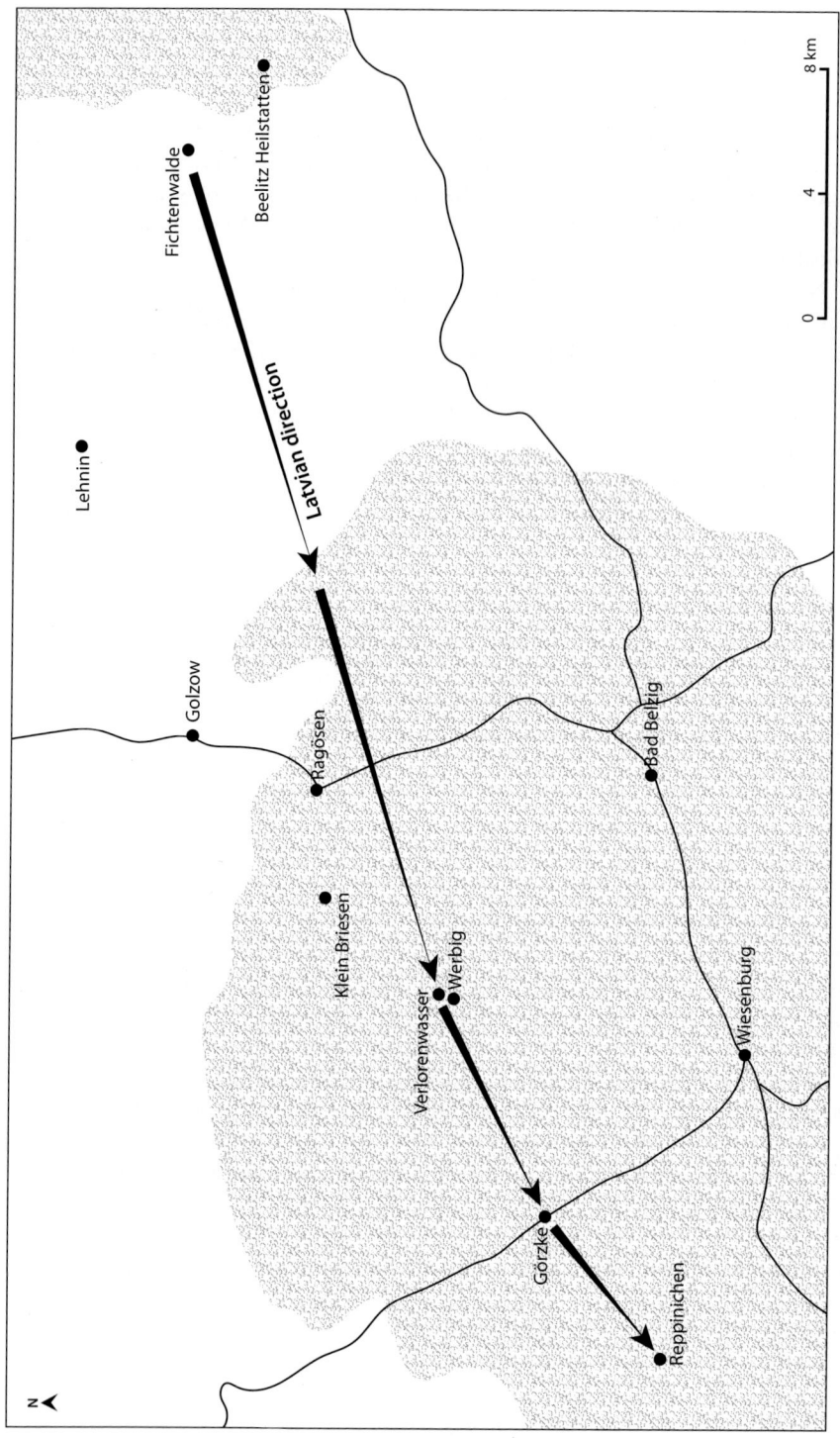

Map 11 The route taken by the Janums Battle Group south of Berlin, moving cross-country at Wildenbruch, encountering Red Army tanks on the Beelitz-Lehnin road and then crossing marshland at the Plane river to reach Verlorenwasser.

On 22 April at 0900 we reach the village of Wildenbruch. At this village my map runs out, which is why I am in great ignorance about the future direction of the march. During a short rest, I enter a local tavern with some officers. A map of the area is attached to the wall in the guest room. After waiting for an opportune moment, when the innkeeper goes out into the next room, one of my officers deftly collects the map. After this deed, we say goodbye in a hurry. When the village is already far behind us, we start to see to what extent this map could be useful to us. Although this map is fly-blown and dirty, it is possible for me to determine the future route of the march.

We move slowly, because my sons are tired, and our walking speed no longer exceeds three kilometres per hour. We learn from German refugees that enemy tank spearheads are already approaching Potsdam. In order for the tanks not to cut off our route of retreat, we must still reach the deep forest west of Beelitz this day.

Even though we are tired beyond measure and haven't eaten for two days' running, we continue our journey. Only around 1300 we reach Fichtenwalde, where we rest in the nearby forest. The 3rd and 8th Companies post rest guard on the eastern edge of the forest.

After the 70 km trek, my men's requirements are very minimal. They just want peace and rest. A great many soldiers have rubbed-raw feet. They wash and re-bandage them because we don't yet know how far we have to walk tomorrow.

On 23 April, early in the morning, news arrives that enemy tanks have already been seen near Beelitz. Because of this, I order both battalions to move to the woods west of Fichtenwalde. It is impossible to get food on the spot, so I assign several couriers to go to Potsdam for food. The return of these carriages is not expected before noon, and I am well aware that hanging around near the enemy might result in a surprise. But I also don't want to leave without using the last chance to get food for the battle group.

Having re-positioned the battalions under the cover of the forest and remembering a radio report I once heard in Lichtenberg that the American army had established a position at the end of the bridge at Zerbst, I remind the battalion commanders of this report and indicate that in case of a sudden enemy attack, they should retreat in the direction of Möllendorf-Verlorenwasser.[7]

At 1000 hours, several enemy tanks suddenly break into the village. They are followed by several vehicles with infantry. The battalions are in cover and are not surprised by this enemy attack. The first two tanks are shot up by close guard units, but when the next ones appear, the battalions, following previously given instructions, retreat towards Möllendorf.

As the enemy tanks stormed Fichtenwalde, the retreat to the west was cut off for the units guarding the regimental headquarters north of the Beelitz-Lehnin road. While the security units are gathering up, the messengers of the regiment's headquarters have already found out that the enemy's tanks are blocking

---

7   The Americans had crossed the Elbe a week before Colonel Janums abandoned his positions.

the main street of the resort with their fire, which is impossible to pass without losses. Therefore, I decide to bypass Fichtenwalde, moving along the northern edge of the Berlin autobahn. The 8th Company and part of the soldiers of the 3rd Company are advancing together with the headquarters of the regiment.

At first we walk in the direction of Lehnin, but when we approach the village of Resau, a group of German soldiers comes towards us. They inform us that the enemy has already taken Lehnin, as well as the highway fork five kilometres north-east of it. I see that the enemy's armoured units are moving much faster than us and that we will not be able to bypass them.

In order to unite with the core of the regiment, we therefore turn to the south and, moving through the forest, approach the Beelitz-Lehnin road. When the edge of the forest is already visible, I send out some men to explore the possibilities of further progress.

After returning, they report that enemy vehicles are constantly moving along the road in the direction of Lehnin and that it is currently impossible to cross this road. The whole core of my regiment is south of that road though, and we have to get over it too. Therefore, after leaving the group of soldiers under the cover of the forest, together with Lieutenant Bušmanis, I carefully move towards the corner of the forest where it comes close to the road. We have moved to about 20 metres from the road and, crouched down, each by his own pine tree, we watch the movement of the enemy.

It is broad daylight, and now that I have only one company of infantry at my disposal, it would be unwise to engage the enemy's armoured units. So, we wait to see if there will be an opportunity to cross the road without a fight. For a moment it seems to me that the movement of vehicles is stopping, but then I hear a T-34 tank approaching the corner of the forest from the direction of Lehnin, rumbling and screeching. We don't have any Panzerfausts with us right now. The forest is sparse, and the litle pines behind which we are hiding give little cover. If infantry were mounted on the tank, they could easily spot us.

Having reached the corner of the forest the tank stops, then turns and crosses the road ditch, swaying from side to side. It then turns around again and positions itself so that it can secure the road with the fire of its cannon. As one can see, the commander of the Red Army unit also believes that from this corner of the forest you can threaten movement along this road. It seems, already, that we will not be able to cross the road at this place. I look across at Lieutenant Bušmanis, and I think he is of the same mind.

I want to start to retreat back into the cover of the forest when three enemy cars approach us. As soon as they pass by, a conversation can be heard. Three Red Army men are coming along the road. They are right in front of us when one of them bends down and picks up a pack of cigarettes. Delighted at the valuable find, the three put their heads together, admire the cigarettes – and then smoke them with gusto. We sleep and watch the actions of the Red Army through the pine branches. If it wasn't for that damned tank nearby, one machine gun burst would be enough for us and the way would be clear for our group, but now we are forced to lie down and wait.

Having smoked, the Red Army men calmly continue their journey. No cars are visible on the road anymore either. Just in the corner of the forest, turning its barrel towards us, like a menacing and black beast, Stalin's heavy tank sleeps. Now, behind the corner of the forest, women's cries can be heard. I raise my head and see that, having left some baby carriages on the road, two women are running towards Lehnin. Nothing else is visible on the road.

Now or never, I thought, and gave the agreed sign: 'forwards'. I listen tensely. A few seconds have already passed, but everything is still very quiet in the forest behind us. Could the observer really not have seen the agreed sign? The seconds rush by, and they seem like an eternity. But then the footsteps of running men are heard in the forest, coming rapidly towards us. The men are running with a great noise, branches break, and the ground is reverberating. I so wish that they would be quieter, for I think that the tank crew can't help but hear such a noise.

When they reach the road, we join them. We run as hard as we can across the open field. It seems to me that at any moment a shell from the tank's cannon will crash into a crowd of my men. But the tank doesn't fire. We are rapidly approaching the opposite edge of the forest. We are separated from it by only ten metres. A few more seconds and we are in the forest. The tank never opens fire: the Red Army men haven't noticed us crossing the road.

A few hundred metres into the forest, I give the men a little rest to decide the direction of the march. As I'm looking at the map, two men come up to me and ask for permission to go back to destroy the tank. I point out to them that if they get wounded, it will be very difficult for us to get them out as we have no transport. Besides, Germany will lose the war anyway, whether we shoot this enemy tank or not.

After a few minutes of rest, we continue the march again. When the Möllendorf forester's house is behind us, we come across some tracks. Judging by them, a group of soldiers passed here recently. Soon we find a pack of cigarettes on the side of the trail – exactly the same cigarettes that were issued to us in the last canteen. Further into the forest we find an abandoned coat with a Latvian shield on the arm. Well, it is quite clear that only a few hours before us, the men of my battle group went this way. In the evening, we find them too: in a thicket near the village of Freienthal. Almost the entire battle group is here together: only the 1 Company and the sapper and communication platoons are missing but judging by all the signs, they left here earlier.

The soldiers are visibly pleased to see me and the guard units arrive. The officers gather around me. When they find out that we haven't eaten anything, they treat me with biscuits they have got from somewhere. In spite of the fatigue, some men come from companies that have been placed further away, stick their heads out of the bushes, look, smile and, without saying a word, leave again, having come to make sure that the 'Old Man' really has been found again.

> I'm sleeping under a pine tree and involuntarily I remember Vaiņode. How coldly and indifferently these same men looked at me then, and how happy they are today at my arrival.[8]

Edvīns Bušmanis writes in his diary that by this time, the difficulty of navigating by night with vague maps and the tension were beginning to wear down the men.

> We're still without food. The soldiers who left for Potsdam this morning have to be considered lost, including our German, Obersergeant Ortner. The few bits and pieces the soldiers have managed to scrounge in passing don't change anything: it's a drop in the ocean.
>
> At 2000 hours the reconnaissance group on bicycles sent out by Captain R returns. The enemy hasn't been felt anywhere ahead and the group have found a place to cross the river about five kilometres south of Golzow. At 2200 we leave the forest.
>
> Tonight's march, in comparison to yesterday, isn't so long, only about 35 km. I'm happy that my wound doesn't stop me walking. My leg hurts very little and the only thing I have to carry is my sub-machine gun. My case is in the Squadron Leader's car. I've accepted that all my wordly possessions are in my pockets.
>
> The soldiers march on jauntily. The badly injured man [from the earlier incident with the tanks] is being carried with us, causing him immense pain. It's decided to leave him in the hospital at Freienthal.
>
> This village's inhabitants have decided to stay put. In reality they have nowhere to go. The enemy is on both sides: on one side the Americans, on the other the Bolsheviks. Of course, there's a big difference, only they don't know that. After the village we turn off in the direction of the river crossing, collecting information as we go. A woman tells us that a few enemy tanks appeared in Golzow at lunchtime but they drove off. It doesn't sound very believable but we bear it in mind.
>
> About three kilometres before the river, we turn off the main road onto a smaller one next to the river. The night is quiet and light, with a big, bright moon. It helps with moving but is also a hindrance. Suddenly, in front of us, we hear the sound of tank tracks.
>
> We listen. From the direction of our hoped-for crossing not only the sound of tracks but also engines can be heard. Some think the crossing is being guarded by a German motorised division, others that the enemy has already taken it. Both are dangerous for us. We decide to look for a crossing elsewhere, in the opposite direction.
>
> We turn round and march about five kilometres along the road by the river bank. It's very muddy, difficult to walk. Beginning to think we won't get across

---

8   Janums, *Mana Pulka Kauju Gaitas,* trans. Aivars Sinka. Vainode in Latvia was the location of the first training camp for these men, and Janums was known to be a tough taskmaster.

without getting wet when the companies at the front announce that we have reached the bridge.

In about 10 minutes we are on the opposite bank. There is no fear of a tank following as the bridge is narrow and weak. A bit further on we cross a railway line and again carefully scrutinise our map, as we have to choose a new route to our targeted village. We have a chance to rest while doing this. In reality, we could do with a longer break but needs must. It's 0200 but we still have at least 15 km to go.[9]

The Soviet advance meant the Red Army controlled the main roads and was moving tanks, men and supplies along them. Several villages in the area were now under Russian control, which Colonel Janums took care to bypass. Movement was now only really possible across the fields at night, with the Red Army advancing across the region and the Germans actively looking for Janums. Legionnaire Arvīds Kalupnieks remembers:

> In the night, towards the dawn, the remaining units go through the village under the command of Janums and set up camp in the next village, Verlorenwasser. They had crossed the plain [from Frienthal] overnight. The next morning, 24 April, we move to the same village. Here we have a planned rest until the evening. The inhabitants are much more hospitable than in the Berlin suburbs. They make us lunch; of course we pay them for the ingredients.[10] From now on the plan is to move only at night, as the German military has been made aware of our movements.
>
> That evening, we start our march. The path is through an enormous forest, along small paths. This is where our Colonel shows himself as unsurpassed, because he navigates us through these thickets without the slightest pause, as though he is walking through his own fields – fields that he knows every detail of.
>
> We walk all night, with small rest stops. The Germans have blocked one of the forest roads with wooden blockades. At 0600 hours we reach a German training ground. The Colonel sends a commander to where rations are issued. But news of us has already reached them. They won't issue food until Colonel Janums presents himself at the local commandant's office. Everybody knows what that would mean, so everyone agrees: we have to suffer through until we reach the end.[11]

---

9   The diary of Edvīns Bušmanis, pp.27–31.
10 Silgailis notes that this was the first food the men had had in three days (*Latvian Legion*, p.184).
11 Arvīds Kalupnieks, *Colonel Janums and his Men* in Leitītis (1986).

13

By Compass Through the Forest

The chronicle of a century of Fichtenwalde's history records that life during the Second World War was relatively quiet in the village until 1943, despite rationing having been introduced since the 1936 Olympics. Locals watched streams of American bombers high overhead preparing to unload their cargo of bombs on the capital. Many Berliners took trains to the suburbs in the evening to escape the bombing raids: Fichtenwalde was a refuge where peaceful sleep was possible.

George Zivier, a former Fichtenwalde resident, wrote in 1965:

> Anyone who experienced the war years of 1944–45 in Berlin knows about the exodus of thousands every evening from the bombed-out capital of Germany, the target of barely interrupted massive air raids. The escape began every evening, even in the late afternoon. They were favoured rather than hindered by the authorities at the time.
>
> Squeezed together so that it hurt, the refugees, elderly men, mothers with children and young girls, left the dangerous city miles behind them in their train compartments. Some travelled as far as the Spree Forest and had to return hours before sunrise in order to get to work, because when it came to work there was no quarter. But many people preferred the arduous journeys and the few hours out of danger to the anxious nights in the Berlin air raid shelter.[1]

Some Berliners with houses in Fichtenwalde relocated there altogether after being bombed out, extending their property with verandahs and outbuildings from the plentiful supply of wood nearby. One hot summer's day in August 1944, an American bomber was shot down over the forests and one of the crew who had parachuted to safety was taken prisoner – as a group of locals who had been sunning themselves in their swimwear gathered around and a man who had been bombed out punched the American repeatedly on his back.

In April 1945, the war came to Fichtenwalde. Stray bombs hit the school and houses and as the fighting grew nearer, local people buried their valuables to guard against looters. On 20 April, 37 B-17s from the USAF 384th bomb group

---

1   Memories of George Zivier in *Chronicle Fichtenwalde: 1908–2008,* pp.73–78, edited by Eva Griebel.

Clean and green: Fichtenwalde, near Beelitz in Brandenburg. Picture: author.

significantly damaged the Seddin freight marshalling yards in a daylight raid launched from their base at the Grafton Underwood airfield in the UK.[2]

There was no anti-aircraft fire over the target and no aircraft were lost, but 300 Jewish women and girls who had been used as forced labourers in a munitions factory were trapped in a freight train and killed: they were identified by their red-stained hair and hands.[3]

The local chronicle records that on 23 April Soviet forces moved through Fichtenwalde village but were pushed back to Beelitz. When they returned two days later – a time that tallies with the Latvians moving across that area – a local youth was killed by a rocket-propelled grenade. It was not until 30 April that Fichtenwalde fell under Soviet control. Houses were searched for German soldiers; bicycles were stolen and women harrassed. Ernst Zivier remembered: 'In Fichtenwalde it had become common practice for residents to run into the garden and rattle pot lids when Soviet soldiers came to their house. This rattling was then picked up by the neighbours and sometimes it was still rattling long after "the Russians" had left.'[4]

---

2 Raid details and pictures from the 384th Bombardment Group archives can be seen online at <https://384thbombgroup.com/_content/_pages/mission.php>. This was their last but one mission before the war ended, their 315th out of 316.
3 Presumably due to the chemicals they were handling.
4 Memories of Ernst Zivier in *Chronicle Fichtenwalde: 1908–2008*, pp.73–78, edited by Eva Griebel.

118 ESCAPE FROM BERLIN

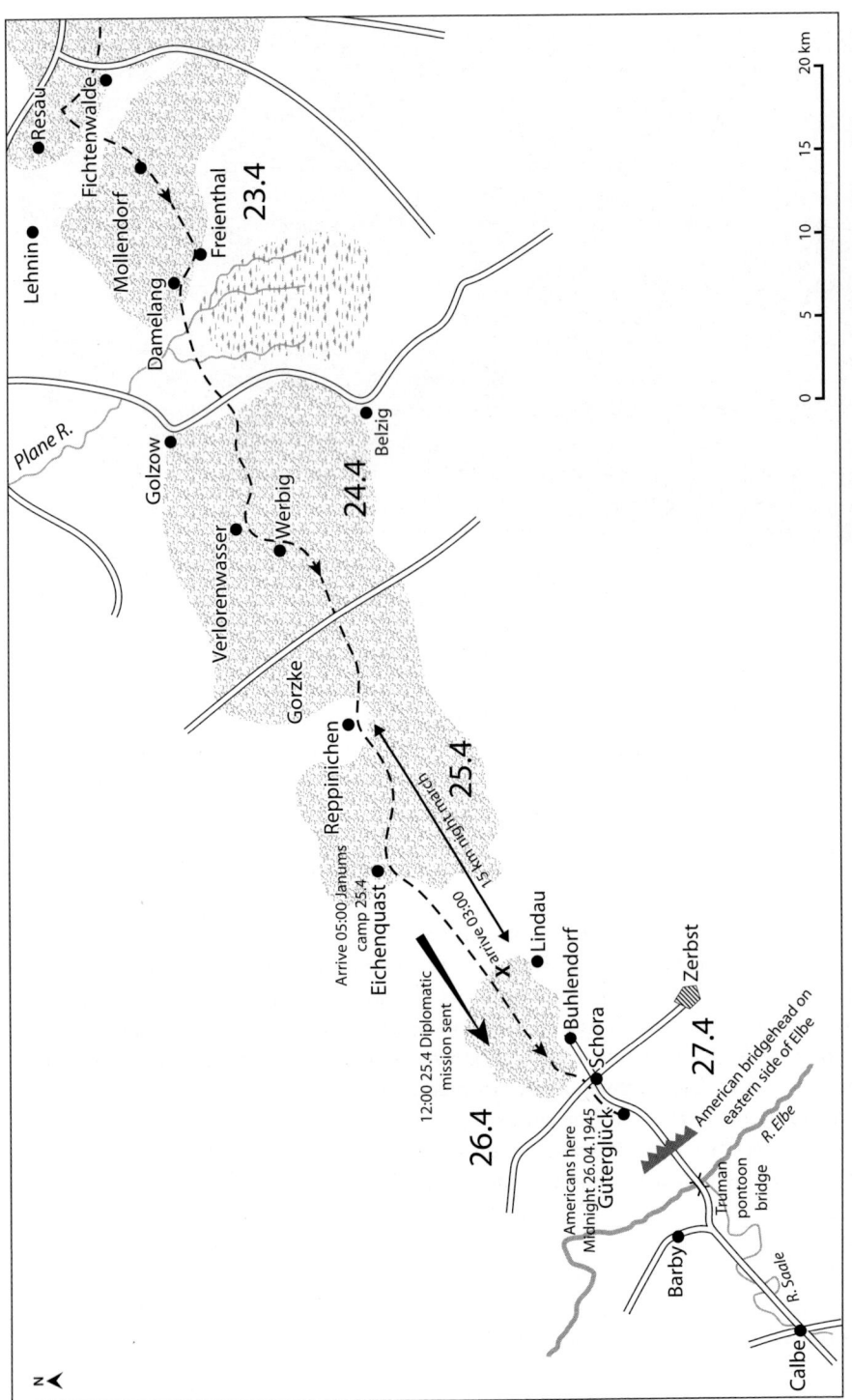

Map 12 Swamps and forests: the Latvians navigated by compass from Fichtenwalde to Verlorenwasser and then to Reppinichen, through forests and across marshland, moving at night.

Post-war reports tell of a mass grave of 23 Ukrainian women who were used as forced labour by local farmers who thought the arrival of the Red Army meant the war was over. They were apparently shot in cold blood by German soldiers from the Wenck Army – their bodies were discovered after the war and re-buried at the Soviet military cemetery at Beelitz (Sowjetischer Ehrenfriedhof), built in 1948 by order of the then-district administrator of the Zauch-Belzig district. The work was supervised by the Soviet commandant's office. Twenty-two Jewish girls were laid to rest there, as well as 854 Soviet soldiers, of whom only 392 are known by name.[5]

For such a beautiful place under a canopy of trees, Fichtenwalde has a dark past.

I have parked in Golzow to have a coffee and work out my next move. It is just over 20 km from Fichtenwalde to Golzow, but in 1945 this route would have been along roads which could have been blocked with checkpoints or were too risky because of discovery by Soviet advance units. So instead, Janums and his men navigated by compass across country, mostly moving through the forests.

The journey into Golzow in 2023 takes the traveller past fields of wheat and tightly-packed sunflowers fringed with pine forests. It's just after lunch on a sunny afternoon and I am trying to pick up the trail of the Latvians from Golzow onwards along narrow country roads on which lorries carrying agricultural goods to Brandenburg whoosh past an old barn that's been bricked up, a church that's been rebuilt and a small settlement of houses. Tractors pick their way from one field to the next, their drivers waving cheerily at my little unthreatening Fiat. I wave back.

Everything is very ordered, very clean and pleasant. My aim is to follow the trail of the Janums Battle Group to Verlorenwasser, Reppinichen and Eichenquast, with the aim of reaching Güterglück tonight. There is no real direct route, so I have to do a fair amount of re-tracing my tracks and finding my way.

Between Dippmansdorf and Lutte the ground falls away to a low-lying area that's now a bird-nesting region. This must be the swampy area the Latvians moved across and I can't get through to Verlorenwasser. I find a tiny left turn off Road 102 towards Ragösen which may take me round to the other side of this marshland and forest.

It's a single-track road that's not very well-surfaced – with potholes, and rough at the edges – so I slow down a little. To the left the fields still look swampy and behind them a stretch of pine forest looms. A sign tells me this is Klein Briesen. There is a house every now and then, and next to what looks like an electricity substation is a guesthouse: the Hotel Restaurant Juliushof. It looks like it has been closed for some time.

To get an idea of what the forest interior looks like, I turn left off the road and into it. Within a hundred metres it becomes quite dense and overgrown with shrubs in the little-used areas and lots of fallen wood between the trees. I nudge the Fiat along the muddy forest track wondering if this is how the Latvians moved during the night: from one tiny village to the next, edging their way closer to the Elbe under the canopy

---

5   Details from Doreen Ryssmann and the Fichtenwalde history group.

The forest at Klein Briesen. There are tracks through the trees for logging purposes, and some of the local paths are marked with paint. Picture: author.

of forest, possibly using the paths through it that only locals would know. Some trees are marked with paint to identify paths.

After a while I've seen enough and, emerging from the forest, I get back on the road through Gross Briesen heading for Friesdorf and Verlorenwasser. The problem is that I find signs warning that this becomes a sand road, more suitable for tractors than hire cars. I don't think I can take a rented Fiat 500 on sand roads for five kilometres. I park up to look at the map and as I do, up ahead a group of six storks flies past an old barn with cracks in the brickwork. They land in the field next to the car. This is real old-fashioned cross-country work. There is no wifi to help, as there is no signal – but Janums managed to get through using only a map pulled from the wall of an inn. I need to get back on a decent road and find a route on my road map that I can follow.

Incredibly – by this afternoon's standards at least – my phone's sat nav suddenly picks up a signal and tells me to turn left towards Verlorenwasser and Werbig. The sat nav hasn't been much help since Potsdam, and it's kicked in just as I was wondering whether I would actually find Verlorenwasser, or if that was just a name the Latvians gave to that place.[6] I take the left, and the road takes me past a care home and nearby

---

6   Ironically, Verlorenwasser means 'lost water'.

The turn-off to Verlorenwasser and Werbig appears unexpectedly. Picture: author.

houses into undulating countryside. After a few minutes it leads me alongside a river – Verlorenwasser – and brings me to a village with the same name.

In his diary, First Lieutenant Bušmanis describes how the Latvians made their way to this place, navigating almost by instinct.

> The thick forest marked on the map is pathetic. Trees are sparse and through the gaps you can see for hundreds of metres. Our map, indeed, is not the best. Firebreaks and forest roads bear no resemblance to those marked on the map. They join and divide so often that we soon lose track of the real one. Only the Squadron Leader's excellent sense of direction and his compass keeps us moving more or less in the right direction.
>
> About 0400 hours in front of us we see yet another village which is not marked on the map. A reconnaissance group is sent out while the soldiers remain on the edge of the forest. They return and say this is [dotted line, no name]. 1 Company is already there and also squadron HQ. It's five kilometres to Verlorenwasser. We get up and with heavy steps continue on our way. We're so tired that our legs won't do as they're told.
>
> We finally arrive but face yet another problem. The village is so small that there is no room for everyone. The Squadron Leader orders 2 Battalion to go on three kilometres to the next village [dotted line, no name].

The centre of Verlorenwasser. Picture: author.

The road from Verlorenwasser to Werbig. Picture: author.

While we are still milling around, two soldiers, dressed in Air Force uniforms, come out of a house. They immediately want to know who we are and what we want. This time the Squadron Leader is very short in his replies – but he, himself, wants to gain lots of information. Because both officers – they are German – turn out to be very boastful, he can find out a lot.

It turns out that both Germans belong to the so-called five-man tank destroyer groups, whose task it is to destroy those tanks which have broken forward. How successful their operations have been up to now is difficult to ascertain. It sounds more like how they have managed to avoid the enemy.[7]

Verlorenwasser, after all the trouble finding it, is a small but charming settlement set within several bridges across the many rivers flowing through this area like the fingers of a hand. The water is ankle-deep and about four paces across, carving trickling channels through the forests of pine. The centre of Verlorenwasser appears to be a wooden carving of a red and white spotted mushroom, close to a bus stop.

There are several thoughts that have been going through my head as I have been tracing the journey of the Latvians through rural Brandenburg. The first thought is that it is quite an achievement to move close to 850 men such a distance with no food and little rest, especially when orders have been issued to find them. Second, to chart a route across country, through forests and swamps, non-stop, at night, with only a compass and a map torn off a school wall or taken from an inn is some feat. But Colonel Janums had got his men out of many tight spots before, and in Verlorenwasser, he was on the verge of doing it again.

---

7 Diary of Edvīns Bušmanis, pp.27–31.

14

Edvīns Bušmanis at Verlorenwasser

On 24 April Colonel Janums, First Lieutenant Bušmanis and 800 Latvian soldiers were at Verlorenwasser, deep in the forests and swamps south-west of Berlin, heading for the river Elbe. The Americans had a bridgehead there, and their goal was to reach them and surrender.

Scouts came back at noon on 25 April with the news that the Americans were at Güterglück, about 50 km away. Everything now depended on what lay in front of them. The men were hungry but their spirits were high. First Lieutenant Bušmanis wrote:

> The Bolsheviks haven't been seen but they're not far off. Yesterday they took Golzow.[1] The Americans are still a way away. The nearest point is Zerbst, where they've dug in at the end of the bridge east of the Elbe. They won't get any further as they're facing strong German forces and artillery. We take this 'story' with a pinch of salt and hope that the Americans approach soon. We reckon them to be about 60–70 km away.[2]
>
> The village is very small. In the middle is a hotel. We choose that as our resting place. Out comes the owner and when we ask if we can rest and eat here, he tells us all the rooms are taken and the hotel is closed. His tone is so provocative that some of the officers present begin to protest.
>
> I try to ignore his manner and attempt to convince him that we don't need anything out of the ordinary, just a room to rest in and some food. He's not having it. He says he doesn't have anything – neither room nor food. No-one is going to come in without his say-so. I inform him that, in that case, we will act according to our judgement and if his rooms are empty, we will make use of them. A significant touch of my pistol makes him relent.
>
> The main room, of course, is empty and there is space for all. We ignore the landlord and set up the room to suit our needs. Meanwhile, the Squadron Leader has called in Captain L and ordered him to go to the local Bürgermeister – or the one in the next village – and obtain food for the soldiers. Captain L

---

1 On the edge of the forest where they entered it, on the present day B102.
2 Slightly less, as the crow flies.

goes off but, looking at the present situation, we don't hold out much hope of a satisfactory ending. I am so tired. I lie down and fall asleep instantly.

About 1100 hours Captain L, smiling happily, wakes us to tell that he has food. He has bought two pigs, four sheep, half an ox, a number of hundred-weight of potatoes and root vegetables. Everything is on its way here. And really!

Half an hour later everything has arrived. Soldiers pour in from all sides, pleased about the forthcoming meal. The canteen staff begin to visit each house, looking for large pans. Some of the food is taken on to the next village, the rest is divided up among the units. Let the cooking commence.[3]

There is more good news before the men eat. A group of 60 Latvian soldiers missing since Fichtenwalde arrives in the village. They are exhausted as they have been walking non-stop. When the main group split to avoid the Soviet tanks entering Fichtenwalde this group was stranded on the other side of the road, unable to cross. By the time they could, they had lost contact with the main group. Led by Major 'A' – Alksnītis – they have walked more than 50 km and only found the main group by chance. Bušmanis continues:

At 1400 the food is ready and for the first time in four days the soldiers can eat properly. There is enough for everyone to have as much as they want.

The German tank-hunters have returned. They say that enemy tanks are nearing Belzig, which is to be defended to the last man. On the map we can see that Belzig isn't far away and we start to get restless. The idea of defending to the last man isn't taken seriously. Decide that today at 2000 hours we will move on.

For our next target, the Squadron Leader has chosen another village in the forest – Eichenquast, about 30 km away. He has decided to stay there longer and when the Americans take the area, allow ourselves to be interned.

Relations with our landlord improve as the day passes. He, as well as all the village inhabitants, can see that we are not savages, as we have probably been described – similar to the Bolsheviks who lay waste and steal. In the evening, as an apology for the behaviour this morning, his wife brings us fried eggs, potatoes and a bit of bread.

We've almost forgotten this morning's altercation, as similar events have happened before. Even though our dinner was filling, we don't need to be asked twice and tuck in – with the thought that while there's food, eat.

When the evening begins to draw in, the soldiers start getting ready for departure. When everyone is together, the Squadron Leader tells of his plan to go over to the Americans. The soldiers are delighted. The opportunity to end the war in such an acceptable way gives everyone an extra dose of energy.

Many, including Major A, have badly-blistered feet and can barely walk. We therefore requisition horses and carts from the village. Everyone else marches

---

3 The diary of Edvīns Bušmanis, pp.27–31, unpublished. From the archive of the Latvian War Museum, Rīga, translated by Daina Vītola. Captain L is Captain Lapainis.

on cheerfully, having had a good rest. As we leave the village we are joined by 2 Battalion, squadron HQ and 1 Company.

The route, as on previous days, takes us along small roads. We avoid main roads and open spaces. The night is dark, as there is no moon. We stop on a number of occasions and, thanks to the Squadron Leader's sense of direction, keep on the right road.

In the interests of safety, a strong reconnaissance group is sent about 500 to 1,000 metres ahead. They carefully check roads, crossroads and villages that we go through or pass. We meet long lines of refugees coming from Belzig. They say that the enemy has almost taken it.

We march through the night at a fast pace. We come across a group of women in striped clothing. I find out that they are inmates from a concentration camp, Jews from Czechoslovakia, who have been released to go where they will. Like us, they are now making their way to the west. Taking into account our recent experiences, we are low on energy and liveliness, but the women are even weaker. As we get up to move on, they remain resting.

At 0500 we are nearing Eichenquast. Another surprise. On our map it is shown as a small, lonely village in the middle of the forest. Not so. In reality, it's at the edge of an aerodrome and training ground. That's very unwelcome news for us but it isn't possible to choose another place to stay at the moment.[4]

As every available bed and resting place in the village has been taken, the soldiers are forced to sleep in the forest. Overnight the temperature drops to zero degrees, Bušmanis writes, and the soldiers wake to a chilly morning.

We are shivering because the Squadron Leader has strictly forbidden the lighting of any fires for us to be as unobtrusive as possible. The soldiers of course can't understand this and the officers have their work cut out to stop them lighting fires and wandering around. At last the sun rises and it gets warmer. We lie in the moss and look at the sky.

The Squadron Leader calls for our remaining administration officer Lieutenant Zv and orders him to sort out the food supply. Major A is ordered to choose a reconnaissance group from his battalion: one officer, two NCOs and two soldiers.

The Squadron Leader gives them their task: *Check out the overall situation. Where are the Bolsheviks, where are the Americans? Are the Americans advancing? If not, why not? Who is in their way? What are the possibilities of crossing over to the west of us? Are there more forests where we could hole up, in case of necessity? Where would be best?* I fill in the necessary order slip with a fictitious reason and off they go on bicycles.

Having rested, together with the Squadron Leader we take a walk round the local area. We come to the nearby aerodrome, which doesn't seem to be in use at

---

4   Bušmanis, pp.27–31.

present as only a few damaged aeroplanes can be seen. There are soldiers living in the house by the airfield. We find out from them that their commander is a squadron leader – a lieutenant – who is also the commander of this area. We're not sure what to do next.

How long will we have to remain here? When will we be able to carry out our plan? If we're here for longer, we need to consider housing the soldiers under some kind of shelter. As well as which, it will seem suspicious if a unit were to set up camp here and its leaders not announce themselves to the local commandant.

Having mulled this over, we decide to announce ourselves. The commandant keeps us waiting for a considerable time and, on meeting us, does not look at all happy about a strange unit's arrival and intention to stay. Perhaps he has an idea that our plans are not crystal clear. However, he does not say anything and lets us have all his empty premises – Finnish model tents. When we examine them later on, we immediately refuse them as they're filthy.

We go back. Meanwhile Lieutenant Zv has returned with the news that he has found an army food distribution station about seven kilometres away, where it's possible to get something. He has already organised transport here in the village to bring the food. Hearing that lifts everyone's spirits. We will be fed today, too!

While we are still talking, we notice a car coming in our direction. We can't believe our eyes when, as it gets near, we recognise our Squadron Leader's car, which has been missing for two days. The driver, Private Z, is overjoyed to have found us and shares his truly incredible adventures in a long story. He only knew of our [vague] plan to march to the west and, in so doing, to use the larger forests. He just drove at random.[5]

I'm happy too as I get back my property, which I had written off. Now I've got more than just what's in my pockets and, in addition, a blanket to cover myself with. I swear never to let the little case out of my hands again; to carry it with me at all times.

Now that we have a car, the Squadron Leader puts it in the charge of Lieutenant Zv in order to move the food faster from the supply station.

At 1700, the reconnaissance group returns. The news they bring isn't very uplifting. The Americans have dug in at the end of the bridge on the right bank of the Elbe at Zerbst. They have remained in position for some time without an apparent reason.

You would imagine that they are facing strong German forces which are holding them back but information collected so far doesn't confirm this. It's clear the Germans don't have artillery. Rumour has it that the Americans are letting women and children go over to them. The group confirms that there are forests ahead and it's possible to hole up there.

---

5   Private Z becomes an even more significant figure later in this story. Lieutenant Zv is Lieutenant Zvirgzdiņš.

We sit for ages discussing what to do and how long to stay. *When will the Americans start to expand their position and move forward? How long can we stay here without arousing suspicion?* Most of us agree that it should be possible for a few days.

Whilst we are sitting and pitching ideas, the car returns with Lieutenant Zv. Agitated, he tells us that something unforeseen has happened. The order slip to obtain food had already been filled in and signed. The only thing left was to receive the food itself, when suddenly, by telephone, the order was halted.

When he asked the reason, Lieutenant Zv was told that the unit commander has to first present himself at 20th Army HQ, Human Resources leader (IIa). Not being able to do anything further himself, he has returned.[6]

For a moment we freeze. Everyone knows what this news means. We have begun to attract interest at HQ: *why are we here and on whose orders?* Under these conditions, if the Squadron Leader were to obey this order, his head would roll.

The Squadron Leader is thoughtful. He understands the threatening situation very well but knows too that without supplies he won't be able to carry out his plan. After a short silence, he suggests that maybe it won't be too bad, that he won't lose his head immediately on arrival at HQ, that supplies are seriously needed, the soldiers won't last for long, etc.

All the officers begin to protest immediately. To their way of thinking, it's not on that the Squadron Leader risks himself for the sake of one day's rations. Yesterday everyone ate very well. They can manage for a day or two. Maybe, in the meantime, it might be possible to obtain rations elsewhere? Seeing our attitude, the Squadron Leader calms down, gives up the idea of going to see the Germans and begins to think of other possibilities.

The lack of provisions has radically changed our position. If we were going to wait for the Americans approaching, then now, whether we want to or not, we have to go forward to meet them. We have to go to them, and if necessary fight our way through. As a result, it's decided that tonight we will move the frontline forward by another 15 km, survey the situation from there and only then make a final decision as to what to do. As our march this time isn't very long, the Squadron Leader decides to leave at 2300 hours.

At the appointed time, the forest comes alive. Companies and battalions line up on the road. The driver wants to use the road and tries to start the engine, but to no avail. It turns out there is not a drop of petrol in the tank. Our recently re-acquired car will have to stay here. Private Z doesn't give up that easily. He asks the Squadron Leader for permission to remain until the morning as he hopes to get petrol from somewhere. On the map I show him the area in the

---

6 Aivars Petersons corrects this to the HQ of the Twelfth Army – General Wenck's – which was fighting in the area after Hitler ordered Wenck to break through from the west to Berlin. The headquarters of the 20th Army were in Berlin.

forest in which we are planning to rest, shake his hand and, clutching my case, march in pursuit of the others.

The route takes us down small roads and paths again but the reconnaissance group has memorised the way very well. Therefore, by the light of the moon, we keep our bearings as if by day. About 0300 we reach our destination without any incidents. Our new resting place has been chosen in a wood by the side of a road, about five kilometres north-west of Lindau and a good distance from the nearest houses.

The Squadron Leader settles the battalions into sectors and commands absolute silence and lack of movement. Only in the most dire emergency should anyone come out of the forest. Lookouts are posted in the corners of the undergrowth at the side of the road.

The morning is cold again. In order not to freeze completely, the Squadron Leader and I decide to sleep next to each other. My blanket goes underneath, his blanket on top, together with our coats, giving us some hope that we won't freeze.

Empty stomachs don't allow a long sleep. By 0930 we're up again. Jumping and moving about helps to bring back some kind of warmth. The most dissatisfied is the stomach, but nothing can be done there.

The Squadron Leader wants not one reconnaissance group but two, as he wants to send them in two directions. Again both groups are on bikes. One is led by Lieutenant B, the other by Private P. The task for both groups is the same, about the same as yesterday: to clarify both the American and German frontlines as accurately as possible and – if possible – to find out the German numbers and armament, and to try to find out why the Americans have halted.

Even though we know it will be difficult, we do not doubt for one moment that the groups will succeed. The scouts ride off on bicycles: Lieutenant Zv goes in search of food. The rest of us stay in the forest, making lots of plans about crossing over and trying to guess why the Americans have stopped.

We listen to the boom of artillery in the distance and wonder whose it is. Everybody is hungry again. The soldiers can't understand why they're not allowed to leave the forest and go, so to speak, 'on the scrounge'. The officers, following the Squadron Leader's orders, have their work cut out to stop them from wandering around.

Suddenly, round about lunchtime, 2nd Company commander Lieutenant V turns up to see us, to inform us that there has been an unpleasant incident in his company. Precisely on the spot where the company had set up camp, the soldiers had noticed suspicious dug-up ground.

Wasting no time, they set to checking it and found a pit with all kinds of things: tinned goods, chocolate, cigarettes, cigars, drinks, men and women's clothing. By the time the commander learned of this, the goods had been shared out and the food eaten.

Then the most unpleasant bit happened. Two German soldiers with a horse and cart turned up, ready to dig up their goods and take them away. Finding the hole open and empty, they kicked up a tremendous fuss and, if they didn't get their property back, were going to call the military police.

We agree that the incident is very unfortunate. Not because any of us have a bad conscience about digging up an unknown owner's property, sharing it out or eating it but that the German soldiers chose that moment to collect it and could really carry out their threat to call out the military police. The Squadron Leader sends Captain A to the incident to sort the matter out peacefully.

Returning a little while later, Captain A informs us that he has not been able to reach an amicable resolution. Very few goods were recovered, not to mention the food. Both Germans were dissatisfied with what was recovered and promised to complain to their superiors, i.e., the owners of the property. What they would do is hard to tell.

It turns out the goods belonged to a couple of German officers, who, at some time earlier, had ordered them to be buried. We are cross about the coincidence that made the company set up camp exactly where the goods were buried.[7]

---

7 Bušmanis, pp.31–34. Lieutenant V is Lieutenant Vaivads, who secured the bridge at Schmöckwitz.

15

Fiat 500 at Werbig

I make a tactical stop at an inn in Werbig to have a coffee, a good look at the map and read what Bušmanis wrote about these final stages. It's a nice feeling to be sitting outside the Gasthof zur Erholung eating cake and drinking coffee in the sunshine of a summer afternoon. The occasional tractor goes past the 13th century church opposite, but there is nothing much else to interrupt the day.

That's not always been the case here. Werbig is a hamlet that has seen its fair share of history since it was founded in the 1200s – being almost destroyed by fire in 1558, suffering the plague in 1638 and being assigned to Prussia in the Congress of Vienna in 1815.

As I pay for my coffee and cake, I notice a map painted on a wooden panel fixed to the wall in the entrance hall. It has a timeless quality that could date back hundreds of years. Deep in the German countryside, this shows Werbig as part of an interconnected network of small villages with Gorzke as the focal point, showing the local churches, the types of trees in each forest, the manor house on the Schmerwitz estate established for Carl Friedrich Brand von Lindau in 1736 … I almost laugh out loud as I remember how the Latvians came across a similar map and distracted the innkeeper so they could rip it off the wall. I feel almost the same way, but this would have to be jemmied off with a crowbar. Fortified with the local delicacies, Reppinichen is my next destination.[1]

The road to Reppinichen through the countryside turns into Dorfstrasse – 'Village Street' – which is lined with two-storey houses opening out straight onto the pavement along one side of the road. Some houses have big gates which look like they may be barn conversions. Near to the bus stop there's a fire station dating from 1924 with a fire hydrant added three years later. On the other side of the road the buildings are single-storey, so may have been – or still are – used for storing vehicles and equipment.

---

1 Like at Cölpin Manor, the von Lindau family lost control of Schmerwitz Manor at the end of the Second World War. It was converted into a headquarters for the KPD Communist Party of Germany, then the Socialist Unity Party and later used as a police training area. After the reunification of Germany it returned to private ownership and is now an eco-farm [Source: <www-gut--schmerwitz-de>].

Werbig's 13th century village church. Picture: Natalie Carragher.

Countryside between Werbig and Reppinichen – note the forest treeline offering cover for the movement of 850 men. Picture: Natalie Carragher.

Reppinichen's main street. Picture: author.

The oldest building I can see dates back to 1912 and the village green, planted with trees, has a memorial to the fallen of the two world wars. There's a large church that has clearly been rebuilt and seems to double as a community centre, with a spotlight to illuminate the spire.

Reppinichen looks very much like the kind of place a column of soldiers would march through in the middle of the night. Like many of the villages in this part of Germany, it has a turbulent history.

There's been a settlement here since the 1400s, but that was destroyed in the Hussite Wars of 1419–1434. It was rebuilt in 1571 and about 25 families lived and farmed here until the Thirty Years' War of 1618–1648, when Reppinichen was destroyed again: it was registered as uninhabited in 1651. Over the next 200 years the area was used for family farming: there were 50 houses here in an 1837 census, built around the village green. The church, built in 1703 on medieval foundations, was extended in 1857 and the west tower added in 1880.[2]

On a July afternoon, Reppinichen is a nice place to stop and stretch the legs. The Latvians had been marching for the best part of 120 km to get to this point, and probably moved through here late at night and as quietly as possible to avoid attracting attention, heading towards Eichenquast. They were now just 40 km from the Elbe.

---

2   Neitmann (ed.), *Historical Local Lexicon for Brandenburg, Part V* (Belzig: Zauch, 2011), p.360 ff.

Reppinichen's church and fire station. Picture: author.

Eichenquast: warning signs at the entrance to the training area for the German military. Picture: author.

Colonel Janums and his men had been moving through the forest for nearly two days, staying off the roads and scouting ahead for German patrols, knowing there were orders out to apprehend them. The immediate threat from the Soviet spearhead sweeping round the south-east of Berlin had been left behind on the other side of the swamps south-east of Beelitz and Fichtenwalde. Another 17 km through the forest brought them to Eichenquast, today a restricted military training area backing up to a small housing estate. The road runs out abruptly at the edge of the forest where signs warn curious passers-by to stay out.

The forest ends at Quast, and this now was the most critical part of the operation for Colonel Janums – to navigate the final kilometres to the Americans and avoid any German forces standing between his men and safety.

136   ESCAPE FROM BERLIN

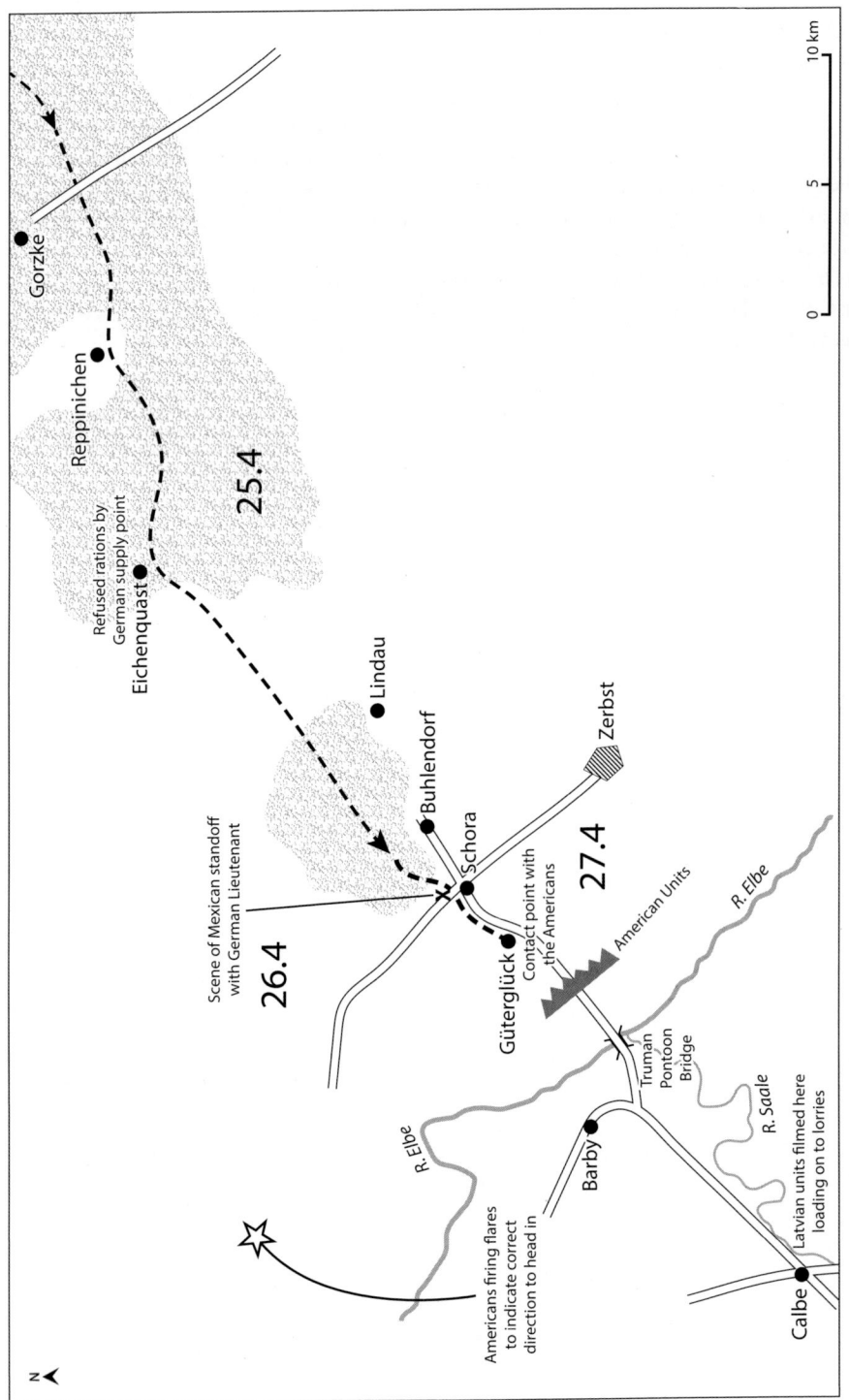

Map 13   The critical final kilometres for the Janums Battle Group: from breaking cover at Eichenquast to the Mexican standoff at Schora.

16

The 'Going Over'

Colonel Janums and his men were very close to the Americans at this point. The Russians were not far away and now the Germans wanted to know why they were there. The slightest mistake could change their lives forever, but doing nothing was not an option. Plans were made to go forward, find the Americans, make contact and surrender.

First Lieutenant Bušmanis describes how the scouts sent out to gather information on how the land lay reported back.

> About 1300 hours the two scouting parties return, one followed quickly by the other. The most useful information comes from the group led by Private P. They have managed to get to the German defence positions, which were being held by very weak forces. They have absolutely no heavy artillery.
>
> The nearest place where the Americans are is Güterglück. Before there is the village of Schora, which is in no-man's land. The Americans seem to have very powerful artillery, as in places the road is ploughed up with small grenade holes. The reason for the American halt most certainly isn't German resistance. The other group's leader gives more or less the same information, though the news isn't as definite.
>
> Our mood lifts on hearing this. So now we have to act. The Squadron Leader calls both battalion commanders and holds a meeting. After a short discussion, it is decided to send a parliamentarian group to the Americans, consisting of one officer, two NCOs and one private as an interpreter. These men need to reach the Americans and notify them of our plan to go over to them and be interned.
>
> We want to go over tonight, unarmed, between 0100 hours and 0300. So that we know where the Americans will be expecting us, we ask that they shoot multi-coloured flares into the air every hour, on the hour.
>
> During the meeting Lieutenant V comes in to say that two military police have arrived in connection with the lost property. They want to speak to the unit commander and, of course, find out what unit we are and under whose authority we are here.
>
> The Squadron Leader gives a deep sigh. The inevitable has happened, then. The owners of the property have notified the police. Thinking what to do next,

we decide that it wouldn't be suitable for the Squadron Leader to meet the military police on his own. That would give away the fact that there is a larger unit here. Therefore, Captain A is to be sent to talk things over and move them along.[1]

It's clear that Captain A isn't at all happy about this, but he is too good an officer to voice his reluctance aloud, plus he understands that he is the only one suitable for the job. In the squadron he is the justice officer, by profession a lawyer and, of all those present, speaks the best German.

As expected, the military police want to know a lot. Amongst other things, they demand to be given the names of all those involved in appropriating the goods. But then we'd have to give the names of all the 1st Battalion! This time Captain A fares better. He manages to avoid this question as well as others so adroitly that as a result the military police are satisfied to leave matters to the next day when, apparently, the unit commander is expected to return. The military police leave.

No sooner have they disappeared on their bicycles round the bend than our abandoned car from yesterday appears from the other direction. The driver, with a great deal of difficulty, has managed to get petrol and is with us again.[2]

He goes straight to the Squadron Leader and says he has come to give news about the situation at the front. In his report he relates how, trying to find us and getting lost, he has got almost as far as the Americans. On the way he hasn't seen a single German soldier. To his mind there shouldn't be any problem from the Germans when going over.

We are really happy to see him. Firstly, for the good news about the situation at the front and secondly, we now have a car at our disposal. Because of the latter, the Squadron Leader changes his previous decision. He gives his car for the use of the parliamentarian group but, due to limited seating, the number has to be restricted.

In due course the car sets off but only the private, acting as interpreter, accompanies Captain A. We come out of the trees and our eyes follow them to the edge of the forest.[3]

By this time, Arvīds Kalupnieks writes, the Germans were actively looking for Colonel Janums.

On the morning of 26 April, we are awoken by the voice of a farmer who is working the fields next to the forest. He is urging on his horses. Around lunchtime, we send out a reconnaissance patrol to investigate the frontline. Our men stand alert, guarding our fellow soldiers from the surprises we may encounter here in the forest.

1 Lieutenant Zvirgzdiņš and Captain Akermanis.
2 This is Private 'Z'.
3 Edvins Bušmanis pp.27–31.

THE 'GOING OVER'   139

We receive news that the Germans are looking for the Colonel. It becomes clear that we can't hang around here. The patrol returns and tells us that the front has very weak German forces [and that] there is no heavy artillery or mortars here in this area. We instantly send out representatives, led by Captain Akermanis, to make contact with the American troops.[4]

Captain Akermanis takes up the story.

After a five-day march and many sleepless nights, the exhausted participants finally reached their planned rest location on 26 April at 0300, in a forest around six kilometres from Lindau. The forest in which the soldiers rested was a thick, young pine plantation, and was extremely useful for hiding from American planes, which dominated the airspace there.

We set up the group's command point at a large pine tree which stood well apart from the young pine plantation, in order to complete preparations for surrendering to the Americans. It was time to find out where and how far away from us the main battle line was. The scout patrol, which had been sent out to discover how powerful the German forces were on the front, how they were grouped, and where the American line might be, discovered that the front was not fortified, even with barbed wire, and only weak German forces were in the main battle lines.

Ahead of us in trenches were a German anti-aircraft artillery unit, and the American units were near the village of Güterglück, around five kilometres west of Zerbst, from which their powerful artillery opened fire on any movement by the Germans.

The Germans had not given up in the search for Colonel Janums, and even now were sending out search squads of military police to look for him.

A group of 20 gendarmes who were looking for Janums turned up in Lindau wood on bicycles. The liaison officer tried to explain to them that the commander had gone to the front. When the gendarmes didn't want to accept that, Janums ordered the Liaison Company to spread out and set up machine guns. The gendarmes understood that much better and hurriedly got on their bikes.[5]

To ensure that we were not destroyed when we began our march towards the Americans, and to avoid potential confusion, Janums decided to contact the Americans directly. Calling the officers to his command point, he gave the order to begin the march to the Americans that day – 26 April. To avoid potential miscommunications and to protect the group from American artillery and air attacks, Janums decided to contact the Americans in advance by sending negotiators to them. To do this, he ordered me and two more soldiers – English speakers – to sort out the terms for crossing the front.

4   Kalupnieks, Colonel Janums and his men.
5   Petersons, *Mums Japarnak*, p.52–55.

On receiving this mission, I was well aware that only surrender to the Americans would save the group's soldiers from capture by the Russians, as Red Army units were fast approaching the Elbe. This task was made much easier by the group's only motor car arriving at our location. While the battle group navigated the area using our compasses, this car's driver [Private Z] was happily able to find and reach the group via the backroads. Our driver, surname Zorgenfreijs [trans: Carefree], truly proved himself to be a carefree and brave soldier, which greatly eased and sped up the delegation's path to the Americans.

We climbed into the car and set off towards Güterglück (Güterglück – good luck!). As we approached the German frontline, a German commander suddenly climbed out of a trench, stepped in front of the car and warned us that moving along the frontline could provoke enemy artillery fire. When I explained that we had been ordered by Kampfgruppe Janums to scout the enemy's positions, this young German commander replied that he was not aware of the battle group being on this front. We got out of further discussions, and I ordered Private Zorgenfreijs to cross the German frontline and continue driving towards Güterglück.[6]

First Lieutenant Bušmanis continues.

In his report, the driver has also told the Squadron Leader that there are some abandoned houses in the direction of the front, about 10 km from us. He thinks there might be something to eat there. On the basis of this, the Squadron Leader orders Lieutenant Zv, who has returned empty-handed, to take ten men and go to see if there really is something to be had. Should that be the case, Lieutenant Zv is ordered to sort things out so that, at 0100, when the squad goes past, there is food ready. He finishes with, 'At least we won't have to go into captivity on an empty stomach.' The detail leaves in a big hurry.

Waiting for the agreed departure time, we spend the remaining hours as each man sees fit. 'Getting ready for captivity', we wash in the nearby stream and spruce ourselves up, as we haven't washed or shaved for two days, not to mention not undressing in that time either. When we have finished, we feel spiritually rejuvenated.

On the way to the stream we notice that soldiers, regardless of the order, are stealing away to the nearest houses to look for food. Being hungry ourselves we understand them very well, but wandering around can't be allowed. We don't yet know how the parliamentarians will have got on and how long we will have to stay here. We have to be as inconspicuous as possible. Therefore the soldiers we meet on the road are quietly but firmly turned back.

The hours pass slowly and it begins to get dark. Suddenly, on the road nearby, we hear the familiar sound of an engine and our car appears back in the forest. We rush to it to check what has happened. Why have the parliamentarians

6   Akermanis, *To the Americans*.

returned? But in the car we see only the driver and the private-interpreter. 'What's happened to Captain A?' we ask each other.

The driver reports to the Squadron Leader that the 'going over' is agreed. Captain A has stayed with the Americans and they have been sent back to notify the 'going over' conditions and time. According to the American instructions, the 'going over' has to take place this very night, with all weapons, up to 0100 at Schora.

The driver also relates that their 'going over' had taken place without any specific hold-ups. On the way there, they had met a group of German soldiers. They had stopped the car and warned them that the Americans were already in the nearest village. Captain A had fooled them, making up a story on the spur of the moment.

The Americans had received them very courteously, as courteously as is possible to expect from the enemy. To begin with, they hadn't wanted to believe that there could be such a large unit in the vicinity – and furthermore, Latvians – but finally Captain A had convinced them.

Then the Americans had decided to send back the car, but not knowing how they would manage to return to the unit, promised to send up the requested light signals on the hour. When the driver had complained that he wouldn't have enough petrol for the return journey, the Americans had filled up the tank and in place of the German pistols they confiscated had given him a big American Colt. 'To be used if a German tries to stop you,' they told him. However, he hadn't met a single person on the way back.

Captain Akermanis had been held by the Americans while the driver was sent back with instructions. In his 1988 account of these final final hours, he recalls the first meeting with them – which did not appear promising at first.

> As we approached the village [Güterglück], we saw white sheets hanging out of the windows of buildings, and when we entered the village, we were stopped suddenly by a group of women and children. They urged us, frantically, to leave the village, the sooner, the better.
>
> An American unit had entered the village the previous day, ordering them to hang out white sheets but with a warning to take them down quickly should any German unit enter.[7]
>
> Not following orders would result in the village being fired on. To calm these people down, we continued our journey. Assuming that the American frontline must be near the village, and we were already nearing their field of vision, I started waving the towel we had brought with us, which was no longer white but rather a grey colour.
>
> After a short drive, near a bush, I saw a well-hidden American soldier, who ordered us with a hand signal to leave the road. We continued driving through

---

7   SS units were known to kill everyone found in a building displaying white flags.

an open field, until we reached and crossed their well-built positions. We drove along the next portion of the road accompanied by American soldiers.

When we entered a small village, which was not on the map, we were suddenly stopped by a smiling group of American soldiers. Although these were not our enemies, we had not expected such a polite greeting, and we also smiled. We felt as though we had met with friends of our people. Sadly, this feeling was fleeting. The next moment, without dropping their smiles, they began searching our pockets, holding up every object they found and calling it a 'souvenir'.

Once this procedure was finished, we were left on the side of the road near a barn wall, now without our watches and valuables, and, as if to calm our anxiety, we were told that we would be taken to the nearest prisoner of war camp at their next convenience. We explained in vain that we had been tasked with negotiating terms of surrender for all the soldiers in our unit. The soldiers paid no attention to what we told them.

Leaving us without supervision, the group scattered, now paying more attention to our car. Getting in, the Americans began a joyride, and it seemed as though our delegation would be unable to complete its task. Knowing the importance of our task, we tried to contact the soldiers' headquarters ourselves.

My soldiers, who spoke English, were able to speak to passing American soldiers and with their help, contact their headquarters. There, I was spoken to by the unit's interpreter, a corporal, but he didn't want to believe that we were Latvians in German uniforms. We were able to convince him that we were Latvian with a certificate of military service from the Latvian Army and a few photos taken during Latvia's independence.

Having heard, with noticeable interest, my assertion and my task of determining terms of surrender, he finally said: 'If you say that you speak Latvian, then let's talk Latvian. I was also born and raised in Latvia, and my family and I moved to America in 1938.' This noticeably improved our mood, and gave us hope of receiving terms of surrender.

From the subsequent, now much lighter conversation, I found out that the interpreter was a young Jewish man. In his time, he was a student at the Jaunjelgava Secondary School, and at school had seen the military calendar for pupils I had published.

Our conversation was interrupted by loud voices and singing next door. Now and then, when the door opened, we could see American officers sitting around a table. With their feet on the table and bottles raised in the air, they were clearly having fun. They could afford to, because for them the war was over. All they needed to do was wait for and shake hands with their then-allies, the Russians, who were at that point fast approaching their positions.

The interpreter didn't have the courage to interrupt these celebrating officers, but made a phone call to ask for advice. As a result of the call, an American major arrived at the headquarters. The major was greatly sceptical of my assertion that we were here to discuss our terms of surrender, and that Kampfgruppe Janums was awaiting news of a time and place to cross the front, and he didn't want to believe us. He was aware of every German unit in this area and had not been notified of our battle group's arrival. He asked for the current location of the battle group and promised to verify this himself. I later found out that a plane was sent to verify this.

Janums later told me of the arrival of a plane at their pine thicket six kilometres north-west of Lindau. They had noticed the approach of the plane in the distance and had stopped all movement, as they had done throughout the march. It had circled several times, and he had taken the appearance of the plane as a sign that we were in contact with the Americans, but he could not have known that their careful hiding could be so decisive in the success of my mission.

Expecting the major to return with good news, I asked the interpreter to start looking for our car, because it was the only way for us to get the news to Janums before nightfall. Luckily, our car was found. It was abandoned on the edge of the village when it ran out of fuel, without major damage. Our driver Private Zorgenfreijs reclaimed it and brought it into driving condition. This pleased us all, including the interpreter, who was on our side, and improved our mood.

Without my watch, which had been taken by the first Americans we encountered, it was hard to tell what time it was, but the sun was starting to set when a Jeep braked hard outside the headquarters, and the major jumped out. In an anxious voice, he told the interpreter that the plane had been unable to see any gathering of soldiers in the location stated, and there was no change along the entire German front. He therefore refused to tell any questionable enemy units a time and place for crossing the front. Watching the conversation between the major and the interpreter, we already knew that it was bad news.

The interpreter then regretfully told us the major's decision, and it seemed like our last hope to complete my mission was lost. Already worried, I asked the interpreter to tell the major again that we undertook our five-day march from the Eastern Front at night, avoiding being seen by planes. Usually, planes, however low they flew, found it difficult to see well-hidden stationary soldiers. It was therefore possible that the plane sent by the major was unable to see our unit, which, on top of this, was waiting in a thick pine forest.

The soldiers themselves were Latvians only, who had fought for their lost country and freedom only on the Eastern Front. We as Latvian citizens had a friendly relationship with the American people, and our only motive was to avoid being captured by Russians at the end of the war.

We could feel that the interpreter, who understood our situation well and was not indifferent to our fate, tried to explain my accounts in full, and also added his own assurance that we really were Latvian soldiers, and that he believed my story in full.

After a while, after some thought, the major finally unrolled a map, and indicated a location for our surrender near Güterglück at 0100 hours, bringing our weapons with us. If my story turned out to be a trick, my companions and I would be held solely responsible. Tapping his pistol holder to let us know the consequences awaiting us, the major began one phone call after another.

After thanking him for the trust he placed in us and the chance to cross the American frontline, I began writing a message to Janums about the conditions for crossing the front, promising that coloured flares would be used to indicate the group's direction of movement. I sent the message to Janums with Private Zorgenfreijs. Over time, the names of the other delegation members, whose good English helped us to complete our mission, have escaped me. On that same day, when the sun rose, the forward-most units of the 30th Russian Army were approaching the American positions.

Luckily, by driving via the backroads and thus avoiding meeting the German commander who could not just capture him but hand him over to the German military police, Zorgenfreijs was able to reach the battle group in good time and pass on the message, giving the battle group the opportunity to start their surrender march promptly.[8]

First Lieutenant Bušmanis describes the scenes in the pine forest six kilometres from Lindau:

By the time the driver finishes his story, the clock shows 2130 already. From us to Schora – that is, the 'going over' point – is about 15 km. In order to make it on time, there is not much time left.

The Squadron Leader therefore gives me the task of informing everyone to form up urgently. He wants the whole squadron to be on the forest firebreak in departure order in 20 minutes. I give the order and messengers hurry off in all directions.

We can see that discipline still rules in our units because almost everyone has already gathered before the specified 20 minutes are up. Without any unnecessary noise, dark figures are grouping themselves into companies and battalions, standing in the usual three-man line.

As soon as the lining-up has finished, the Squadron Leader appears. He is serious, even slightly sad. He has asked for everyone to be lined up because he wants to speak to us all while we are all together and, as squadron commander, to say a final few words of farewell.

The Squadron Leader's speech is very short, without flowery phrases, but heartfelt. He thanks everyone: officers, NCOs, soldiers, for the loyalty and discipline shown to date on this march. Starting out, maybe on our final road together, he invites us to carry it out in just as disciplined a way as hitherto.

He warns us not to see captivity through rose-coloured glasses and not to hope that everyone will be set free within the next few days. To his mind there will be a lot to overcome and endure till the opening of the PoW camp gates.

He also reminds everyone to show our previous excellent Latvian soldier military bearing and discipline in captivity too, for often the value of a whole nation is appreciated through the conduct and behaviour of one man.

---

8   Akermanis, *To the Americans*.

Arvīds Kalupnieks adds extra detail to this moment:

> The Colonel alludes to the difficulties each man had to overcome to make the long journey from Berlin. 'It was all necessary,' he says, 'to save ourselves from certain death. During this time, my worries have been for you all. The Germans wanted to give us up to death, but in spite of the severity of our fate, we have escaped. But all is not over. Don't think that you will no longer face difficulties. The final stretch is ahead of us. Now I can tell you all our final target: it is to hand ourselves over to the Allies. Anyone who doesn't want to do so can remain here. The day will come when we are needed by our homeland, so there was no use in staying near Berlin. Well, sons, now we start our final march as soldiers.'
>
> We all receive orders to remain strictly disciplined and overcome anything that could delay us extremely stringently. Column after column heads towards the front. Despite our exhaustion, the soldiers' pace is fast. The German lines start in about 10 km.[9]

First Lieutenant Bušmanis recounts the final journey:

> Precisely at 2200 the order sounds to move out. The first to show the way, ahead of everyone, is the car. Then we follow at the fore of our HQ, then the units belonging to HQ, 1 and 2 Battalions. Everyone is in formation, with all our weapons.
>
> We leave kilometre after kilometre behind and, as we near the place where the advance group has been sent to prepare food, it is already midnight. We have another five kilometres to go, so it's clear that there will be no time for eating.
>
> Following the Squadron Leader's instructions, I jump in the car and hurry ahead to warn the cooks of the change of plan. As expected, they are up to their eyes in preparation. A whole cow is boiling in a number of pans but the beef isn't ready yet.
>
> With a heavy heart and an empty stomach, I hurry to give the cooks the order to abandon everything and join the march. To begin with they don't want to believe me but then begin to fish out chunks of meat from the pans, even though they are not fully cooked, to hand out to the passing troops.[10]

Bušmanis is aware of the sensitivity of the situation they may be marching into, and so takes steps to signal their intentions clearly.

> Whilst the men are busy, I go into the living room of the abandoned house. I have another mission: to obtain a white flag which, according to the American instructions, has to be visible when crossing. Unable to find a single white sheet or tablecloth anywhere, I pull down a white curtain. Looking at it more carefully, it looks like thin net. I decide that in the dark it will be good enough.

---

9 Kalupnieks, *Colonel Janums and his Men.*
10 Bušmanis, pp.34–37.

On my way through the kitchen, I suddenly grab a knife, forks and two different-sized spoons, not knowing at that moment how valuable these objects would be later.

The house which we had taken over turns out not to be completely abandoned after all. A few inhabitants have stayed behind. Judging by the language, they are Poles. They are standing in the yard and on seeing me with the white flag whisper amongst themselves.

Meanwhile the units have arrived. Marching past, the soldiers grab the discarded pieces of meat and share amongst themselves. Of course, in these conditions, it's not possible to share equally; the smart ones get more, the slower get less or even have to do without. It's not possible to alter anything.

We reckon we need at least 45 minutes for eating and the designated time for crossing mustn't be missed. Marching on, I get a longish pole from a soldier and, continuing to march, I tie half of the torn-down curtain to it. The flag is now ready.

The soldiers, disappointed in not getting time to eat, march on in silence. The road is bad; sandy. That too means that progress is not as brisk as it should be. However, we soon reach the hard surface of the main road and walking for everyone becomes easier. Not far from the frontline, a plane flies over the column.

Instinctively we all freeze under the trees at the side of the road, not knowing who the plane belongs to. In addition, at the moment, we are more wary of German planes than American.

Throughout the whole march, except for one bullet from the German rear (the bullet hit a soldier's hand, lightly wounding him) there hasn't been the slightest noise of battle. We haven't seen a single soldier.

There was to be one final damatic moment, though – a 'Mexican standoff' with the officer commanding the last German line before the Americans.[11]

When we have given up hope of seeing anyone, about a kilometre before Schora village, nearing a fork in the road, a figure appears on the road and in German orders, 'Halt!'

The car that has been ahead of us stops and we stop by it. Coming closer we see that the person giving the order is a German Leutnant. He is holding a pistol, which, upon seeing the Squadron Leader, he waves threateningly at his chest. The soldiers marching behind us catch up and stop.

The moment's silence is broken by the German.

'Where are you going?'

'To the Americans,' replies the Squadron Leader, expressionlessly.

'You're not going anywhere,' the German says, in an imperious voice.[12]

---

11 With its origins in the American West of the 1870s, a Mexican standoff is an armed deadlock that no-one can win – whoever shoots will also be shot.
12 This is Leutnant Geiselhart, an officer in an anti-aircraft artillery regiment, serving under Colonel Albrecht. He took up defensive positions at Schora with four four-barrelled anti

'Don't do anything stupid,' the Squadron Leader replies, and over his shoulder calls to the soldiers who have just arrived. 'Men, load!'

Five to six sub-machine guns slide off shoulders instantly, and simultaneously the safety catches can be heard being released.

The German lowers his pistol from the Squadron Leader's chest and this time his question sounds like pleading. Obviously he has been influenced by the sub-machine guns readied for firing. It seems he has only just noticed the column of soldiers appearing out of the dark and waiting for the hold-up to be sorted.

'Where are you going?'

'Over to the Americans.'

'Who are you?'

'Latvians.'

'Are there any Germans amongst you?'

'No.'

'You can go,' the German says, but this no longer sounds like permission but rather regret that he himself can't cross over with us. The car begins to move and we begin to march again.

I mention to the Squadron Leader that maybe we should take the crazy German with us but the Squadron Leader refuses, saying that it's not worth messing with them. If they want to, let them fight on.

Arvīds Kalupnieks remembers the Mexican standoff this way:

> Suddenly, from a ditch, a German Leutnant jumps in front of the Colonel and points a pistol at him. With his characteristic calmness, the Colonel pushed the Leutnant's arm aside, saying, 'Don't be stupid! We're going over.' Seeing this, the locks of the *Janumieši* guns click, telling the Colonel that we are ready for any surprises. Our automatic rifles are placed in position; these ensure the unit's passage. The march continues.
>
> Along the sides of the road, in dark twilight, we see the figures of German soldiers timidly watching us, shrunk into ditches.[13]

---

aircraft batteries. He and the soldiers under his command were later taken prisoner by the Red Army, and he was released from captivity in 1949.

13 Memoirs of Arvīds Kalupnieks. Trans. Māra Walsh-Sinka from Leitītis (1986).

17

Fiat 500 in Schora

My Fiat 500 chugs through a landscape which is now mostly flat farmland with the occasional copse of trees and farm buildings. Articulated lorries carrying agricultural supplies roar past regularly as I steer the Fiat ever nearer to the Elbe – first through Buhlendorf and then quickly on to Schora. With the sun high in the sky, visibility is very good.

The junction of the L51 with the 184 from Buhlendorf to Schora was the scene of the Mexican standoff with Leutnant Geiselhart. The drainage ditch alongside the major road would have been ready-made shelter for machine gun positions and mortars defending against the oncoming Americans, and beyond that was no-man's land.

Still with the Americans, Captain Akermanis was collected by the major and driven to the rendezvous point.

> The Major, already dressed in battle uniform, drove up to the unit headquarters and invited me and the interpreter to join the drive to the meeting spot. In the note to Janums, I asked him to bring a flare gun. The colourful flares shot every hour on the hour showed that the group was heading in the correct direction.
>
> During the drive, I noticed enhanced movement by motorised units heading towards the front. Evidently, the Americans were attempting to guard against any possible surprises. The Major chose a hillock near Güterglück as his vantage point, and the first colourful flares were shot up at 2200 hours. Several officers and soldier-signallers gathered around the major, keeping contact with the American forces behind us.
>
> Shortly before the agreed meeting time at 0100, we could already hear the sounds of movement, and soon we could see the movers themselves with Janums at the head.
>
> The silence and tension was interrupted by loud conversations between American officers. Clearly, their anxiety had been allayed, and they were convinced that this was not an enemy trick.[1]

---

1   Akermanis, *To the Americans*.

FIAT 500 IN SCHORA 149

Buhlendorf village. Picture: author.

Buhlendorf to Schora. Picture: author.

The last German lines before the Americans at the junction of the L51 with the 184, and the scene of the Mexican standoff with Leutnant Geiselhart. Picture: Natalie Carragher.

18

The Surrender

The diary of Janums Battle Group adjutant First Lieutenant Edvīns Bušmanis records the final stages of the Latvians' odyssey through the forests to safety.

At the fork we keep right in the direction of Schora. On the left I notice a machine gun set up. It's an 08 type with water cooling, the sort the Germans used in WWI. I notice several soldiers lying beside it.[1]

In case they decide to send a few volleys at the tail end of the column, I suggest to the Squadron Leader that he face them off with a few of our automatic rifles. 'Can do,' the Squadron Leader agrees. 'Give the order.'

I pass the order on to 1, 5, and 8 Companies, ensuring against a sudden surprise from our allies-till-now by leaving pairs of machine guns alternately in the ditches at the side of the road. The guns are in position and, as I heard later, the Germans were considerably indignant, accompanied by a lot of swearing!

Carrying on along the road, I notice a soldier here and there in the ditches. They are holding either Panzerfausts or a rifle. How sad, I think to myself, to have to face a superior, technically better-equipped enemy with only a rifle; to fight an enemy with countless cannons with only a Panzerfaust. And to do it when the result of the battle is almost a foregone conclusion.

I hurry forward and give the flag I have made to the soldier sitting in the car at the front. Schora is empty and dark. Here and there buildings can be seen [which have been] reduced to rubble by artillery. After the first bend in the road on the far side of the village, I see the first signs of life from the Americans. There are two red lights, what could be a car, and after 100 metres, four dark figures.

They let the car with the white flag go past and [then] approach us. We stop and wait for them to come near. Behind us the whole column comes to a halt. I look at my watch. It shows 0110. A new day has begun, 27 April. We have arrived only 10 minutes later than the appointed time.

---

1 Most probably a Maxim MG08 water-cooled belt-fed automatic machine gun, in service around 1917.

The four figures are our welcoming party: an American major, two lieutenants as interpreters and our Captain A. Having approached us, the major gives a salute. We reply, not with the Hitler greeting anymore but the same as his: with the hand at the hat, according to Latvian military rules.

Noticing the Squadron Leader, the [American] major turns to him with a request to excuse his squadron commander, who was unable to greet him. He is proud that the honour has fallen to him. The major invites us to continue our journey. Together with one lieutenant-interpreter he joins the Squadron Leader; the other lieutenant and Captain A join me.

To begin with we march in silence. Silent too are our soldiers, marching in strict formation, almost completely in step. Hearing the Squadron Leader talking to his companions, we begin to converse too. The lieutenant asks me about my rank; in return I ask him about his, etc.

He notices a gunner's telescope hanging round my neck, and expresses a wish to obtain it for his battalion commander. I'm not surprised by his wish but by the politeness with which it is expressed. Knowing that sooner or later I'm going to have to surrender the telescope, I happily fulfil his wish.

About a kilometre further on, at a level crossing near Gütergrück, we see the first American soldiers. They too look at us curiously. We are stopped. It turns out that there are mines ahead. Some of the soldiers move us off the road and around the blockade, then back onto the road.

Then we are disarmed. Everyone has to hand in their weapons and other war equipment: telescopes, maps, compasses, torches, etc. The handing over takes place very simply without any ceremony. Soldiers move forward slowly and throw everything in two piles: one for weapons, the other for everything else.

The company commanders stand by and give their final orders. A bit further on a few American soldiers check that in handing everything in, nothing has been forgotten. No-one touches our backpacks or personal belongings. Following instructions, we leave our car at the side of the road. The driver who has driven and looked after the car all this time sadly joins the column.

Everyone is quiet and depressed. Each one of us feels that we are no longer soldiers now but prisoners of war. Though everyone realises that the war is over for them, no-one is happy about it.

I feel very strange. I couldn't say I'm sad but I don't feel any joy either. I'm just satisfied that our plan has been successful and that this was the way my life as a soldier had to come to an end. Physically I'm relieved as I don't have to carry heavy weapons.

A few hundred metres further on from the checkpoint a row of cars can be seen. Upon reaching them officers are commanded to get in. Soldiers and NCOs are left on the road. A moment later the cars begin to move. We just manage to see that the soldiers and NCOs begin to march simultaneously.

Everyone is silent with their thoughts and feelings. We are going forward to a new, unknown future.[2]

In his memoir, Arvīds Kalupnieks describes the surrender:

> We go through a village, behind which is no-man's land. Behind that, along a railway, start the American lines.
>
> The time is 0120 hours when we put down our weapons. This is the tenth encirclement from which the Colonel has rescued his regiment. He never thought about himself, only his soldiers. We have walked about 100 km to reach the American lines. And the words he said to Major Ķīlītis when saying goodbye came true: 'If someone tells you that I am dead, don't believe them until you see my corpse.' The Colonel and his soldiers are one body: that is also what he said in his final farewell.
>
> Every man has followed his Colonel in this march, and every one of the *Janumiesi* is willing to fight with the legendary Colonel again for the freedom of our beloved homeland, Latvia.
>
> Latvia will exist as long as we are willing to make sacrifices for its future.[3]

---

2   Bušmanis, p.37.
3   Kalupnieks, *Colonel Janums and his Men*. Trans. Māra Walsh-Sinka. His memoir was written while Latvia was still occupied by the Soviet Union.

19

78 Years Later

Beyond the junction of the L51 with the 184 where Leutnant Geiselhart challenged the Latvians in an ill-judged Mexican standoff lies Schora village: a small place, not really much more than a cluster of houses alongside the L51 road. By now the Latvians would be navigating by the stars and by the direction of the flares being sent up by the Americans a kilometre or so away.

After a journey of almost 100 kilometres on foot through the forest and cross-country the Latvians reached Güterglück. The Americans had halted just outside the village and were waiting for contact from them. Andreas Baumgart, a teacher in nearby Zerbst – fascinated by the story since his father told him about the Latvians as a boy – wrote an article about their journey for the local paper in 2022.

> The village seemed to be abandoned and had suffered much under the artillery. The unit walked along the cobblestones with their footsteps echoing in the silence of the night. When they reached the western part of the village they were greeted by an American major with his adjutant. Janums stopped the column and as the commander of the American group approached, the battle group put down their weapons. They exchanged courteous greetings.
>
> A few moments later Colonel Janums saw 12 tanks about 50 paces away, with their guns pointing down the street at them. The Americans obviously didn't want to risk anything.[1]

The contact point itself today is unremarkable – it's unmarked and that's not surprising. While the incredible escape of the Janums Battle Group was a journey of stamina, determination and resourcefulness – as well as considerable luck – it was a minor footnote to this chapter of the war.

As First Lieutenant Bušmanis notes in his diary, the Latvians met the Americans just past the bend in the road from Güterglück, with tanks in position by the treeline in the photograph below and the river Elbe behind that.

I turn the car around at the contact point and re-set the trip meter to zero, then – according to Bušmanis' diary – drive a kilometre back in the direction I had come, to the point where he said the Mexican standoff with Leutnant Geiselhart took place.

---

[1] A. Baumgart, *1945: The Odyssey of Battle Group Janums* in Zeitung Volksstimme, 17.06.2022. Trans. Tania Kibermanis.

His measurements were exactly right: this corresponds to the junction between the country roads and the 184.

I drive back through Güterglück, past the contact point again and on to the Elbe, where first I come across warning signs showing a car plunging into water, then – slowing down – find a cable ferry across the river. The river is not very wide, but these are the sandbanks and island banks where refugees gathered when the Americans came across. Somewhere along here there would have been the Truman Bridge. On the other side of the river is the town of Barby and beyond that Calbe, where the US Army filmed Colonel Janums marching his men into captivity.[2]

There's electricity rigged up to the bridge and a timetable but there doesn't seem to be anyone around to operate it. The sun is setting and I've had a long day, so as I have a meeting in Zerbst tomorrow with Mayor Andreas Dittmann, I think my journey, like that of Colonel Janums and the Latvians, ends here.

When I get back to my hotel, I look up Bušmanis' final tally of what happened to the Latvians during this period.

The total number of men left behind in Berlin with the Recce Battalion was 307, comprising 13 officers or cadet officers with 294 non-commissioned officers and soldiers. Most of these men were killed or captured in the final days of the Battle of Berlin, but some survived.[3]

Of the men who surrendered to the Americans, 29 were officers, 11 deputy officers – presumably promoted in the field; 126 were instructors (the equivalent of non-commissioned officers or NCOs) and 658 were private soldiers.

The losses from the entire escape episode are categorised in Table 1.

Table 1. The tally of losses by First Lieutenant Bušmanis from Erkner to the surrender on 27.4.45

List of Regiment Losses from Berlin to Güterglück	
Battle group battalion that hadn't arrived in the place they had been ordered to	13 officers and cadet officers; 294 NCOs (instructors) and soldiers
Stayed in Herzfelde with the battle group supplies	11 NCOs and soldiers
Sent to the Berlin commander	3 officers and cadet officers
Disappeared in the action with the enemy at Erkner	1 officer/cadet and 31 NCOs and soldiers
On their own initiative left the unit and went to Berlin	1
Killed or wounded in the accident (Panzerfaust explosion) at Dahlewitz	1 officer/cadet and 13 NCOs and soldiers
Suffered an accident at Fichtenwalde (run over by a tank)	2 soldiers and NCOs
Went to Potsdam for food	4 soldiers and NCOs

Source: Bušmanis diary in Leitītis, p.95

---

2 This remarkable film was discovered by chance during the research for this book, and can be seen at the author's website at <www.vincenthunt.co.uk> and also at the US Holocaust Museum Memorial online at <https://collections.ushmm.org/search/catalog/irn1004700>.

3 This is the subject of the author's forthcoming book for Helion, *Sent to Die in Berlin – the Latvian 15th SS Recce Battalion, 20 April–8 May 1945*.

Schora village, summer 2023. Picture: author.

Passing through Schora village and its well. Picture: author.

78 YEARS LATER 157

Where the war ended for the Janums Battle Group – the contact point in Güterglück where they met the Americans just after 0100 hours on 27.04.1945. Picture: author.

The Elbe, a symbol of safety for the Latvians. Picture: author.

The Elbe at sunset. Picture: Natalie Carragher.

Part Three
Janums' Captivity

20

'We are Latvians, and we consider that the war has finished' – the Handwritten Diary of Colonel Janums

I am in Rīga, in the back office of the War Museum in the Old Town, looking through a pile of folders and envelopes. This is part of their collection of material from the 15th Division in Pomerania and Germany and has been assembled for me by the curator, Jānis Tomaševskis.

Inside the envelope he has given me is a booklet of typewritten pages. This is the diary of Colonel Janums, possibly in its second form, having been typed up from the original handwritten diary. That's here too.

The handwritten diary covers the period 22 January 1945 to 27 April 1945 and is written in blue ink with a fountain pen on A4 size paper. It dates back to the days when Janums was a prisoner of war at Camp 2227 at Zedelghem in Belgium. It's bound in covers made from thick cardboard once used for shipping wholewheat biscuits, as the print in English reveals.

Janums' version follows the story told by Bušmanis very closely, but adds detail about events on the last day, as the Latvians prepared for the 'going over'.

Janums had sent Captain Akermanis to make contact with the Americans and agree that flares of different colours would be fired every hour on the hour so the Latvians knew the right direction to head in. As he waited for the car to return, his attention was distracted by news of food nearby.

> In the afternoon Lieutenant Zvirgzdiņš tells me that civilians have already abandoned Buhlendorf, leaving behind cattle, potatoes and other food. The men haven't eaten in two days so I order the kitchen staff and cooks to go down there and get busy. At 2145 Captain Akermanis sends back a messenger.
>
> The US Army is convinced that it has detailed information about German units in this sector but they don't know anything about a 'Kampfgruppe Janums'. Their spotter plane has returned from a mission not having seen any evidence of

The handwritten diary of Colonel Vilis Janums, commander of the 33rd Regiment of the Latvian 15th SS Division, at the Latvian War Museum, Rīga. Picture: author.

the group in the place where Akermanis said they were.[1] However Akermanis has convinced the Americans we are genuine and we have been given directions to cross at Güterglück at/before 0100 hours. It is 10 km to Güterglück. If we want to eat, we had better get a move on.

We have just left Buhlendorf when, in the direction of Güterglück, a number of different coloured rockets are fired. It's 2300. The Americans are showing us the way to go. It is a bright moonlit night, and our column marches quietly, without singing. The men are serious but not nervous.

When the head of the column reaches Schora, we see German soldiers hunkered down in their dugouts by the side of the road. We go past them, but suddenly out of the ditch jumps a German lieutenant, Geiselhart. He runs up to me.

'Where are you going?' he demands.

'To the Americans,' I say.

The lieutenant sticks a pistol in my chest and orders: 'You will immediately come with me, or I shoot.'

With a strong, sudden movement I push his pistol away. Behind me I hear the sound of weapons being cocked and pointed towards him. 'Don't do anything stupid,' I say to the lieutenant. 'We are Latvians, and we consider that the war has finished.'

1   Because the Latvians were too well-hidden in the forest when it went overhead.

The lieutenant says: 'OK. I will submit to a superior force.' He steps aside. As if broken, he sits down by the ditch.

To make sure they don't fire us from behind, I put four machine guns down to cover them as we cross. Then we go over to the Americans.[2]

They were met just after 0100 hours by Akermanis and the Americans, where the surrender took place of 40 officers, 126 NCOs and 658 men.[3] The military records for the US Army units in the area at the time add further detail to how Janums' men made contact with the Americans.

The 83rd 'Thunderbolt' Division had been in constant action since landing at Omaha beach, fighting their way through the Hurtgen Forest and then repulsing the German attack in the Ardennes. They had been dubbed 'the Ragtag Circus' as they raced at full speed for the Elbe, which they reached on 13 April at Barby.

Advance units crossed the river in assault boats to secure the opposite bank while engineers towed pre-prepared sections of floating Treadway bridge into position, throwing a 624 foot (190 metre) bridge across the Elbe overnight, which was named the 'Truman Bridge' after the new US President, Harry S. Truman.

By 0730 the next day tanks were crossing it to establish bridgeheads on the Berlin side.[4]

Contact from the Latvians came as the Americans were trying to persuade the German garrison at Zerbst to surrender. The Russians were not far away, and the war was a lost cause. For several days the local commander refused to surrender but eventually agreed the German garrison would not resist if the Americans came in. The Latvians made contact just before this point. Their surrender was to the 330th Infantry, part of the Thunderbolt Division. The unit log for the 330th for the period 22–30 April reads:

> The sector remained generally quiet throughout this period. Patrols were sent nightly to N and NE. No indication of enemy reinforcements was discovered; in fact it appeared the enemy was withdrawing forces from their positions to our front. We continued to improve our defences and additional AT and AP mines [anti-tank and anti-personnel] and tactical wire was laid.
>
> On the nite [sic] of 26 April K Company was contacted by a Captain of the German Army sent to arrange details for the surrender of a Regiment. The Captain accomplished his mission with the result CT JANUMS [15 Latvian SS Div] commanded by Col. Janums, with a strength of 41 officers and 856 EM [enlisted men] were marched to our PW cage. This Regt had marched from the vicinity of BERLIN to surrender to our forces.[5]

---

2 Janums, *Mana Pulka Kauja Gaitas*, translated (Self-published, 1953), pp.281–287.
3 Silgailis, p.186.
4 Article *Truman Bridge Built at Night*, The Thunderbolt 5 May 1945 page 2 at <https://83rdinfdivdocs.org/documents/newspapers/83rd_Thunderbolt_May_5_1945.pdf>.
5 Log of 330th Infantry Regiment, 83rd Division for April 1945, at <https://83rdinfdivdocs.org/units/330th-ir> (accessed 10 July 2020). By Dave Curry, 83rd Division historian.

The Truman Bridge over the Elbe, photographed by US Army soldier Louis Drucker in April 1945. Image credit: the US Holocaust Memorial Museum collection at: <https://collections.ushmm.org/search/catalog/irn501808#?rsc=170115&cv=73&c=0&m=0&s=0&xywh=-1%2C-212%2C1790%2C1696>.

```
      Co B, 643d TD Bn, was attached.

22 - 30 April 1945

     The sector remained generally quiet throughout this period. Patrols were sent
nightly to N and NE. No indication of enemy reinforcements was discovered, in fact,
it appeared the enemy was withdrawing forces from their positions to our front. We
continued to improve our defenses and additional AT and AP mines and tactical wire
was laid.

     On the nite of 26 April, K Co was contacted by a Captain of the German Army
sent to arrange details for the surrender of a Regiment. The Captain accomplished
his mission with the result CT JANUMS (15 Latvian SS Div) commanded by Col Janums,
with a strength of 41 officers and 856 EM were marched to our PW cage. This Regt
had marched from the vic of BERLIN to surrender to American forces.

     The 1st Bn (-B Co) reverted to Regtl control on 28 April at 1200. B Co was atchd
to TF Hawkins and remained under Div control. The 1st Bn (-B Co) occupied positions
vic of GUTTERGLUCK (924857) at 2000, vacated by the 3d Bn 329th Inf. The 1st Bn (-B Co)
was relieved by 3d Bn 329th Inf on 29 April and reverted to Regtl Reserve.

     The Regt was assigned to a zone of responsbility in the Div rear area for purpose
of collecting, feeding and housing displaced personnel as well as maintaining order.

     On 28 April, Col Montague, Regtl S4 and Regtl S1 set up headquarters in STASSFURT
(6568) for this purpose. On 30 April, the 1st Bn (-B, C and D Cos) moved to STASSFURT
to assist in administration and policing the area.
```

Detail of the surrender of the Janums Battle Group in the US 83rd Division log. Picture: author.

The news was announced in the 83rd Division's newspaper, the *Thunderbolt*, in the next edition, titled 'East of the Elbe':

> A dramatic midnight excursion behind German lines in the neighbourhood of Schora by Major Bedford Foster of Kenmore, (Wa) and three enlisted men from the 330th Infantry resulted in the mass surrender of a Wehrmacht regiment numbering 41 officers and 896 enlisted men from Latvia.[6]
>
> First indication of the large-scale capitulation came when S/Sgt Stanley J. Kiel of Hamtramck, Mich; and S/Sgt Cort C. Braught, Des Moines, Iowa reported to Lieutenant Warren W. Witt of Tonca City, Okla. that a German Captain had driven up to their K. Company outpost under a flag of truce and told them that his commanding officer wanted to surrender his regiment to the Americans.
>
> Witt established contact with regimental headquarters and Foster hastened to the outpost to investigate the capitulation offer. Several minutes' conversation with the German officer convinced him that the offer was *bona fide*.
>
> The signal suggested by the Latvian Captain to advise his commander to come to the rendezvous point was a green and white flare fired every even hour. Advising Witt to shoot the flare as prescribed, Foster, accompanied by Sergeant Grover Crawford of San Antonio, Texas, and two German-speaking non-comms, Sergeant Kurt Rittner of Buffalo, NY and Sergeant Fred Kramer of New York City, went out to meet the German commandant.
>
> 'It looked bad when we ran into a German road block after we had gone a couple of miles,' said Crawford, 'but the Nazi Captain succeeded in making the 30 men manning it hold their fire.'
>
> The white and green flare was fired at midnight. About an hour later the Nazi Colonel and his regiment approached the appointed meeting place. Negotiations took but a few minutes with Kramer acting as interpreter.
>
> The Wehrmacht regiment was permitted to keep its weapons until it reached the American lines because there was some danger that other German troops in the vicinity might contest the mass surrender.
>
> According to the Latvian Colonel, his regiment had been ordered on line east of Berlin, but he had no desire to continue the fight so he had proceeded to fake orders and move his men toward the Elbe. According to his story he had, at one point, been stopped by German troops and had admitted his desire to surrender.
>
> 'I threatened to fight them if they did not let me pass through,' he said. 'They let us pass.'
>
> The mass surrender was completed without hitch, and the colonel and his regiment were soon safely out of the war in the Division PW cage.[7]

---

6   NB: The correct figure was 824.
7   Article *330th Receives Surrender of Nazi Regiment* in The 83rd Thunderbolt, Vol 1, number 2, 5 May 1945 at <https://83rdinfdivdocs.org/documents/newspapers/83rd_Thunderbolt_May_5_1945.pdf> page 2. By Frank DeCarolis, Co. E, 331st Infantry Regiment and son-in-law Tom DePiano.

I am browsing through the online archives of the United States Holocaust Memorial Museum one night when I find a film in the catalogue. It's shot in a town called Calbe in Germany on 27 April 1945 and titled 'Mass Surrender PWs'. The shotlist begins:

> *Two battalions of Latvian troops march through the streets of Calbe after surrendering to US forces. Several men in arm slings. Civilians and army personnel watch surrender.*
> *01:04:18 Roll II slate. Latvian soldiers and officers load into US trucks.*

I recognise the officer leading them. That's Janums, without a doubt; a wiry, bird-like figure in an officers' coat, on the half-turn. The men march past the camera position, all in caps; without helmets, and no insignia. Certainly there is no SS insignia to be seen.

There is a sequence filmed from an upstairs window or a church tower that shows the scale of this surrender. Janums leads the march, ahead of a group of 24 men, probably the officers, with the ordinary soldiers marching ten abreast, filling the road.

As the film continues, I pause it and take a still so I can look at the picture in greater detail. There are small groups of unarmed GIs watching from the side, some leaning casually against trees with their hands in their pockets. For them this is not a formal occasion.

In another sequence trucks are pulled up at the side of the road while Colonel Janums in his officer's cap walks in what looks like a group of officers. Perhaps they're being taken to their own vehicle. Alongside Janums is a man carrying a briefcase who looks quite relaxed. As I stare as these images from seven decades ago, there even seems to be the faintest hint of a smile on his lips. I wonder if this is First Lieutenant Bušmanis, re-united with his precious briefcase and happy to have survived the war?

The shotlist continues. Seeing German soldiers surrendering was obviously quite an event for the local children, who turned out to watch.

> *01:04:56 A caravan of trucks filled with POWs move out. CUs [close ups] of children watching. More Latvian troops loaded into trucks.*

Another shot from the centre of the road shows transport lorries loaded with soldiers parked up along the side of the street.

The camera then moves round to the back of the trucks to show the process of counting and loading the prisoners. The shotlist records:

> *01:05:23 Roll III slate. Latvian POWs are counted and loaded into trucks in front of a church. Civilians and soldiers watch.*

With the human cargo loaded the trucks leave, followed by the camera.

> *Camera pans civilians talking about surrender. A crowd of women and children. A woman cries as soldiers are loaded into trucks. 01:06:29 Roll IV slate. More US*

THE HANDWRITTEN DIARY OF COLONEL JANUMS 167

Colonel Vilis Janums leads men of the 15th SS Division Latvian Legion through the streets of Calbe, Germany, after surrendering to the Americans at Güterglück on 27 April 1945. Still picture by author from newsreel footage in the collection of the United States Holocaust Memorial Museum at <https://collections.ushmm.org/search/catalog/irn1004700>. Used with permission (accessed 26 June 2020).

March past of the Latvian 15th Division in Calbe, prior to loading up for transport to PW cages. Still taken by author from US Army film. From the collection of the United States Holocaust Memorial Museum (see previous plate), used with permission.

168 ESCAPE FROM BERLIN

This image shows the scale of the surrender of the Latvian 15th Division. Still from US Army newsreel footage.

Colonel Vilis Janums (centre left) in Calbe. The officer (centre) with the briefcase is probably Edvīns Bušmanis. Still by author taken from US Army newsreel footage see timecode.

Children watch as the Latvians prepare to leave Calbe. Still by author from US Army newsreel footage, USHMM archives.

A convoy of trucks prepares to take the Latvians to holding camps. Still by author from US Army film, USHMM archives.

Men of the Janums Battle Group are counted onto trucks by the Americans. Still from US Army film, USHMM archives.

US soldiers get the last of the 824 Latvians onto trucks at Calbe, Germany, April 1945. Still by author from US Army film, USHMM archives.

trucks move out. A Red Cross Flag hangs from the church. Civilians watch. CU, children and women. Trucks leave.[8]

Later, at the conclusion of his handwritten account of his final months as a soldier – then a prisoner of war – Colonel Janums recalled the moment of surrender:

> At 2100 hours on 27 April, Janums' fighting group has ceased to exist. Together we have broken free from ten encirclements, together have suffered cold and starvation. At the moment of surrender my fighting group consisted of 40 officers and cadets, 126 NCOs and 658 soldiers.[9]
>
> We have to wait for transport, which will take us to the division HQ, which is somewhere on the other side of the river Elbe. We officers have been separated from the other soldiers and I feel a prisoner, just the same as all the other soldiers in my squadron, as all the cares and responsibilities have been taken off my shoulders.
>
> I soon had to change my mind because it turned out that even in captivity, there was many a time when it was possible to care for and support my men, even if only morally.
>
> After more than an hour's wait, transport finally arrives. According to the stars, we are travelling in a southerly direction. In a few minutes we reach the Elbe, which has a pontoon bridge built for the use of the army.
>
> A soldier stands guarding it. Every now and then he fires into the air. But why he's doing that we can't understand. When the transport is driving over the bridge I can't help but think of the many times I have racked my brains thinking of how to get my fighting group across the river.[10] And now we've solved the problem. We cross in American vehicles.
>
> It's getting near morning when we reach Calbe. All the officers are separated again and put into the basement of a house. A soldier remains on guard on the steps. The basement is fairly large and there is room for everyone. Having had a look around, to my surprise I find another exit leading to a side street. It has been provisionally nailed shut with thin, off-cut pieces of wood.
>
> It's early morning and there is no guard on the street. It seems the Americans are not particularly bothered about guarding us … and where would we escape to? All around is a foreign land and foreign people. More voluntarily rather than guarded, we remain prisoners in our cage.
>
> At about 1000 hours on 27 April, I am called for questioning/interrogation. It is carried out by an American Army captain in German. To begin with he is

---

8 US Army film in the collection of the United States Holocaust Memorial Museum at <https://collections.ushmm.org/search/catalog/irn1004700> (accessed 26 June 2020). Historical specialist Matthias Hille in Calbe has identified the road in the film as what is now Magdeburger Strasse. The marching soldiers were filmed from the east side of the street, while the loading pictures were taken from the other side.
9 Red Army tactics of encirclement were used extensively in Pomerania. For more details on this period, see the author's book *The Road of Slaughter* (Helion, 2023).
10 That is, the river Elbe, which represented safety.

interested in the German forces in this district. I explain to him that I have come from the Eastern Front and have no knowledge of the German forces hereabouts.

To prove to him that we really have come from the Berlin district, I show him the fighting group's diary, only it is written in Latvian. Our interrogation goes on and on. Dinner time arrives. The officer leaves us in his office and goes off to eat.

After about an hour he returns with a general – the commander of this division – and another two officers. The general asks me why we have come such a long way to surrender to the Americans. We surely had the opportunity to cross the front and surrender to the Red Army. I reply that to surrender to the Bolsheviks means certain death for us.

And I add: 'I think that in the future we will be useful to you, because many of us speak Russian, know the local conditions and the way the Red Army fights.'
General: 'Why do you think we will need your people?'
Me: 'The Soviet Union is already preparing for the third World War. The time will come when you too will have to fight the Bolsheviks.'
General: 'They are our allies and what you are saying is pure German propaganda.'
With this statement our conversation was over. The interrogation is carried on by the captain, who asks: 'Did you know that the Gestapo operates in Germany?'
Me: 'Yes I did, as many Latvians were arrested by the Gestapo.'
Captain: 'You knew that but you still fought together with the Germans?'
Me: 'We defended our country because we were afraid of the terror which we experienced in 1941 from the NKVD. They acted with more savagery than the Gestapo.'

On hearing this reply the captain begins to laugh, translates my reply into English and all the American officers begin to laugh, as if I had said something extremely foolish. I am offended by their loud laughter. I shrink into myself and think, *God be with us. Are all Americans so naive?* My look stops their laughter. The general gets up and, together with his companions, leaves.

Now on his own, the captain begins to question me about the Red Army's strength and organisation. I tell him that in the Red Army a company usually has about 30 to 40 men but a battalion about 100 to 120. Only punishment battalion companies have up to 200 men in each.

The American officer again doesn't want to believe these numbers and I have to point out places where I have taken prisoners and obtained the information.

It's late afternoon by the time my interrogation is over. An American instructor takes me back to the basement.

As from today, I am prisoner number A879489.[11]

---

11 Vilis Janums, *Mana Pulka Kauju Gaitas* (*My Regiment in Battle*).

Part Four
Zerbst

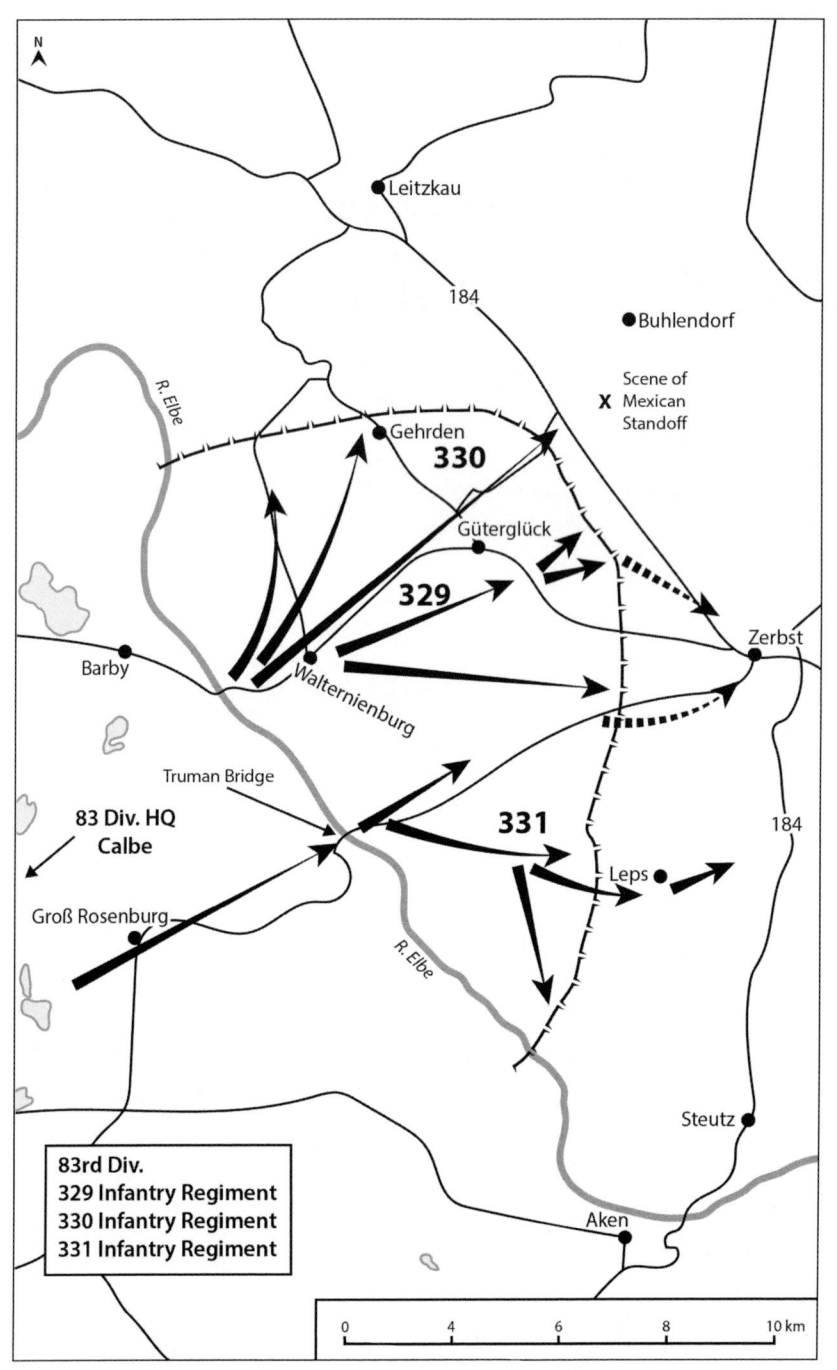

Map 14 The advance of the US 83rd Division across the Elbe in April 1945, broken down into regiments: 329th, 330th, 331st. The 329th moved towards Zerbst while the 331st recced ahead to connect with the Red Army. Based on the original in *Brückenkopf Zerbst* by Udo Pfleghar.

21

The Bombing of Zerbst

Another article in my list of background reading is titled 'Why Eisenhower's Forces Stopped at the Elbe', published in 1952 in the journal *World Politics*. The author, Forrest C. Pogue, charts the development of Allied strategy from D-Day in June 1944 – when Berlin was 'the ultimate goal' – to the advance on the Elbe of April 1945. By then the Russians had made considerable advances towards the German capital and lay just 35 km from the city.

What happened to a defeated Germany after the war, and also an occupied Berlin, had been decided by the US, Britain and the USSR more than 12 months earlier in January 1944. There had been no guarantees then on the fate of Prague and no decision on whose armies would take Berlin.

Pogue writes that from mid-September 1944, the Allied Supreme Commander believed strategy needed to be coordinated with the Russians. If the Red Army beat the Allies to Berlin, the British should push forward to take Hanover and the ports around Hamburg. Depending on the progress of the Russian advance, General Omar Bradley's forces should take as much of the area around Leipzig and Dresden as they could.[1] Eisenhower made it clear, Pogue says, that he was more interested in advancing into the Ruhr than on Berlin.

Germany, he believed, had two hearts: one industrial (the Ruhr), and the other political (Berlin). He wished to attack the Ruhr, for if the industrial heart stopped, the political heart would also die.[2]

General Bradley thought a breakthrough from the Elbe towards Berlin could cost 100,000 American lives: he told Eisenhower this was 'a pretty stiff price to pay for a prestige objective' – one that would have to be returned in line with previous agreements that the Russian occupation zone would run within one hundred miles of the Rhine.[3] British chiefs of staff were concerned that Eisenhower had already told Stalin the Allies planned to stop at the Elbe, and asked Allied representatives in Moscow not to say any more until they had a chance to discuss the matter further.

---

1   Pogue, *Why Eisenhower's Forces Stopped at the Elbe* in World Politics, Apr 1952, Vol. 4, No. 3 (Cambridge University Press), p.350.
2   Pogue notes that this figure of speech was used by Lieutenant General Walter Bedell Smith in an interview with the author in November 1951 explaining SHAEF'S policy.
3   Pogue, quoting Bradley op. cit., pp. 531–37, 544.

While Churchill stressed the political and psychological importance of Berlin as a prize, Eisenhower argued that the city was in ruins, and militarily it was more politically important to push on along the Baltic coast near Lübeck to prevent the Red Army from establishing a hold on the Danish peninsula.[4] In a letter to Field Marshall Bernard Montgomery dated 8 April 1945, he said he regarded the decision to make Berlin a major objective as 'militarily unsound [...] particularly in view of the fact that it is only 35 miles from the Russian lines.'[5]

Whether he knew it or not, Colonel Janums led his men directly into the centre of the US Army's consolidation of power south-west of the German capital. Bridging the Elbe removed the last natural obstacle before Potsdam, with the Soviets now across the Oder and eyeing up the prize of Hitler's citadel. The medieval town of Zerbst – considered 'the Rothenburg of Central Germany' – lay directly in the path of the American advance.[6]

The crossing of the Elbe was filmed by the Special Coverage Unit (SPECOU) of the United States Army Signal Corps, a team of cameramen and sound recorders created to photograph the Americans landing in Europe on D-Day. The unit was embedded with American and Allied troops as they moved through France, Luxembourg, Belgium and Germany headed by film director George Stevens (1904–1975).

Stills from their archive film in the Library of Congress reproduced here show how the Elbe was bridged.

Zerbst's pre-war population of 23,000 had been swollen by refugees fleeing the Soviet advance to upwards of 30,000 by April 1945, meaning the town was overcrowded and all the available accommodation had been taken. The military field hospitals were overflowing with casualties from the war while around 400–500 poorly-equipped Wehrmacht troops formed a garrison. *Arbeitsdienst* (labour service) men and pioneers from nearby Rosslau built anti-tank barriers on the roads leading to Zerbst which consisted of two layers of tree trunks filled with rubble and stones. Guarding these barriers were local men from the *Volkssturm* who were too old or too young for the Wehrmacht.[7]

The Berlin side of the Elbe became a strategic target for the advancing American forces, as crossing the river would bring the end of the Third Reich a significant step closer. Important targets in Mecklenburg and the Brandenburg region were bombed as the intensity of Allied air raids stepped up across Germany. On 10 April 1945, 75 B-17 Flying Fortresses bombed the Luftwaffe base at the airfield near to Zerbst, damaging the runway badly enough to stop the new Messerschmitt Me-262s parked

---

4   Pogue, pp.362–363.
5   Pogue, p.363 quoting personal papers from Eisenhower to Montgomery, 8 April 1945 from Eisenhower's personal file.
6   Zerbst's beautifully preserved medieval streets and houses prompted enthusiastic comparisons with the walled city on the Tauber river in Franconia, Bavaria.
7   Claus Blumstengel, *Zerbst im April 1945* Extrapost – Verlag für Heimatliteratur, (2009: 15) and Udo Pfleghar, *Brückenkopf Zerbst*, Anhaltische Verlagsgesellschaft mbH Dessau (1998: 75).

THE BOMBING OF ZERBST 177

A still from the SPECOU film of the crossing of the Elbe, showing the newly-named Truman bridge. From the Library of Congress archive, online at <https://www.loc.gov/item/2020600757>.

A wide shot showing the pontoon bridge across the Elbe, with vehicles and GIs crossing. SPECOU film details as above.

178 ESCAPE FROM BERLIN

The pontoon bridge enabled advance units of the 83rd Division to move closer to Zerbst and establish control over the northern side of the river Elbe.

Troops in assault boats land on the Zerbst side of the Elbe.

The bridge meant US troops, supply vehicles and tanks could cross to support offensive operations against Zerbst.

The bridge crossing appears to be relatively unchallenged, with GIs in deckchairs as messengers on motorcycles cross the Elbe.

there using it but not enough to shut it down: the hangars remained operational and other fighters could land there.

At 1345 hours on 13 April 1945, men from the 1st Battalion of the 329th Infantry US Army began crossing the Elbe in assault boats from Barby. With no resistance reported, the 2nd Battalion followed. Work began assembling a pontoon bridge across the river to move men, tanks and equipment to support the spearhead units.

Around 1600 hours. the advance troops came under small arms fire two kilometres east of the crossing. The push forward was stopped within range of the supporting artillery and Army engineers focused on getting the bridge complete before dawn the next day.

German counter-attacks during the night were repulsed, and the bridge opened for traffic at 0500 hours. Captured soldiers said the Germans were forming a new division in Zerbst, nine kilometres east of the American advance. The daily action records for the 329th note on 14 April:

> 0940: An ultimatum is being given over the telephone to the Bürgermeister of Zerbst. If the city does not surrender, an air mission will be carried out on it. Arrangements are being made for the air mission.[8]

Ninety minutes later, the telephone lines to Zerbst were cut. The town was bombed, and people ran for the air raid shelters. The next day Zerbst police gave orders to evacuate and people formed up in columns to leave. Some got lifts into the forest on trucks provided by the Wehrmacht and *Volkssturm*, but most walked. Claus Blumstengel wrote on the basis of eyewitness reports:

---

8   Unit Journal for the 329th Infantry, 14 April 1945.

The street scenes on this Sunday afternoon were almost indescribable! Columns, groups, families, individuals, old and young, men and women marched until late in the evening and into the night. Packed with rucksacks, suitcases, bags, panniers, baskets, bundles on their backs and in both hands [...] with large, small and tiny handcarts, prams, bicycles [and] makeshift vehicles of strange construction.[9]

That night, phosphorous grenades were dropped on Zerbst, lighting up the market place 'as bright as day'.[10]

Having postponed the previous day's attack, the Americans again moved towards Zerbst at 0900 hours on 15 April. The first US troops met heavy resistance as they approached Güterglück at 1100. This slowed the advance and Güterglück was not in American hands until 1545. As the command posts moved up, the decision was made to delay any further advance until after an air operation against Zerbst the following day. Closing its entries for the day, the journal records, '2300: 253 prisoners were taken today. Most of the prisoners were quite young and put up very fanatical resistance.'[11]

The morning of 16 April 1945 began with a strong German counter-attack against Güterglück at 0600, which needed the help of tanks switched from nearby Gehrden to the north. Three German tanks and an assault gun were knocked out. One large tank survived despite being hit eight times. At 1000 – an hour after the counter-attack was beaten off – the bombing began.

The huge raid changed Zerbst's history. Five waves of B-26 Marauders and Douglas A-26 Invaders from the USAF 9th Tactical Air Force dropped 116 tons of high explosives and 90 tons of incendiaries, which ripped the heart out of the medieval town.

Udo Pfleghar's 2007 account of the bombing – *Brückenkopf Zerbst* – records the operational order for the attacking bomber crews. 'The target is the city of Zerbst in the grid square D-988830. This city is a defended transportation hub, very strong in terms of its facilities, its supplies and its personnel, according to tactical intelligence reports...'

Pfleghar describes the impact of the incendiary bombs, dropped by the fourth and fifth waves:

> These devilish things had a special detonator setting. At an altitude of 1,500 metres, the containers opened and scattered incendiary bombs and phosphorus canisters over a wide area. There had been no air raid alarm. The population rushed into the air raid shelters, into the palace gardens or tried to get out of the city. As part of the air raid protection, the city wall was breached in several places as a precaution.

---

9 Blumstengel, pp.68–69.
10 Udo Pfleghar, *Brückenkopf Zerbst*.
11 329th Infantry records, 15 April 1945.

THE BOMBING OF ZERBST 181

An aerial picture of Zerbst before the USAF bombing of 16 April 1945 shows the three sides of the castle intact and a densely populated centre built around several main roads. Picture courtesy of Juliane Bruder from the Stadtarchiv Zerbst_Abt. XF Nr. 56.

A second aerial shot shows the castle intact. Demolition work by the East German authorities on the bomb-damaged structure post-war meant the castle could not be restored, and all that remains now is the eastern wing. Picture: Stadtarchiv Zerbst_Abt. XF Nr. 59.

The houses shook and collapsed under the detonations. Not all air raid shelters held: people were crushed and buried. When incendiary and phosphorous bombs fell in large numbers, the flames found plenty of fuel in the covered, windowless and partially destroyed [half-timbered] houses, and the heat became unbearable.

The fires merged into wildfires from which there was often no escape. People suffocated and burned to death in the cellars. Low-flying aircraft circled overhead and fired as they fled into the open and crouched in the bomb craters. In the cellars of the *Hereditary Prince* which had become a reserve hospital, around sixty to eighty soldiers were killed in a direct hit out of 150 wounded, including doctors and nursing staff.

In the large brewery cellar at Breite Straße 32, 117 people sought protection: women, children, evacuees, refugees, soldiers and 30 Soviet prisoners of war. After a direct hit, only three of the 117 could be saved; most of them suffocated.

The Heidetorfriedhof [cemetery, with a chapel], where many people had fled, was not spared either. The castle and other buildings in the castle gardens became burned-out ruins. The Franzisceum was saved through determined extinguishing. Even during the attack, ongoing assistance was provided by the fire brigade, emergency rescue teams and police. There was no water to extinguish the fire because the pipes had burst.[12]

The city was a smoking sea of flames even at night and shone like a gigantic torch into the surrounding area. A firestorm developed. Charred corpses lay on the streets, and even the asphalt was burning. After the bomber attack, the accompanying Mustangs hunted down fleeing people and the rescue workers.[13]

The attack killed 484 men, women and children, 80 percent of the city was obliterated and more than 1,400 houses – mostly half-timbered houses that burned like firewood – were destroyed. Pfleghar notes, 'It was the greatest catastrophe that Zerbst has experienced in its thousand-year history.' The dead included 247 women, 209 men, nine children and 19 'unknown'.[14]

However, there are claims that casualty figures from this catastrophe were inflated in some reports 'for political reasons' and include deaths which were not as a result of the bombing. According to one account by Claus Blumstengel, the official record of bombing victims compiled in Zerbst in 1948 should be corrected because some of

---

12 Anhalt's oldest Latin school – the equivalent of a grammar school – the Franzisceum dates back to 1246 when it was founded as a monastery. The damage was so severe the building was not restored until the 1990s. The school's website considers the Franzisceum as 'an architectural monument and a cultural site of national importance; it represents the history of the city of Zerbst.' Source at <https://franzisceum.de/>.
13 Translated account of Udo Pfleghar, *Brückenkopf Zerbst*.
14 Hehne and Kirchner. Article for *Zerbst Actuell* 16.04.2020 *Commemoration: Zerbst was destroyed 75 years ago today – contemporary witnesses remember* online at <https://zerbstaktuell.wixsite.com/zerbstaktuell/single-post/2020/04/16/gedenken-heute-vor-75-jahren-wurde-zerbst-zerst%C3%B6rt-zeitzeugen-erinnern-sich>

THE BOMBING OF ZERBST 183

People standing in front of the remains of the St Nikolai Church in Zerbst. Picture: Stadtarchiv Zerbst_Abt. XF Nr. 318.

the people on the list died after the war in internment camps.[15] Annemarie Lüdicke, author of the books *Bittere Nachkriegsjahre – Zerbst 1945* (*The Bitter Post-war Years*) and *Vergessene Schicksale – Festnahmen in Mitteldeutschland 1945–1961* (*Forgotten Fates – Arrests in Central Germany 1945–61*) says the original death toll of slightly more than 300 deaths were correctly listed by city officials. Later, another 100 or so names were added to the list due to reports of buried victims. But, she believes 'the list was subsequently inflated for political reasons.'[16]

Luise Orlicek spent that day in a cellar in the city centre. She was interviewed by the local paper *Zerbst Actuell* for the 75th anniversary of the bombing in 2020, and shared the memories she wrote down for her sons aged one and two years old at the time:

> I was alone because your father was a soldier on the Eastern Front. At the beginning of March he was here for a few hours on the way back to Hungary in a truck loaded with tank parts. In his opinion, nothing would happen here in Zerbst. As soon as he left, Zerbst was declared a fortress and anti-tank barriers were set up on all entrance and exit roads, with tree trunks placed across them.
>
> On 15 April the population was finally told to leave the city. But to go where? For days we – including all the other residents of the house, such as the Drews, Gerstemann, Frässdorf, Lehmann, Jäckel, Zehle families and two students from the building school – lived in the basement under the most difficult conditions. But since we didn't know where we could go, we agreed to stay.
>
> In the morning hours of 16 April, despite low-flying bombardment, I went to Bäckerstrasse to get released food. I met a group of women who were on their way to the tank barrier on Breite Strasse. They wanted to persuade the guard squad stationed there to open the barrier. I would have gone too, but I didn't want to leave you two alone with your grandma for so long. However, the women returned after a short time. They had been threatened with being shot.
>
> I was finally back with you around 1000 hours. Only a short time later we heard the booming approach of the wave of bombers and just a few seconds later the unforgettable inferno began. Detonating bombs, never-ending crashes, bursts, tremors, countless vibrations. We literally sat with our backs against the wall with you children wrapped tightly around us. Terrible fear and trembling came over us, and you clung tightly to us.
>
> And it crashed and crashed and crashed and crashed and crashed … And it shook and shook and shook and shook and shook: the earth, the walls, everything. Apart from the noise of the bombs falling and detonating, there was not a single sound to be heard far and wide, not a word – dead silence.
>
> Suddenly there was an impact in the immediate vicinity. The open cellar holes were darkened by smoke. Everyone thought everything had collapsed on us. Smoke was coming into the basement. One of the construction students

---

15 Blumstengel, *Zerbst im April 1945*, pp.7–8, trans. H. Witte.
16 Correspondence with Prof. H. Witte, 2020, shared with author.

The ruins of the St Nikolai Church in Zerbst. Picture: Stadtarchiv Zerbst_Abt. XF Nr. 175.

suddenly jumped up and ran up the stairs to investigate. When he came back he said, with a stunned expression: 'The whole city is a sea of flames.'

We tried to make our way to the castle through bomb craters, huge piles of rubble and thick black smoke. But we couldn't stay there for long because the castle also started to burn. Finally we had to leave the city and were taken to Grimme. It was only after days that we were allowed back into the city. There were horrific images in front of our eyes. We were assigned emergency accommodation.[17]

Another witness, Lisa Winetzka, had a narrow escape when she could not get into a popular shelter in the cellar of the Pfannenberg brewery, which had a large vaulted ceiling: 'We wanted to go into the basement in the event of an attack but we were turned away. The basement was full. A short time later we had to watch as everyone who had sought shelter in the cellar was pulled out dead.'[18]

The ceiling had collapsed in the bombing, suffocating everyone inside. A military field hospital (*lazarett*) had been set up across the street at the Hotel zum Erbprinzen,

---

17 Hehne and Kirchner. Article for *Zerbst Actuell,* 16.04.2020. Grimme is a village 17 km northeast of Zerbst.
18 Hehne and Kirchner in *Zerbst Actuell,* 16.04.2020.

Lisa told the newspaper, but the same thing happened there too: 'The soldiers were found holding hands with nurse Traudchen Lehmann. Everyone was dead.'[19]

Buildings on both sides of Breite Straße were reduced to rubble, and it became known as 'The Street of Mourning'. Ruth Tschersich was twelve years old at the time. Her voice trembled as she told her stories to the reporters: 'We had to watch as the many dead people were recovered. Many Zerbsters who passed by while the dead were being retrieved stopped, paused and thought of the dead. I had to think about whether I should call and tell you all about this, but at some point there will be no one left who can tell the stories.'[20]

The battle log for the 329th Infantry for 16 April notes at 1250 that plans to attack Zerbst had been shelved. The regiment was ordered to take up defensive positions after rumours of an imminent counter-attack against the bridgehead. German aircraft attempted to bomb the area late the following evening followed by a series of attacks throughout 18 April.

On 20 April, Ninth Army commander Lieutenant-General William Hood Simpson visited the command post. He told 329th commander Colonel Edwin B. Crabill that his orders were to hold the present position and wait for the Russians to advance to the area. A civilian was sent to Zerbst with an ultimatum for the town commander. The 329th log notes: 'We are giving them an opportunity to surrender the city and save it from further shelling and bombing. If they choose not to surrender, the city will continue to be shelled and bombed.'

Two days of waiting followed. The Germans in Zerbst could not get permission to surrender and there was no contact from the Russians. At one point, American commanders sent a civilian on a motorbike to Zerbst to ask if anyone in the town knew where they were. The Americans were wary of moving forward without knowing what lay ahead, especially towards the town of Lindau. Reconnaissance indicated new troops arriving, the presence of assault guns and even two Tiger tanks.

On the morning of 22 April, a rapid reaction task force was put on standby to roll out to meet any Russian advance. A Red Army officer being held as a prisoner of war by the Germans, First Lieutenant Theo Prissjaschnjuk, was brought in to contact Red Army advance units by radio.

Herbert Witte writes in his account of this time *Zwei Tage im April* (*Two Days in April*):

> The Soviet officer sat in front of the radio for more than twenty-four hours, tirelessly searching for radio contacts without interruption. He managed to make two connections (1235 and 1440), although the Soviet side again refused to give any location details. The Red Army soldiers wanted to pass on the information, but they were not authorised to transmit their location. The higher-ranking staff also remained silent.

---

19 Hehne and Kirchner in *Zerbst Actuell*, 16.04.2020 (accessed 28.12.2023).
20 Ibid.

Colonel Edwin B. Crabill (left), commander of the 329th Infantry Regiment, with Russian prisoner of war 1st Lieutenant Theo Prissjaschnjuk (centre) during the attempt to make contact with the Soviets. Picture credit: George Stevens and the United States Army Signal Corps, Special Coverage Unit. World War II colour footage; SPECOU at Remagen and the Dora concentration camp, 1945, video. Retrieved from the Library of Congress online at <www.loc.gov/item/2020600757/>.

Towards evening, the civilian who had been sent out on a motorbike came back and said that he had been told that the Red Army was in Treuenbrietzen, about 55 km north-east of Zerbst. He had also learnt that the Soviets had reached Wiesenburg, about 26 km north-east of Zerbst. They would presumably turn northwards to complete the encirclement of Berlin.

The radio contact was continued until 2100 without success. The chances of a meeting dwindled, as the Soviet side had completely different problems at this time and the Red Army soldiers were still far away from the proposed meeting points.[21]

Throughout this time, the German garrison at Zerbst refused to surrender, despite repeated requests from the Americans. Psychological warfare teams broadcast messages to the remaining German troops in the area, and they started to give themselves up the following morning in groups of 25 and 30, but Zerbst refused, saying

---

21 H. Witte, *Zwei Tage im April (Two Days in April)*, p.26.

The attempts to contact advancing Red Army units were filmed by the SPECOU crew, which also filmed the meeting of the US and Red Armies at Torgau shortly afterwards. Online at <https://www.loc.gov/item/2020600757>.

the senior officer did not have permission to surrender. At 2310 on the night of 26 April, reports came in that a large number of German soldiers wanted to surrender to the 330th Infantry.[22] At 0910 the following morning the log reads, 'The surrender of 896 German soldiers and 41 officers, including a Colonel, to the 330th Inf. was effected early this morning after the approval of Div. The unit was a regiment minus one battalion.'[23]

It took several days of talks involving senior German officers and two civilians who had been given the authority by then-Mayor Helmut Abendroth to see if they could find a solution – Heinrich Gelzenleuchter and local doctor Hermann Wille – to break the deadlock and prevent further bloodshed. Eventually, the two men promised on their lives the soldiers in Zerbst would not open fire and the Americans advanced cautiously towards the town.[24]

The agreement held. The German garrison did not surrender but neither did the soldiers open fire, and the Americans moved in and took 800 prisoners of war. This became the signal for a general capitulation, with hundreds of refugees 'apparently fleeing from the Russians' trying to enter American-occupied Zerbst.

---

22 This is the Janums Battle Group.
23 329th Infantry log for 26–27 April 1945.
24 Hehne and Kirchner, article for *Zerbst Actuell*, 16.04.2020 (accessed 28.12.2023).

By the afternoon of 29 April, American reconnaissance units sent out to establish contact with the Russians reported from Rosslau, 20 km east of Zerbst, that hundreds of Germans were surrendering to them. The unit log notes that, 'Along the cavalry's route of advance, large groups of German soldiers have been walking in to surrender and then wait by the road for someone to pick them up. In some instances the Germans have loaded their own trucks with troops and have driven in to surrender.'[25]

The German collapse continued. By lunchtime 4,000 soldiers were prisoners of war, including 2,500 in hospitals. The 113th Cavalry Group took 4,200 PoWs in a cautious advance east of Zerbst, even though there was concern about pockets of resistance in towns and villages in the area. When contact was made with Red Army forces 36 km away to the east at Apollensdorf on 30 April, the war around Zerbst was effectively over. Continuing it would now be pointless.[26]

But danger still lurked. Locals questioned by the Americans said that there was a military hospital and supplies of ammunition and food as well as German patrols in Buhlendorf, with mines laid in the fields surrounding the village, and that the village of Deetz, five kilometres north-east of Lindau, had been prepared for defense.[27] On the evening of 30 April 1945, the Americans received information that there were approximately 300 German soldiers with some tanks and self-propelled guns that had withdrawn into the forests north of Lindau with the entrances to the town mined.[28] Ensuring that these units surrendered without further bloodshed became the aim.

25   329th Infantry log for 26–27 April 1945.
26   Ibid.
27   Witte quoting Hermann Graf, *Das Deutsche Unheilsjahr 1945 in den Gemeinden des Kirchspiels Lindau*, entry for 1 May 1945 and G2-Journal 83. US-ID, 30 April 1945, timed at 2115 and 2120. Trans. Tania Kibermanis.
28   Witte, *Zerbst Ende II – Helle Funken in Schwarzer Nacht* (Bright Sparks in the Black Night) quoting Selbstfahrendes Geschütz (Räder-oder Kettenfahrgestell) mit Panzerung, zumindest für den Motor – und den Fahrerbereich and G2-Journal 83. US-ID, 30 April 1945, timed at 1355.

22

A Meeting with the Mayor of Zerbst

Seventy-eight years after the Latvians passed briefly through this region, I drive my rented Fiat 500 carefully into the centre of Zerbst and park outside the town hall. This is a town most famous for being the childhood home of Catherine the Great (1729–1796) who grew up living at Zerbst Castle and became Empress of Russia from 1762 until her death. She was born Princess Sophie of Anhalt-Zerbst. The castle is now a shadow of its former self due in part to the catastrophic bombing of the town on 16 April 1945 and then a disastrous decision by the Communist authorities several years later to demolish most of what was left. Only the eastern wing remains.[1]

Once through the big heavy wooden doors I walk up to the first floor and turn left, stopping outside the Mayor's office. A man sitting at a table by the door gets to his feet and introduces himself: this is local teacher Andreas Baumgart, author of one of the articles in the town's archive about the Janums' Battle Group passing through the area near Zerbst.

As we introduce ourselves, another man arrives. This is Herbert Witte, a retired professor from the University of Jena. He has written an extremely detailed and thorough account of the Latvian foray into Brandenburg. The door opens and we are greeted by archivist Julianne Bruder and Mayor Andreas Dittmann. We sit down at a very large table and offer drinks to each other while I explain that I'm tracing the movements of Colonel Janums' 800 men towards surrender, survival and ultimately freedom.

I start my recorder and explain that I have found a spot by the main road at Schora that matches the descriptions of the Mexican standoff between Janums' men and Leutnant Geiselhart, and then traced the movements through the village to the surrender to the Americans at Güterglück. Andreas Baumgart is the first to speak.

> Yes, Schora is the place where the Leutnant stopped them. Then they went through the village, met the Americans, went together to Güterglück where there were Sherman tanks. There they laid their weapons down and went in the direction of the pontoon bridgehead by the river. My father told me about this.

---

1 Friends of Zerbst Castle website, online at <https://www.schloss-zerbst-ev.de/html/geschichte.htm> (accessed 17.03.2024).

A MEETING WITH THE MAYOR OF ZERBST 191

The reconstruction of civic buildings in the centre of Zerbst, including the town hall at Schlossfreiheit 12 which was badly damaged in the 16 April 1945 bombing raid. Picture: Stadtarchiv Zerbst_Abt. XF Nr. 328.

A meeting at Zerbst town hall with Mayor Andreas Dittmann (right), the author, town archivist Juliane Bruder, Professor Herbert Witte and Andreas Baumgart (left). Picture: Natalie Carragher.

> 3. **Surrender of CT JANUMS:** 27 April 45
>
> On the night of 26 April, three enemy officers reported to the 330th Inf Regt with an offer to surrender a Combat Team of 896 men (41 officers and 855 EM) who were at the time in the woods N of SCHORA (D9367). The surrender was agreed upon and the group proceeded to march to our lines, arriving at 0300, 27 April, at the outposts of 330th Inf Regt.
>
> This group of men was detached from the 15 Latvian SS Div which was doing construction work in POMERANIA, and was selected to go to BERLIN to aid in the defense of that city. 1 Bn, 32 SS Gren Regt; 1 Bn, 33 SS Gren Regt; and the Fusilier Bn were sent to a point N of BERLIN where they received weapons. CO of this CT was SS Standartenfuehrer (Col) JANUMS. Col JANUMS decided to save his group and proceeded to march towards American lines. He did not take the Fusilier Bn along since it was commanded by German officers whom he did not trust. With his two Latvian Bns he moved around the E edge of BERLIN to BLANKENFELDE, which is 3 of the capitol. Then the clm proceeded to march westwards towards POTSDAM. The Col marched at the head of his clm and due to his rank, was never challenged by enemy. He also carried faked orders. Once during the trip, vic FICHTENWALDE, SW of POTSDAM, they were engaged in a short struggle with the Russians, during which they suffered approx 100 casualties. However, the bulk of the force escaped the Russian prong and arrived vic SCHORA where it billeted in the woods while negotiating surrender. A German Lt commanding a Co vic SCHORA attempted, at pistol point, to force the Col not to surrender. The Col threatened to give battle to the few Germans if they attempted to interfere, and the Lt meekly withdrew his objection.
>
> Col JANUMS is an officer of long standing. He was an officer of the Russian Czarist Army and later of the Latvian Army. When the Russians conquered Latvia in 1940 Col JANUMS escaped to Germany. There he was one of the first to join the SS
>
> - 1 -
> **SECRET**

US Army G3 intelligence report detailing the surrender of Combat Team Janums and the apparent loss of 100 men in a battle near Fichtenwalde. From the divisional records online. Picture: author. Courtesy of Professor Herbert Witte.

He's dead now, but he was 17 at the time. It's part of local legend: that's why I wrote my article.

I say, 'Some of these places are difficult to find with a car, let alone marching through a forest at night with a map torn off a school wall to guide you. It's an incredible achievement with German patrols trying to find them and the Russians sweeping east to west to encircle Berlin.'

Professor Witte has read US Army intelligence reports about the journey of the Latvians based on post-surrender interrogation. He says, 'They [the Latvians] started with about 1,000 soldiers but lost 100 men in the fights with the Soviets and the German army along the way.'

City archivist Juliane Bruder pinpoints these losses to combat near Beelitz, just south of today's Autobahn 10. 'They lost the majority of the men south-west of Potsdam in a small battle with the Russians near Fichtenwalde.'[2]

---

2   Detail from the G3 report of the US Army 83rd Division (see above).

Professor Witte explains the complicated and chaotic situation on the ground less than 100 km from Zerbst.

> The situation was the following. On 23 April Hitler ordered the whole German Twelfth Army – the Wenck army – in the direction of Berlin, to relieve the city. The Latvians came from Berlin so perhaps there were also fights between the Latvians with the troops of the Wenck army as well as the Soviets. It was a very complex situation, but here – Zerbst – there was a very weak defence roster.

Andreas Baumgart leans forward. He is quietly spoken.

> In the village of Dornburg there was a concentration of very strong German SS troops in the forest and it would not have been possible for Janums to pass through that way. The only way they could get through was to take the way they did. They were very lucky to get through to the Elbe.[3]

I did not know that. Janums does not mention it, and perhaps he did not know. In those circumstances, they were very lucky indeed.

> VH: What about these concentration camp prisoners they come across? Who are these people?
> HW: No. There was no concentration camp here. There were five thousand German prisoners of war here from 29 April till 1 May. There some Hungarians who had been in the Pioneer School in Rosslau, east of Zerbst.
> JB: There were no big concentration camps near here, so we don't know. Perhaps they were from a little Jewish camp at Zerbst airfield, on the north-east side of the town near Lindau.[4]
> HW: There were lots of small camps so it's difficult to have an overview. The prisoners were used in agriculture and manufacturing, but the situation was one of great chaos.
> JB: Then there was the very heavy bombing in the air raid of 16 April which added to that chaos.
> VH: It seems unnecessary at that time of the war to drop so many tons of high explosive, and incendiaries – phosphorous – on a town like Zerbst. I'd be interested in your thoughts on that?
> HW: There is an interesting theory about this. There was an order given to bomb Zerbst and at the same time Eisenhower issued the 'Stop' order. The

---

3   The Schloss Dornburg castle 10 km from Gütergluck was an SA and SS stronghold from the earliest days of the Nazi regime, used as a training facility and prison and torture centre for political opponents. At the war's end, it was used as a Soviet storage archive for sensitive files on Nazi and Wehrmacht officers.
4   This was a labour camp of around 700 Jews apparently not considered 'Jewish enough' to be killed, so they were used for construction projects and peat digging.

theory is that the air attack on Zerbst was probably ordered at a time when the American commanders on the ground were not yet aware of the stop order on the Elbe and Mulde rivers.[5] The bridgehead here was what they called 'The Gateway to Berlin': it's 80 km to Potsdam. There was agreement between Eisenhower and Stalin that the bombing would stop on 14–15 April. But the theory is that the aircraft were not informed of the order, so therefore they bombed Zerbst. It makes no sense to bomb Zerbst: there was no military power here. That is the theory. Zerbst was evacuated.

VH: Seventy or eighty years later, we can look at these incidents through different eyes. The 'Stop' order lets the Soviets take this area as well as Prague. Zerbst was described as a 'communications centre' – what communications were here? The logs say: 'bombing of Zerbst communications centre'.

HW: There was no communications centre here. Maybe that was an error. In Zerbst there was a training school for non-commissioned officers of Army communication troops. Town commander Oberst Paul Koenzgen was the commander. This may have been what was meant in Zerbst.[6]

AD: If Koenzgen had said 'Come in' [to the Americans] then we would have had no bombing of the city.

VH: The town was absolutely flattened, at a time when Germany was clearly defeated. And they used incendiaries; phosphorous.

HW: Koenzgen could not say to the Americans 'come in', so the town was bombed. He was willing to do this. Koenzgen was in communication with his Corps centre XXXXVIII Armoured Corps, a Panzer Corps. The commander was General von Edelsheim.[7] The answer for Koenzgen was 'No'. It was impossible. The information was not to fight the Americans, but there was no option to surrender. It was a very complex situation.

VH: I'm following the Latvians, who are going through the forest trying to escape Russian captivity and the prospect of spending ten years, maybe more, in Siberia. But they're walking into an international incident involving the Americans, the Soviets and the end of the Third Reich...

HW: There was a plan: a systematic, organised retreat of the troops from the Elbe and the Mulde rivers to the north. Therefore Zerbst must be held for one day, two days, as that was the plan. So it was impossible for Koenzgen to capitulate and surrender. The orders came from the Army Corps. The town was evacuated, although there were plenty of people who didn't want to go to local villages nearby. Not everybody left. It was a marvellous town. It's a pity.

---

5   Olaf Groehler, *Anhalt im Luftkrieg Anhaltische Verlagsgesellschaft mbH Dessau* (1993), p.167.
6   *Heeres-Unteroffiziersschule für Nachrichtentruppen.*
7   Maximilian von Edelsheim, a Wehrmacht general and recipient of the Knight's Cross with Oak Leaves and Swords, who negotiated the surrender of German forces on 2 May 1945 at Tangermünde on the Elbe.

VH: Going back to the damage – eighty percent of a beautiful medieval town destroyed, hundreds of innocent people killed – for no good strategic reason. The history of the town was changed forever. Is the bombing of Zerbst a war crime?

HW: That is a discussion in the historical literature, indeed. But the Germans started the war. There are so many crimes. That is war.

VH: Some of these beautiful places are saved, while others aren't. Zerbst was destroyed, and that's cultural vandalism, isn't it? It's a cultural crime for a beautiful town to be destroyed when it didn't need to be.

HW: There is also the bombing of London…

As I circulate the pictures of the Latvians in Calbe after the surrender, Professor Witte explains that there was agreement between Eisenhower and Stalin that troops captured by the Americans who had fired on the Soviets were to be handed over to the Soviets. 'And if they were SS, that meant death,' he says. There were also Vlasov troops in the area, he adds: Russians who fought against Stalin.[8]

I ask Mayor Andreas Dittmann what this period means to people in Zerbst and what he thinks about what happened to his town.

> For us, this is our history. 16 April 1945 was a disaster for this town and the people living here. My grandfather lived here at the time and he went to a nearby village, Bone. My family was lucky: we lived outside the city walls and there was only one bomb that landed near to them. Inside the city wall there was a great disaster; for people, for our castle, and also for our culture. The historic town hall, the market, St Nikolai's church – all destroyed.
>
> Schoolchildren grew up knowing about the massive bombing and the destruction of our city, but this story about the Latvians moving around here is not a well-known topic. It is new to me.

Professor Witte leans forward.

> It is a short and mostly unknown episode in our history. The liberation of the prisoners of war at the camps at Altengrabow [Stalag XI A] and Luckenwalde [Stalag III A] was commanded from the bridgehead here. The bridgehead was the centre of all operations and actions. It was more important than the meeting at Torgau – it is a little piece of world history.[9]

8 There are many accounts in Second World War literature of Vlasov men being shot by the Red Army the moment they were captured.

9 On 25 April 1945, soldiers of the US First Army and the Soviet First Ukrainian Front met at the bridge over the Elbe at Torgau. On 1 January 1945 there were 60,000 Allied prisoners at Altengrabow: Australian, French, British, Belgian, Serb, Russian, Italian, American, Dutch, Slovak and Polish, held in separate compounds. Operation Violet was launched on 25 April 1945 to ensure the prisoners were protected as the war ended, but the team of US, French and Commonwealth paratroops were captured and transferred to the camp. They persuaded

Juliane Bruder nods. For her, the loss is of irreplaceable historical records.

> JB: The castle was destroyed, along with more or less everything in it. Most of the archives were lost, including the original taxes from Martin Luther's time. Some boxes in the basement of the castle were rescued, and what is in them is fabulous – but it is only ten percent of the material we had. So people grew up in this war-damaged city, and we had to build places for living. They built what we call prefabricated *Plattenbauten*, or 'blocks of houses' – lots of units – and they are very…
>
> VH: East German?
>
> JB: Right. But it destroyed the historical structure of the town. And you see this wide main street, 184th Street? There was not such a street before 1945. They were all little houses: lots of little places to live. It was a really medieval city: a medieval jewel. In the 1950s and 1960s this street was really built up with living apartments and shops.[10]

We move over to a map on the wall of Mayor Dittman's office showing the layout of the city in 1714. It is a dense network of human habitation over many hundreds of years – narrow streets and passages clustered together, weaving past brick houses and without the uniformity and calculated structure of the post-war redevelopment under Soviet control.

'The war came home,' Mayor Dittmann says with a sigh.

Trying to pin what happened to Zerbst somewhere between a war crime and a pity is a difficult exercise, but there is no doubt that the city was devastated and the face of it was changed forever. So were the lives of the people living there and growing up under Soviet control, education systems and lifestyles.

> VH: You have taken a very different path to the rest of Germany, haven't you?
>
> HW: Very different. The difference between now and the Communist time cannot be described. Now we can travel, we have a much higher living standard, but to be free – that is the most important.
>
> AD: I am younger, but I agree. I was 21 in 1989 and for 18 months before that I was standing on the border as a guard with a Kalashnikov. Now many

---

the Commandant to contact Robert Macon, the US commander in Zerbst, who arranged to shuttle the Allied prisoners out. When the Russians arrived on 4 May 1945, Polish prisoners were not allowed to leave. Source: Hughes, *The Special Allied Airborne Reconnaissance Force* (SAARF), (1993) online at <http://www.insigne.org/SAARF-I.htm>.

10 Historically important buildings and districts in Latvia were destroyed by the occupying Soviet authorities post-war as well. The House of the Blackheads in Rīga was blown up instead of being restored. The old town of Jelgava was destroyed in the fighting in summer 1944, but, after the war, a Soviet film was shot there and the film crews were given permission to blow up what was left for realistic footage.

A MEETING WITH THE MAYOR OF ZERBST 197

Inspection of a medieval map of Zerbst showing the densely developed town centre. Before the bombing, Zerbst was considered 'a medieval jewel'. Picture: Natalie Carragher.

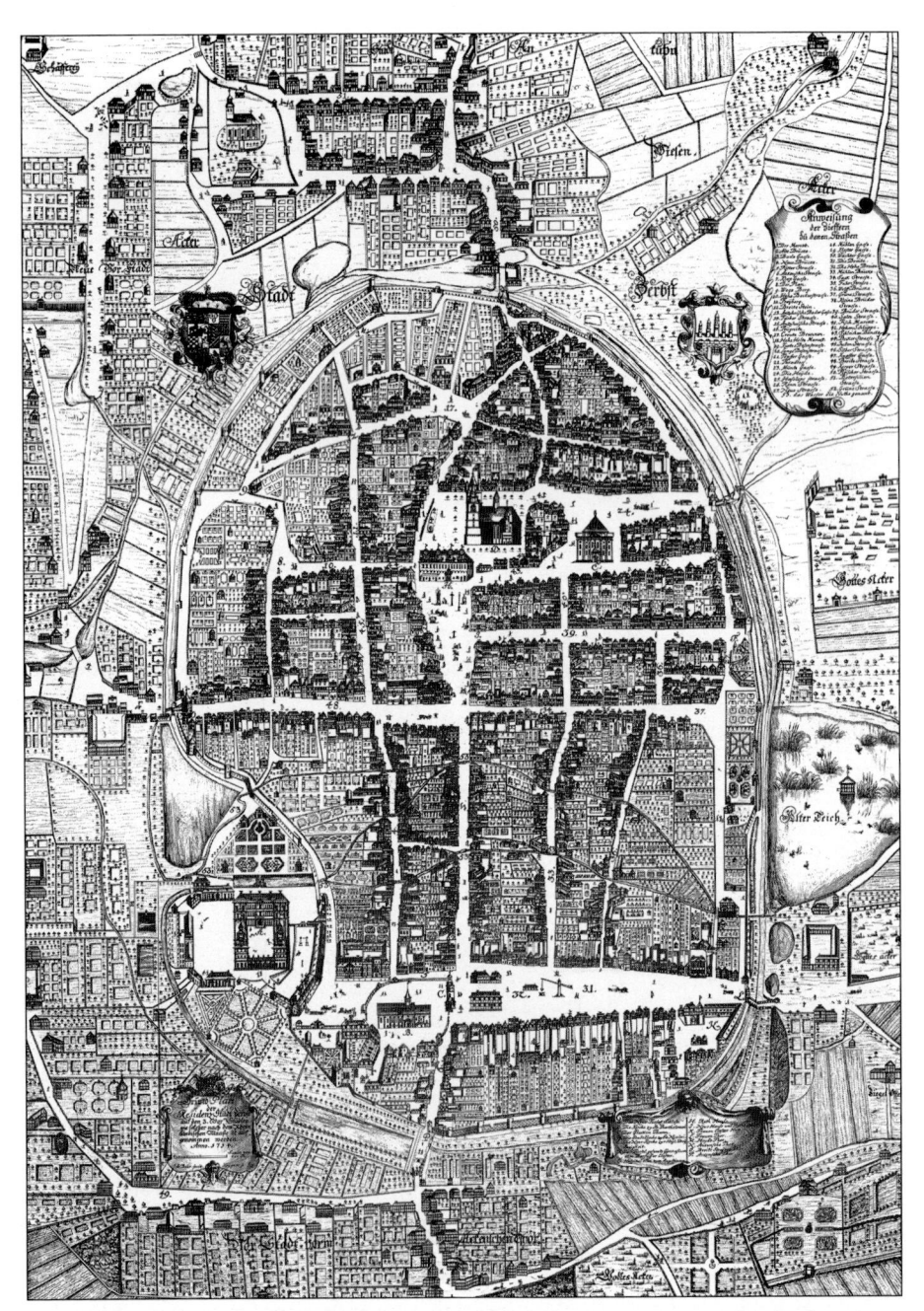

Detail of the centre of medieval Zerbst in 1714, showing a concentration of timber houses congregating around natural meeting points, such as markets and churches. Picture courtesy of Juliane Bruder, Zerbst town archive.

The author thanks Mayor Andreas Dittmann, Professor Herbert Witte, Andreas Baumgart and city archivist Juliane Bruder before leaving Zerbst town hall. Picture: Natalie Carragher.

people say this time was good, but they have forgotten the reality; the lack of freedom.[11]

JB: Nowadays if you have your grandfather's bicycle in your garage it is like gold. People will pay a lot of money for that old bicycle. They don't know anything about the GDR, but they will buy these old bicycles.

AD: My father remained friends with an American GI for fifty years, and he came and stayed with us in 1993. He told me about the times in 1945. The GIs were very kind: they gave us chocolate, cigarettes, something to eat. There are good memories.

VH: That time wouldn't have lasted very long though, would it? Because the Americans handed Zerbst over to the Soviets very quickly.

HW: Yes, on 5 or 6 May.

VH: Was the handover peaceful? Because I've read accounts, in Berlin for example, that women were raped, watches were stolen. Did that happen in Zerbst?

---

11 During the Cold War, East German men were required to perform military service which involved guarding the border with the West.

HW: You asked for the difference between the Americans and the Russians. In German there is a special word – *Wilde Horde* – a marauding horde. It was a very bad time for the Germans here, for the women…[12]

VH: So it did happen?

HW: Yes.

JB: There was chaos in the government, no information was collected, no crimes were judged. There are no records.

HW: But they captured many of the people who were involved in the governmental system of the Nazis. Mayors, for example. Most of them died. Buchenwald was also active in the four years after the Second World War ended. The gulag system was the same system as the concentration camp system, but there is no comparable place for death camps like Auschwitz – except hell.

After our meeting ends, I have a look around the town. The shell of St Nikolai's church remains, open to the elements with several display cases showing what stood here in the past.

The ruins of St Nikolai's church, with GDR-era blockhouse flats built alongside. Picture: author.

---

12 Germans understand 'Wilde Horde' to mean chaos, savagery; without control or behaviour.

Inside the shell of St Nikolai's Church. Picture: author.

Zerbst's rebuilt homes: modern flats, but a little out of keeping with the original medieval city. It's a legacy of the destruction of the Second World War. Picture: author.

A hundred metres away, the pre-fabricated *Plattenbauten* 'block houses' begin – the homes and living spaces of Zerbst rising from the ashes, rebuilt in the GDR time. There are apartment blocks with parking spaces, wide roads, shopping areas and supermarkets. It looks nice, and it's clean and taken care of. But every now and then, like a crack in this modern façade, there is a single old building, or a turn round a corner that leads to the remains of an historic district.

Driving and walking round Zerbst makes me realise what 'eighty percent destruction' really means. Jagged, discordant, incoherent remnants of medieval Zerbst protrude awkwardly into the modern city like a restless memory that will not be restrained. Single ancient buildings stand metres from vast supermarket car parks and there is a sense of wide open space for no real reason - other than what stood here before was obliterated. It's among the most schizophrenic places I've ever visited.

Zerbst is a town which has had its celebrated medieval past blown away by high explosives in a last-minute and possibly unnecessary act of cultural vandalism – justified perhaps as an act of saving lives and hastening the end of the Third Reich. It now stands as yet another legacy of the enduring destructive power of Adolf Hitler and the Nazis.

An aerial shot of Zerbst at the turn of the 21st century, showing the remains of the castle (mid-left), the ruins of St Nikolai's Church (top centre) and the scale of the post-war rebuild with 'block houses'. Picture: Stadtarchiv Zerbst_Abt. XF Nr. 146b.

The discrepancy between the two deaths reported in the diary of Latvian Legion Adjutant Edvīns Bušmanis and the figure of 100 men lost in the post-surrender American intelligence report cannot be easily explained. In correspondence after our meeting in Zerbst, Professor Witte dug deeper into the records of the time.

> HW: I have looked at the general staff map of the 1st Ukrainian Front commanded by Konev from 24–25 April 1945 and the war diary of the base commander of Belzig from 21–26 April. The war diary contains information from a radius of at least 50 km, which includes Zerbst, Wittenberg, Brandenburg town and Jüterbog. On 22 April, the first information from the vicinity of Fichtenwalde comes from Lehnin:

22 April, 1410 By order [of] General Höllzner, Base Command Brandenburg, Lieutenant Scholz calls from Brandenburg and reports that the Russians are advancing on Lehnin from Beelitz with 150 men and eight tanks. Lehnin holds its ground.

> HW: This is the first enemy report in this area. With his soldiers, Standartenführer Janums could have destroyed the 150 Red Army soldiers. However, no

fighting is reported near Fichtenwalde, so no major casualties are possible on 22 April. There is an entry on 23 April at 1730:

Enemy near Lehnin has advanced in the direction of Nahmitz, south-east of Brandenburg [on the highway] and has taken Nahmitz.

HW: And at 1840:

Area to the east of Golzow and area to the east and forest between Golzow and Lehnin enemy-free in the afternoon. Detected by reconnaissance troop from Golzow to the south-west edge of Lehnin. In Lehnin one tank and some Russian infantrymen observed.

HW: The next entry comes 24 hours later, the following evening.

24 April, 1950 hours: Six enemy tanks coming from the direction of Golzow in the direction of Ragösen. Infantry fire audible in the direction of Ragösen.

HW: This could have been a small skirmish between Red Army soldiers and the troops from Janums, but that is just speculation. It can be assumed that the battle group of Janums passed Belzig and reached Lindau unnoticed and it seems very likely that there were only a few casualties. A battle with 100 casualties would have been recorded in the war diary.

Even on 24 and 25 April there is no record of fighting or a retreating larger battle group. The war diary is very accurate, including daily situation reports from Zerbst and the surrounding area. Colonel Koenzgen reported personally in Belzig.

I cannot resolve the discrepancy between the information on the soldiers killed in the G3 report and later statements, i.e., 100 against two. It is possible that Standartenführer Janums wanted to dramatise his escape route for the Americans.

The more I think about the question of two or 100 casualties at Fichtenwalde, the more I become convinced that there was no major fighting and therefore fewer casualties. I think the Latvians would have avoided any contact with the enemy, because as a Latvian, being taken prisoner by either the Soviets, the SS or the Waffen-SS would have been a death sentence.

The Germans were not squeamish when dealing with retreating soldiers – they hanged them as deserters. In the eyes of the Soviets the Latvians would have been Nazi war criminals and in the eyes of the Germans they would have been deserters.[13]

---

13 Correspondence with Prof. Witte, 4.2.2024.

Part Five

Postscript

23

One of Janums' Men: Henry Vītols

I meet Henry Vītols the day after his 94th birthday at his home in West Bridgford, Nottingham. Henry is a remarkably sprite man, wearing a T-shirt and check shirt; friendly and sharp-witted. His real name is Henrijs Teodors Vītols, but everyone calls him Henry.

He is a full-time carer for his wife, who is confined to bed in the back room after having had a serious stroke. Despite visits from health care workers four times a day, this is a demanding workload for someone his age. He's in good spirits though. As we sit down to talk in his conservatory I turn on my tape recorder to record our conversation and tell him to ignore it.

'Ignore? Ignore?' he says, laughing. 'And finish in jail?'

We look at the map showing the places the Latvians passed through in Pomerania. Jastrow, Nakel, Neustettin, Neustrelitz. He follows my finger and there's some recognition of places but nothing that triggers any specific memories. Some people have warned that I'm ten years too late doing these interviews. Most of those who were there have now died, and in some cases the memory has gone. Henry admits it himself.

> We got to Berlin. Somewhere in Berlin. We finished up there. There was a river, the Rhine I think and Janums – a marvellous fellow, like a father.[1] I didn't see him very often but he was like a father. He was so kind. Like when he says, 'It's over, boys.' A very fatherly tone.
>
> We had a Panzerfaust – you know Panzerfaust? – and he said, 'Boys. We're going to give ourselves up. You don't need it anymore. Put it in the river.' So we threw it over the bridge into the river and at night time we walked over to the Americans. There were some youngsters in uniforms, Germans, who said, 'Where are you going?' And we said, 'To the front.' So they came with us. I don't know what happened to them. There were arrangements. Our officers went to the Americans and they made arrangements. The 15th Division was something like 600 people with 40 officers.[2]

---

1   The river was probably the Elbe at Güterglück.
2   Bušmanis counts 824 men: 29 officers, 11 deputy officers, 126 instructors (the equivalent of non-commissioned officers or NCOs) and 658 private soldiers.

Former Legionnaire Henry Vītols, a veteran of Pomerania and the incredible escape of the Janums Battle Group, at his home in Nottingham in May 2019, aged 94. Picture: author.

They had a place they were going to put us. 'One there, one there…' There were 600 of us! It was completely flat, and we were caged in with wires. The food was just a tablespoon of dry potatoes with some margarine. My mate had dug a little hollow in the ground so we could dodge the wind and the rain. We could pull a coat over us. Otherwise you woke up and you were wet. There was no shelter at all – the sky was our shelter.

Then after that we were sent to Zedelghem in Belgium and I was there nine months. We went to Zedelghem and travelling through Belgium the train went slowly and of course we are wearing German uniforms, and the Belgians were all shouting rude things at us. I think there were three *lagers* [camps] there. At Christmas the Red Cross sent us 300 cigarettes. The Russians came to say, 'Come home.' One of my sister's boyfriends said, 'I'm going home.' When he arrived in Latvia he was sent straight to Siberia.

After nine months we could go to England, to America, to Canada. I saw a map and I said, 'Latvia is nearer England.' There were only two jobs a man could do: coal mines or working on the land. For women, hospitals or domestic help. After two years you could go wherever you want.

England was fantastic. Freedom. The policemen were your friends. If you did something wrong they just gave you a clout. Nowadays you'd have a criminal record. Completely different. You never locked your door. I like the British people but I don't like the government. They couldn't run a toffee shop.

For a long time I did three jobs. I worked at Stanton Ironworks, blacking the pipes for tar. Then I was a gardener at the camp at Edwinstowe, in Robin Hood country. We were going to go to Canada but then they found I had TB, just like a pin, so we didn't go. After six months off work in bed having injections, they said I could go, but we didn't. All my friends did.

One of my friends was an electrician. He went for four weeks and he was knackered! He says: 'They work and eat! They eat while they're working! I couldn't keep up. It's a different lifestyle.'

Henry had warned me that his memory had gone, but we persevere: he had been with Janums for the surrender to the Americans, after all. I show him the route, but he shakes his head.

> VH: Battle Group Janums went from Berlin to over here [I trace the ring road to the south-west] then into the forest to the Americans.
> HV: It was actually a nightmare really, but you get used to it and you take everything that comes. I was lucky. A bruised leg and I survived. If I'd been with my mate … he was killed. Bombs dropping … I was on the wagon, not far from him … There's an English word for it… [he struggles for while to remember] when what's happened has happened…
> VH: Destiny?
> HV: That's it! Destiny. You're in the forest … [he makes a whizzing noise] it's quite an experience. It made me grow up.
> VH: Did you go through the forest much? There was some terrible stuff in the forests [in Pomerania].
> HV: I can't remember. We didn't write anything down, we didn't have time. And the food…
> VH: You're cold, you're hungry, you're tired, you're scared?

HV: The scaredness goes. What happens, happens. You're not bothered. You're here, you're there … [he makes a whizzing sound again.] We were in Germany, in Bytow and we wanted to go back to Kurzeme to fight with the 19th Division. We were patriots. We would die for Latvia.

VH: Did you volunteer to go back?

HV: No.

VH: Did you see any action?

HV: Not really. Everything was dropping down.

VH: You were being bombed?

HV: Yes. Coming from heaven! My memories are more of the nights. And the walking. We were sent to Bytow. We were supposed to train as the light artillery – 8mm – but all of a sudden we started to move.[3] We started to move and all the time the Russians were behind us. For a youngster – 18, 19 – it was something new. We walked and walked and walked. I fell asleep and was nearly left behind. We fell asleep while we were walking.

VH: With your hand in the belt of the man in front, and if someone didn't take a bend in the road you'd all end up in the ditch?

HV: Yeah! [He laughs, warmly.] Yeah. Now it seems funny, but it was… [he drifts off]. We had transport as well for people who couldn't walk. I lost the skin on my feet and I couldn't walk any more. They put me on a wagon and my friend was left and he was hit in the stomach and chest [by shrapnel]. If I had been standing there I would have been dead as well.[4]

Henry was the last Legionnaire on my list of men in the UK to interview. As an eyewitness his stories had the potential to be brilliant, but he just couldn't remember. We have a pleasant chat and run through some encounters the 15th Division was involved in, but quite quickly we both realise that further talk is futile.

Henry shows me to my car, and we stop to have a look at his garden. West Bridgford is a lovely suburb of Nottingham, and Henry worked as a gardener for many years. It shows. His garden is immaculate, with flowers of all shapes and colours blooming in the summer sun. We shake hands.

'I'm sorry I couldn't be more help to you,' he says.

I smile. 'Don't worry. It was worth the trip for the Panzerfaust story.'

'Are you going to ask me how many I killed?' he says. 'I can't remember. It's gone. And it doesn't matter.'

I smile, and shake his hand again.

'No, it doesn't matter. Thanks, Henry,' I say.

---

3 Henry was in the 33rd or 34th Regiment. He couldn't remember exactly.
4 Interview with author, May 2019. Some of Henry's account has similarities with stories told by other Legionnaires about their experiences of forced marches to escape Russian encirclement in Pomerania. I have reproduced the interview verbatim rather than attempt to separate his memories.

24

The Post-Surrender Diary of Edvīns Bušmanis

The surrender of the Janums Battle Group to the Americans ensured that those 800 men would survive the war, but their involvement in that war has been controversial ever since. Although the vast majority of the Legionnaires were conscripted, as a unit of non-Germans they had the designation 'Waffen-SS' and wore Waffen-SS uniforms to help the Nazis avoid Clause IV of the Hague Convention of 1907, which forbade the conscription of citizens of an occupied country into the military forces of the occupier. Some, but not all, Latvians had the SS tattoo noting a soldier's blood group.

Their memories are of being drafted and given little or no choice about reporting for duty. Dire consequences were threatened if they did not obey. They state repeatedly that their motivation was to defend Latvia from a second period of Soviet occupation following the 'Year of Terror' between 1940–41. This period – described as a 'class war' by historian Andres Kasekamp – culminated in the deportation of 15,000 intellectuals, government officials, opponents of Communism and those resisting the new ideology.[1] The pre-war Latvian Army was absorbed into the Red Army following the killing of its officer class.

The order to form the Legion was given in February 1943. This occurred after the mass killings of the Holocaust in Latvia but former members of the Arājs Kommando, a collaborationist Latvian auxiliary police unit, were transferred into the 15th Division in late 1944, including its leader, Viktors Arājs.

Under Nazi orders, the Arājs Kommando participated in the 'Holocaust by bullets' in Latvia in 1941–42, executing Jewish civilians, burning synagogues and taking part in massacres of Jews, including the massacre of 25,000 Jewish civilians at Rumbula on 30 November and 8 December 1941. Later the Kommando was used in anti-partisan operations in Belarus.

Viktors Arājs was attached to the 15th Division in Pomerania in February 1945, arriving with the rank of major and an Iron Cross. He lasted eight days before the Latvian officers had him transferred out to a reserve unit for his unreliable

---

1   A. Kasekamp, *A History of the Baltic States* (London: Palgrave MacMillan, 2018).

The diary of First Lieutenant Edvīns Bušmanis, which charts both the incredible journey of the Janums Battle Group and also the Latvian period in captivity post-war. The original is kept in the War Museum in Rīga and was made available to the author by Second World War curator Jānis Tomaševskis. The diary was translated into English for this book by Daina Vītola. Picture: author.

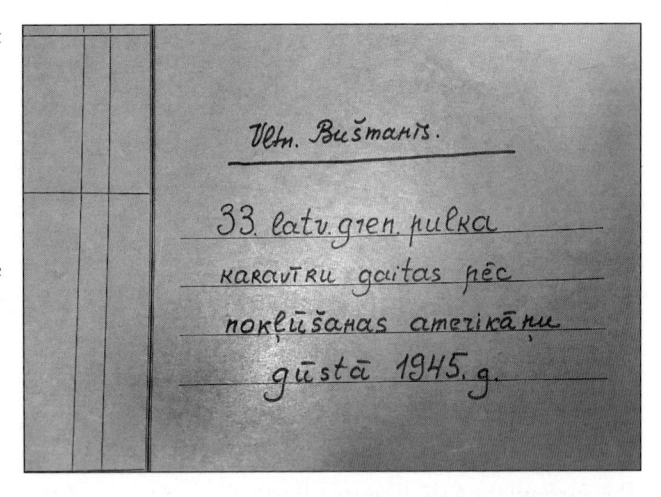

behaviour and lax attitude towards orders. At the end of the war he used the name 'Ābele' (Abols) in the post-war camps and was recognised and identified by the Latvians to the British. Despite knowing his real name and the crimes he had been involved in, the British put him back into the camp system as 'Ābele' where he was again identified to the British by Latvians, at Zedelghem in December 1945.

Arājs was released by the British in Christmas 1948 and promptly disappeared, adopting another false name – Zeibots – and living in Frankfurt until he was tracked down, arrested and convicted in the mid-1970s. He died in prison in 1988. The British also searched the post-war camps for Herbert Cukurs, who acted as adjutant to the Arājs group and was therefore a key figure in its operations. Wanted in connection with the murder of thousands of Jews in the Riga ghetto, he fled to Brazil, where he was granted permanent residency in 1945.

Cukurs had fought in the Latvian War of Independence and was an Air Force officer and pilot whose adventurous feats had made him famous – his CIA file from 1988 notes his name 'was known to every child in Latvia'.[2] He set up a boat rental business in Brazil but soon faced opposition from the local Jewish population, who demanded he be thrown out of the country. In 1965 Cukurs was lured to Uruguay by Israeli Mossad agents and killed.

The men of the 15th SS Division spent a year in British and American custody, seven months of which – from September 1945 until May 1946 – was in Zedelghem. British historian Bob Moore writes:

> The Latvians in British captivity in Camp 2227 at Zedelghem are part of a complex narrative on prisoners-of-war that encompasses both the negotiation between the Allies and the Axis as the war came to an end on the one hand,

---

2 De-classified CIA files OGC-88-51906 on Arājs and Cukurs dated June 1988 online at <https://www.cia.gov/readingroom/docs/CUKURS,%20HERBERTS_0012.pdf>.

and the increasingly fraught relationship between the Western powers and the Soviet Union on the other.³

The Soviets considered the Latvians who surrendered to the Western Allies as their citizens and demanded their return. The Latvians were moved out of Germany to camps in Belgium where around 11,500 were held at Camp 2227, known as Zedelghem. Soviet officers visited these camps several times and invited men from the Baltic states to 'return home', but few accepted these offers – despite the freezing conditions and poor food at the camp.⁴

In a letter to Field Marshall Montgomery of 19 November 1945, Marshall Zhukov demanded that units such as the Latvians, not held as prisoners of war, be disbanded. Subsequent disbandment discussions confirmed that the Balts would not be transferred to the Russian zone 'Under instructions of HMG' and diplomats having contact with their Soviet counterparts were briefed on the British decision.⁵

The Krīpens incident occurred nine days later after Zhukov's letter, on 28 November 1945 – the day before Colonel Janums and his men were to be moved there. SS-Standartenführer (Colonel) Arvīds Krīpens had been commander of the 15th Division's 32nd Regiment until he resigned his position in June 1944 after a disagreement with his German divisional commander Nikolaus Heilmann over 'the Battle for John's Hill' – Hill 228.4 on the Velikaya river in Russia – in which many Latvians died. He assumed a leadership role in the PoW camp at Putlos before becoming the commander of the Latvians at Zedelghem.⁶

When a Soviet mission arrived at Zedelghem to arrest him, Krīpens plunged a knife into his chest in an attempt to kill himself but survived and was hospitalised. The British were apparently 'not aware' he was Latvian and the Soviets had provided no details of specific crimes, other than he was the commander of an SS unit and allegedly 'a furious Nazi'.⁷ Diplomatic moves behind the scenes ensured that future

---

3   An Emeritus Professor at the University of Sheffield, Moore considers the 2021 removal of a plaque and 'Beehive' monument commemorating the Latvians at Zedelghem on the advice of a historical commission he was part of in a 2023 article titled *The British and Their Latvian SS Prisoners: Zedelgem 1945–1946* (Source: The Journal of Slavic Military Studies, 36 (2) pp.179–198).

4   Questions were raised in the House of Commons on 16 July 1946 by Richard Stokes, Labour MP for Ipswich from 1938–1957, about the nature of British 'protective custody' at the camps. Men shipped to the UK from there arrived 'in a dire state of starvation' and 'unfit for work, due to malnutrition,' he said. (Source: Hansard, Volume 425: 'Belgian Prison Camp allegations' online at <https://hansard.parliament.uk/Commons/1946-07-16/debates/6ad7189e-39bd-4e95-8075-fc40cc560e6e/BelgianPrisonCamps(Allegations)?highlight=belgian%20camps#contribution-4ad36db7-155b-48e9-8273-5f2ec0e91bc7>).

5   Zhukov letter from British National Archive at Kew (FO 1038-140) and briefing notes on Baltic detainees from 'Brief for British representative at Control Council 18th December 1945: 1HQ/2857/Sec C in (FO 1038-140).

6   Silgailis, p.92. The retreat at Kalininko followed the Battle of John's Hill and is covered in more detail in Chapter 25.

7   The British did not regard Krīpens as a war criminal. One diplomatic telegram reads: 'Krīpens is not, I repeat not, a member of the SS'.

Soviet approaches for individual detainees would be accompanied by evidence of their crimes, and the British would no longer allow the Russians to enter the camp uncontrolled to address the Latvians. Colonel Janums took over leadership of the Latvians in Zedelghem after the 'Krīpens incident'.

Another officer, Captain Arnolds Laukers, did surrender and was extradited to the USSR. At his trial he was accused of killing civilians as a member of the Arājs Kommando, found guilty and sentenced to ten years in prison. He died behind bars within two years.

In a statement to a meeting of the Allied Control Council on 30.11.1945, Montgomery said he was 'astonished' to receive Zhukov's letter of 20 November as 'this is the first occasion on which one Zone Commander has openly challenged the administration of another.'

The reasons for the Latvians not being designated as PoWs had already been explained in a letter of 26 November to General Sokolovsky, he said, but he would repeat them here:

> If we were to declare these men prisoners of war we would have to accord them certain privileges in conformity with the Geneva Convention. We should be debarred from using them for certain tasks. We should have to feed them on a relatively high scale of rations. Therefore instead of describing them as prisoners of war, we have given them the status of 'disarmed enemy forces'.
>
> They are completely disarmed and will be disbanded as soon as possible bearing in mind our need for labour and our policy on inter-zonal transfers. I should be surprised to hear that there is any difference between our policy in this matter and that of our American colleagues, since the policy we are following was originally established during the period of combined command under General Eisenhower.[8]

While the British stressed that they were concerned to see justice meted out to 'genuine' war criminals, they were reluctant to hand over Balts they did not consider as falling into this category. After the Krīpens case, the Russians would be asked to supply *prima facie* evidence of crimes lest this set a general precedent for the handing over of Baltic SS men, some of whom were being used by the British as intelligence agents.[9]

After a week of talks at Halle in Germany at the war's end, an agreement was signed on 23 May 1945 regarding which prisoners would be returned. The British and

---

8 National Archives FO1038-40.
9 B. Moore, *The British and their Latvian SS Prisoners: Zedelhem 1945–46* in 'The Journal of Slavic Military Studies, 36:2, 179–198'. However, in *War Criminals Welcome: Australia, a Sanctuary for Fugitive War Criminals Since 1945* (Black, Inc: 2020) Mark Aarons argues that the case against Krīpens was well-established and that the British had already agreed to hand him over to the Soviets but backtracked to avoid setting a precedent or to protect a useful intelligence source. However, no evidence was found against him by the British, despite a second investigation in 1947.

Americans insisted that soldiers from states occupied by the Soviets after September 1939 would not be included. Moore examines memos in October that year from the Foreign Office to the Political Division of the British Control Commission for Germany which state that soldiers from the Baltic:

> ...were not to be regarded as Soviet citizens and thus would only be returned to Soviet hands voluntarily. This also meant that they were not to be regarded as citizens of the 'United Nations' (the alliance that had fought against Nazi Germany) and could, theoretically, be tried for criminal acts in German courts.
>
> More favorable treatment for Baltic prisoners-of-war captured in German uniforms was not to be countenanced, as it was 'impossible to distinguish between those who had enlisted voluntarily and those who joined up under duress'. [...] Moreover, decisions taken elsewhere in the Foreign Office had already determined that in any future discussions about the formal recognition of Soviet control of the Baltic States, '...it has been our intention to make the non-return of Balts in British hands against their will a condition of recognition'.[10]

Moore writes that although Soviet military missions visited the camps under British control in Belgium to interview any men claiming Soviet nationality, these were conducted under supervision and those wishing to be repatriated were transferred to Soviet control. In the case of Krīpens, who would not have considered himself 'a Soviet national' there was a breakdown in this process. In reality, according to Latvian sources – including London ambassador and de facto head of the Latvian government-in-exile Kārlis Zariņš – these rules were broken all the time.

Keeping the 19,000 Baltic soldiers in Allied hands at the end of the war in camps in Belgium came at a cost the British considered unsustainable and within six months solutions were being looked at to free them from the camps while avoiding repatriation. With the behaviour of the Baltic servicemen regarded as 'disciplined and cooperative' the British Control Commission for Germany in Berlin suggested in December 1945 they be moved to Displaced Person (DP) camps as civilian refugees.

By January 1946, the success of pilot schemes moving young female Balts to Britain to fill gaps in the labour market was considered a success, and the European Volunteer Workers (EVW) scheme was extended to include ex-servicemen.[11]

The adjutant of the Janums Battle Group, First Lieutenant Edvīns Bušmanis, was one of the prisoners held in the camps in Belgium during this time – as were all the veterans interviewed for this book – and his diary of captivity is reproduced here.

---

10 Moore, *The British and their Latvian SS Prisoners: Zedelhem 1945–46*.
11 Moore writes that a total of 175 prisoners from these camps were handed back after a visit by Soviet missions on 10 October 1945. There were further visits on 28 November 1945 (the date of the 'Krīpens incident') and 22 January and another 175 prisoners were transferred on 1 April 1946, 'but by that time most of the Balts in the camp had already been returned to Germany.'

The Post-Surrender Diary of Edvīns Bušmanis

27 April 1945: Taken by transport to Calbe. Everyone, except officers, is herded into a big yard. The officers are put into a cellar. The Colonel is called to an HQ before midday. He returns, and I go, taking my diary with me. I translate it into German, then that is translated into English. In the HQ I am treated well, but not offered any food. In the evening we are ordered into transport with other prisoners. We go through the Harf hills – Wernigerode-Goslar-Hildesheim. When we get there we are put into a big yard, already full of thousands of prisoners. The officers are put into school classrooms. We are not fed again.

28 April: The next day at lunch Red Cross nurses give us a bowl of soup. In the afternoon we are again loaded onto transport. A lot of our men are left behind, and we are joined by many Germans and civilians and taken to Herford. Here we are herded into a square, which is surrounded by barbed wire. We are finally fed. During the night we are joined by those we left behind.

29 April: The Colonel is called to interrogation, then me. Again we have to recount who we are and why we were fighting with the Germans. The Americans seemingly don't believe we surrendered voluntarily. As they consider us to be a political group.[12]

The radio news tells us that the Russians have taken Neustrelitz. The officers are transported to Paderborn, the former Staumuhle concentration camp. We are put in warm barracks. The Colonel goes on the offensive with the camp commandant to insist that we were not captured, but that we surrendered. He demands we are sent to an internment camp, not kept here as war criminals. The Colonel suggests we send a letter to Dr Bilmanis in Washington to obtain our freedom.[13] Later we found out that the letter had to be in English, but we didn't have any English speakers in our group. The camp is full of Hitler's top officers, and that is apparently the best place for us, as 'we are SS'.[14]

5 May: The letter is ready. The commander says we'll be sent elsewhere. What about our men who were left behind in Herford? There is no news.

---

12 On account of having an SS designation.
13 Dr. Alfreds Bilmanis, Latvia's ambassador in Washington. No. 5 CIC (Civilian Internment Camp) at Paderborn-Staumuhle was a British Army detention centre in occupied Germany for disarmed enemy forces, suspected Nazis and 'unfriendly witnesses'.
14 Bušmanis made several copies of his diary and in various other publications, the exact remarks differ. Leititis (1986) quotes an entry for 29 April 1945 as: 'the soldiers are upset at being put together with SS prisoners and, with that and the non-stop rain, their morale is being completely wet-through'

In another extract in a different book headlined "In mud pits near Herford", he writes of 29 April 1945: "The weather is unpleasantly cold, and there is fine rain. To save ourselves from the cold, in the same way as others are doing, we dig into the ground like moles. But that still doesn't save you from the rain. Slowly we become rained through, wetter and wetter." (Source: Auseklis Zaļinskis. *Bez Ienaida un Bailem* [*Without Hate and Fear*] Latviešu gūstekņi Otrā pasaules karā. Laikmeta liecības, dienasgrāmatas, vēstules, atmiņu skices. Apgāds GAUJA 1991.)

8 May: News comes through of the German capitulation. Rumours that a group surrendered near Schwerin with Latvian shields. Could they be ours? The Colonel is also worried about the III Battalion and those left in the Danzig siege.[15] We march to a new camp at Esselheid, seven kilometres away. It's dirty and full of bedbugs.

28 May: The first Latvians – invalids – are freed to Detmold. The Colonel is told that camp is to be taken over by the English occupiers. That happens on 30 May.

5 June: The foreigner group in the camp is to be taken over by a German officer.

7 June: The German officer can't cope, so the Colonel once again takes over command of the camp. On the same day we have contact with the outside world – two women who were passing who learned of our presence. They promise to make contact with the management of the Latvian camp at Detmold to report that we are here.

10 June: The women return. Detmold already knows we are here.

14 June: Everyone receives five cigarettes and three cigars. The Colonel says, 'The price of a watch is going up.'

19 June: We meet a nurse looking for her brother. She tells us our letter was sent to the envoy in London.

17 June: The Colonel's wife turns up. They are allowed to meet for a short while. We are to be sent to a different camp – our sixth. We travel Dortmund to Essen, cross the Rhine and reach Rheinberg. There are about 50,000 prisoners there. Not long ago there were three times that. Waiting for us there are the men we left behind at Herford. We can't meet but we know they're safe. It turns out there are about 1,300 Latvians in this camp.

25 July: Visit from Latvian Red Cross.

26 July: Told to prepare for departure the next day.

27 July: Loaded into wagons.

28 July: We read notices in French and Flemish and realise we are in Belgium. We march to our seventh camp.

31 July: Joined by 12 new officers from other sectors. We are about seven kilometres north-east of Brussels. Together there are about 20,000 soldiers. We, along with 40 other officers and about 1,300–1,500 soldiers are a large number of Legionnaires.

10 August: Heavy rain and wind. Some tents collapse.

16 August: Everyone is vaccinated against typhus. This affects everyone.

23 August: We are told we will be transferred to a new sector.

1 Sept: We have moved, and erected tents anew.

7 Sept: We are joined by two men separated from units which left the camp at Putlos on 1 Sept. Colonel sends letter to envoy Valters in Brussels describing the situation and asking for a visit.

---

15 Janums' son Linards was an artillery officer (Untersturmführer, the SS equivalent of lieutenant) with the III Battalion of the 33rd Regiment, and almost certainly died of wounds received in the siege of Danzig on 20 March 1945. He is listed as Missing in Action.

11 Sept: Rev. Grikmanis from Brussels visits. Tells us that there is to be a large camp in Belgium for Legionnaires.[16]

17 Sept: Rev. Grikmanis visits again with news that Camp 2227 near Bruges contains about 10,000 men – basically the whole of the 15th Division. A troop train with men from Putlos arrives.

21 Sept: The train and soldiers are sent on to Camp 2227.

25 Sept: The Colonel is arguing with the camp commander that we should be sent to Camp 2227 to be with the others.

5 Oct: Given extra blankets. Looks like we'll be here a while.

9 October: Life is hard. There is too much time to think.

19 Oct: The Balts, along with Romanians, are addressed by four Russian officers. We are invited to go home. Everything is forgiven. No Balts accept the invitation. About a dozen Romanians do. It is not a nice feeling with the Russians being around and knowing that they know where we are. We write to the camp commandant Capt. Greten that we are very unhappy with the Russian arrival. The English are not happy either. The next day the Colonel is told we will not be delivered up to the Russians.

27 Oct: We have been six months in captivity, with no idea of what the future has in store.

6 Nov: Ex-Minister [Alfred] Valdmanis arrives unannounced.

8 Nov: Valdmanis comes again. He has been to Camp 2227 to see Colonel Krīpens. It is not good there either.

11 Nov: Celebrate Lāčplēša festival [Lāčplēsis Day, commemorating the men who fought for Latvian independence].

16 Nov: First frost. The pipes freeze.

18 Nov: Our national day. We sing the anthem.

22 Nov: The full-blown colonels are separated to the 'generals' paddock'. We lose Janums, Skurbe, Lasmanis.

23 Nov: Janums has permission to come and see us. Says we need to keep the men occupied. Rations are very poor.

29 Nov: All Balts are to be moved to another sector. That's everyone except our three doctors – about 240 men. We have to hand in all our blankets. Next door, unguarded, is another pile of blankets. Everyone helps themselves. We journey through half of Belgium and arrive at Camp 2227 to rejoin the other Latvians. The Russians try to take Colonel Krīpens, who attempts suicide, and [Captain Arnolds] Laukers, who disappears without trace.[17]

---

16 Moore writes that request for visits from the Latvian representative in Belgium, Dr. Miķelis Valters, or the Baptist Minister Rev. Grikmanis were considered by the British as 'attempts to politicise the prisoners' and so rejected.

17 Pol Denys in his online article *The Prisoner of War Camp Zedelghem 1944–46* includes the account of Egils Kalme (1909–1983) in his consideration of this incident: 'The Russians requested the extradition of two Latvian officers and the British agreed. One of the officers, Colonel Krīpens, stabbed himself in the abdomen with a knife and was taken to hospital. The other, Captain Laukers, was taken by the Russians [...] Captain Laukers did not return.

6 Dec: In an empty barracks. It's depressing, with bad food and no cigarettes.

13 Dec: We are moved into a barracks with 62 officers. I am writing my diary and want to finish it by the Colonel's birthday on 7 January.

21 Dec: Conditions are bad. I am making four copies of the diary in the hope that we can get one of them out of the camp.

24 Dec: Some get parcels. I get some mail. 'Return to sender'. The Colonel's wife and daughter have been injured in a train crash. Both are injured.

26 Dec: Many in the camp didn't celebrate Christmas. The Colonel is down – his daughter had to have her leg amputated after the train crash.

1946

2 Jan: New Year arrived. Everyone got 126 cigarettes and 10 grams of tobacco.

7 Jan: We celebrate the Colonel's birthday and give him small presents and the diary. The atmosphere in the camp has improved. The Daugavas Vanagi organisation has been formed – a new soldier association meant for collectively helping one another. We are proud that on the eve of his 52nd birthday, the Colonel was elected as the first chairman. The English say we need to do more exercise. There is not enough food: we get a half-litre of milk soup in the morning, a litre of soup at lunch and in the evening 300g of bread, 5g of butter and 10g of sausage or cheese.

10 Jan: Very warm weather. That's good, as we have nothing to provide heating.

17 Jan: Now it's freezing again. Rev. Grikmanis brought eight loaves of bread; two each for Janums, Skurbe, Lasmanis and me. We don't know who sent them, but we share them out. Lasmanis at first refused to share his bread and in the end, only shares one of his loaves.

19 Jan: The biggest event and surprise for all of us is that we have been officially informed that we will soon be set free and sent to Germany. That isn't the usual camp rumour but a true and honest statement. The Colonel and I have agreed that, after being released from imprisonment, we will firstly go together to his family, and then we'll see what will happen next.[18]

Two years later he died in Siberia. Colonel Krīpens was sent to the 105 British PoW General Hospital in Ostend, about 20 kilometers from our camp.' Captain Laukers was extradited from Belgium to the USSR, where he was sentenced to 10 years in prison for killing civilians as a member of the Arājs Kommando. The Latvian historian Uldis Neiburgs notes that the Soviet investigators 'were more interested in the fight against the Red Army and partisans, and less the possible crimes of the Holocaust. Furthermore, no specific crimes were proven against Laukers.' Sources: Elita Weideman's interview with Uldis Neiburgs: *Jāpēta ne tikai Arāja, bet arī NKVD un SMERŠ noziegumi (Not only the crimes of Arājs, but also of the NKVD and Smersh should be investigated)* online at <https://neatkariga.nra.lv/intervijas/313504-uldis-neiburgs-japeta-ne-tikai-araja-bet-ari-nkvd-un-smers-noziegumi> and Pol Denys webpage at: <https://zedelgem--jabbeke--powcamp-com.translate.goog/zedelgem-powcamp/?_x_tr_sl=nl&_x_tr_tl=en&_x_tr_hl=en&_x_tr_pto=sc>. (accessed 24.04.2024).

18 On 25 January 1946, despite public protests, Sweden complied with Soviet demands for the return of 149 Legionnaires who had escaped Courland by boat, along with nine Lithuanians and nine Estonians. Desperate to avoid extradition as they would be regarded as traitors, some mutilated themselves in advance and some committed suicide. The majority were released on

31 Jan: All paperwork is being finalised.

4 Feb: We are told we are going soon. The other camp is being cleared after its previous use. The English have come to arrest Captain Cukurs and Major Arājs. Cukurs hasn't been seen in this camp but everyone knows that Arājs has been living under the name ABELE. The English know this. They first take Major Arājs-Abele, then just in case deputy officer Arājs and one soldier called Arājs, together with Oberltn. Cukurs and a soldier called Cukurs.

7 Feb: Waiting to be set free, apparently in Hannover.

12 Feb: Rev. Grikmanis brings food parcels and says our being set free is hampered by floods in Germany.

24 Feb: I re-read my diary about the first days of our captivity when we were in Herford, Rheinberg, etc. Then we had a sense of humour and optimism, and thought we'd be set free in a month. Now, ten months later, it's not clear if and when we'll be freed. We have become nervous, impatient and short-tempered.

1 Mar: Rev. Grikmanis brings more food.

3 Mar: It's deep winter, there's snow and it's freezing. We have lost all patience.

7 Mar: The freeing-up begins. Today 1,200 men left. Our destination is Münster, in Westfalen. The past few days we have seen our envoy Dr. Valters from Brussels, but he didn't come to us.

11 Mar: Today is our day. It's my birthday and a year since we made it out of the siege of Pomerania. What a coincidence. We are 40 men in the wagon and in the coming darkness we are travelling through Holland. So, tomorrow we'll be in Germany. Strange. It feels like going home.[19]

---

return but at least 50 were arrested subsequently and sentenced to between 10 and 15 years in prison. Two officers were sentenced to death but served 17 years in gulag labour camps instead, while three ranking soldiers were sentenced to death and executed in 1946. In 1994 the Swedish government invited survivors back to meet King Carl Gustav, and announced it 'regretted' the decision.

19 Post-surrender diary of First Lieutenant Edvīns Bušmanis. Translated by Daina Vītola. Alexandrs Edvīns Bušmanis died aged 92 in Belleview, Florida on 26.04.2001. The announcement of his death was headlined 'A friend of ours from the old days'.

25

The Life and Legacy of Colonel Janums

Colonel Janums remains one of the most significant figures in Latvia's 20th century military history. His career spanned some of Latvia's most turbulent years, from joining the Tsarist Army in 1914, fighting the Bolsheviks in the battles for independence post-First World War, then fleeing the Soviet occupation of 1940–41 and returning to lead a Latvian Legion regiment. He was decorated both by the Russians during WWI and the Germans during the Second World War and also – though circumstances were slightly different in each case – deserted from both armies.

Janums was born in 1884 in Codes parish in Courland, western Latvia, and was mobilised into the Imperial Russian Army in 1914 as an artilleryman. In WWI, he fought in the 4th Vidzeme Latvian Rifle Regiment in battles near Riga, being awarded the Cross of the Order of St. George (IV Class), and the Order of Saint Stanislav with spears and bows (III Class). He was demobilised in February 1918 and stayed in Latvia.[1]

The Latvian Red Riflemen were a significant force in the 1917 Bolshevik Revolution which removed the Tsar and were instrumental in suppressing anti-Bolshevik opposition in Moscow and Yaroslavl in 1918. A month after Latvia declared independence in November 1918, the Bolsheviks sent the Red Riflemen across the border to establish Soviet rule in their homeland.

In January 1919, Janums was mobilised into the Soviet Latvian army, this time as commander of a machine gun battalion. He deserted on 6 June 1919 to join the Latvian National Army, commanding a company in the Cēsis Battalion as a lieutenant in the Balodis Brigade. After six months of fighting, supported by Estonian and Polish forces and the British and French navies, the Bolsheviks were pushed out of Latvia along with the German-backed 30,000-strong West Russia Volunteer Army. Peace talks began with the Bolsheviks in April 1920 and a Latvian-Soviet peace treaty was signed on 11 August.

---

1   He later donated these medals to be melted down and added to Latvia's post-independence gold reserves.

After the war, now a first lieutenant, he stayed in the military, eventually joining the General Staff in 1930 as a lieutenant-colonel. He was chief of staff for the 1st Kurzeme Infantry Division when the Soviet Union occupied Latvia in June 1940 and was demobilised with the rank of colonel that autumn.

Janums was already highly-decorated before the Second World War started, having been awarded the Order of the Three Stars, Latvia's highest civilian honour, in November 1928 (fifth class) and the fourth class in November 1935. In May 1940 – a month before the Soviet occupation – he was awarded the Order of Viesturs for his efforts strengthening state security, defending Latvian borders and promoting patriotism.

He managed to slip out of Latvia to Germany during the Soviet occupation but returned soon after Operation Barbarossa in June 1941 working for the Latvian Self-Administration. In June 1943, he was appointed as a regimental commander of the 15th SS Division of the Latvian Legion with the rank of Waffen-Standartenführer.

This put an experienced combat leader in charge of the mostly-conscripted Latvian soldiers who were sent to the Eastern Front in November 1943, although the commanding officers were German SS men. He developed a reputation as a Houdini-esque commander who could get his men out of seemingly-impossible situations and cemented that status as he led the 15th Division through the chaos and carnage of repeated encirclements between January and March 1945 in Pomerania, sometimes in defiance of the orders of his German superiors, and sometimes with good reason.

One incident on the Russian Front at Kalininko stands as an example of Latvian deaths due to muddled Nazi command. Two weeks after the Latvians suffered heavy losses in the Battle of John's Hill on 22 June 1944, Colonel Janums was defending a line around Lake Kamennoye. Minsk had fallen and fighting had reached Latvian territory at Daugavpils. Orders were given on 9 July for a 'secret' retreat the following night of 10–11 July, but any element of cover was blown when the supply units set fire to everything around them that day and headed west on wagons loaded with tables, mattresses and even pigsties, choking the roads.

Seeing this, Soviets tanks and infantry attacked after an intense artillery barrage on the morning of 10 July. Unable to push them back, Colonel Janums organised a tactical withdrawal. The next morning he was visited by Divisional commander Nikolaus Heilmann, whom he describes as the former chief of a police station in Germany, without military education, who was 'brutal and nervous' and in that position simply because of his Nazi party membership card. Colonel Kripens had resigned after falling out with Heilmann after many Latvian lives were lost at John's Hill.

Having applied the tactics of retreat he'd lectured on pre-war at military college, Janums had a whole battalion in reserve. In the face of Janums' misgivings, Heilman ordered him to hold the line Melenka–Stolbovo. Heilman issued orders to all the command points then countermanded them, creating confusion and chaos in his wake. In his autobiography, Janums notes that finally even he didn't know what he was supposed to be doing.

The defensive plan was a disaster, and as his men were armed only with Panzerfausts, Janums withdrew when Soviet tanks overwhelmed his lines. He pulled his men back to a wood in the south-west corner of Lake Kamennoye, and wrote a scathing summary of Heilmann's judgement:

> During such a heavy fight for the 15th Division, the Division's commander could not come up with anything cleverer than to order a number of soldiers to be arrested, of which four had abandoned their weapons and were therefore ordered to be shot. All the men of my regiment saw the corpses of these soldiers by a sauna in the village of Filevo.

After another day and night of retreat, the Latvians set up a new command post in woods at Kalininko. Again Soviet tanks broke through the defence line and had to be fought off. That night, when infantry and tanks attacked again, Janums withdrew his men across the Velikaya river.[2]

In August 1944, Heilmann was transferred to the 14th SS Galicia Division which was being rebuilt after taking huge losses in the Brody pocket. Reinforced with new volunteers and reserves, the Galicia Division was sent to suppress the Slovak Uprising, fought Tito's partisans in Slovenia and took heavy losses fighting the Red Army on the Austrian front. During this time Heilmann was wounded and also awarded the Knight's Cross for his command of the 15th Division.[3]

Another of those superiors was Oberführer Adolph Ax, who commanded the Division during the initial stages of the Pomeranian campaign, including along 'the road of slaughter' when as many as 5,000 Latvians were killed in a Red Army encirclement between Jastrow and Landeck. Disagreements between Ax and Janums were common, as Janums objected to the Latvians regularly being the first and last on the frontline. One time he told Ax, 'We are not Germans and we are not men of the SS. For years and with pride we had worn the Latvian uniform. As soon as this war is over we will take off our current uniforms.'[4]

---

2 Janums, *Mana Pulka Kauju Gaita*, Chapter 7 'Retreat', pp.128–132. Trans. Aivars Sinka.
3 In September 2023, the speaker of the Canadian Parliament was forced to resign after inviting 98 year-old Galicia Division veteran Yaroslav Hunka to attend an address by Ukrainian President Volodmyr Zelensky. Professor Lubomyr Luciuk, a senior research fellow at the University of Toronto, specialist on the Second World War and Ukrainian diaspora and scholar at Canada's Royal Military College believes this row was generated by Russian Federation propagandists and their 'fellow travellers in the West' to distract from the war in Ukraine and cause discord between Ukrainian and Jewish communities in Canada. On 10 May 1945, 9,000 Division men surrendered to the British and 1,200 surrendered to the Americans. As PoWs in Rimini, Italy, they were screened by American, British, Canadian and even Soviet interrogators who determined they were not implicit in war crimes. The 1987 Deschene Committee Inquiry on War Criminals concluded that charges of war crimes against Division members had never been substantiated; in 1950 when they first arose, in 1984 or before the Commission. In September 1950, the Canadian High Commissioner to the UK Dana Wilgress described Soviet narratives about these alleged 'war criminals' and 'quislings' as nothing more than 'Soviet propaganda.' Source: Luciuk, *The Galicia Division – They Fought for Ukraine* (Kashtan Press, 2023).
4 Janums, *Mana Pulka Kauju Gaitas*, p.51 in Major Edmunds Svencs, *The Latvian Legion (1943–1945) and its Role in Latvia's History* (2103).

Once across the Oder into the German heartland, he activated a plan agreed with his fellow officers and General Rudolfs Bangerskis, the Inspector-General of the Legion, to lead the entire division westwards to avoid capture by the Soviets, but German orders to split the division up and send the best fighters to Berlin put paid to that.

Although mutinous, his decision to abandon his positions in Berlin in late April 1945 and march 125 km to surrender to the Americans at Güterglück saved 800 men from death in pointless combat or years in Soviet captivity. They eventually joined around 11,500 Latvian Legionnaires held at Camp 2227 in Zedelghem in Belgium designated as 'disarmed enemy combatants' on Montgomery's orders.

Janums was decorated several times for his bravery in action with the 15th SS Division. He was awarded the Iron Cross Second Class in February 1944 and the First Class six months later. In March 1945 he was awarded the German Cross in Gold for a series of defensive battles in Pomerania which extricated his men from ten Red Army encirclements.

He became the first president of the Daugavas Vanagi veterans' organisation when it was founded at the Zedelghem camp in Belgium in December 1945. After being released from captivity in 1946 he lived with 300 other Latvians in a camp for DPs (displaced persons) in Augustdorf, West Germany.

Seeing so many of his men sign up to the European Volunteer Workers' scheme in 1947 and move to England – about 18,000 up to 1950 – Janums applied too but was turned down by the Immigration Board on the grounds that he was too old to start work in the UK.

The Latvian envoy in the UK, Kārlis Zariņš (1879–1963), the ambassador in London from 1933 until his death and de facto head of the Latvian government-in-exile, tried repeatedly to get approval for Janums to move to England,stressing how popular he was with the younger Latvians as a 'symbolic leader' who would help knit the Latvian community together.[5]

On 1 March 1949, Zariņš asked the Foreign Office for Janums to be interviewed by 'a person knowledgeable in military matters'. War Ministry official Lieutenant-Colonel R.F.G. Stoney subsequently met Janums and reported back to the Foreign Office that the Colonel's main aim appeared to be to train Latvian officers in British Army methods, before they 'rust' – that is, go stale.

'It's not our policy to train anyone, apart from for guard duties, so I couldn't promise anything,' he concluded. 'I passed the information on to GCHQ [Government Communications Headquarters].'

---

[5] Before the Soviet occupation of Latvia in 1940, the Latvian Cabinet of Ministers granted Zariņš extraordinary powers to supervise the country's diplomatic missions abroad, with the title Envoy Extraordinary and Minister Plenipotentiary. While the British never recognised *de jure* Latvia's incorporation into the Soviet Union, there were restrictions on the official activities the ambassadors from the Baltic States could undertake.

His biographer Jekabs Leititis wrote, 'He had this idea of training up an army of 100–150 officers to fight against the Soviets. The British decided they wanted no such thing.'[6]

In mid-September 1950, Zariņš applied for Janums to join the Latvian Embassy in London as a member of the staff. This was refused on the grounds that it would then be impossible for the British to get him out of the country, he would bring his wife and family, and there was no proof of the benefits his presence would bring.

There were further attempts to get approval for Janums to come to the UK but the reluctance of the British to approve his immigration application was becoming obvious, and eventually the Latvians decided that 'it seems best for Janums to stay in Germany'.[7]

When the Augustdorf camp closed in 1957, Colonel Janums moved to Münster to join the Latvian community there, which had established a high school. He became the chair of the board of the Latvian community in Germany between 1950 and 1970, with the aim of keeping the school running, which it did, from 1946–1998.

During his time in Germany, Janums – along with several other senior Latvian Legion officers – gathered intelligence for the Americans and West Germans in his role as head of the Latvian Central Committee (LCK).

The LCK had developed a close relationship with the West German Büro für heimatvertriebene Ausländer (BfhA or Office for Exiled Foreigners) which was set up to observe and report on emigrants from the East – their organisations, activities and outside connections – in effect, spying on them.

Historian Kārlis Kangeris, who worked at the LCK in Germany and lived in the same Latvian community as Janums, writes:

> From to 1955 to 1964 the BfhA was a valuable instrument in the Cold War offensive against communism and communist activities among refugees. It provided highly useful information to West German ministries and the Federal Office for the Protection of the Constitution.
>
> In the end the BfhA had become a typical Cold War institution, which, on the one hand, gathered and published information about the Communist bloc countries, while, on the other hand, it followed the activities of the East European refugees, assisted the German government and the refugee groups in their efforts to stop the repatriation policies, thus taking an active part in combating communism in the ideological battle of opposing world views.[8]

---

6   Leititis, *Pulkvedis Colonel Janums*, pp.146–150.
7   Leititis, *Pulkvedis Colonel Janums*, pp.146–150.
8   Kangeris, article for the University of Latvia website Büro für heimatvertriebene Ausländer (1952–1964) *Latvian Refugees in West Germany and Their Role in Functioning of the Office* online at <https://www.lu.lv/en/par-mums/lu-mediji/zurnali/akademiska-dzive/arhivs/56-numurs/buero-fuer-heimatvertriebene-auslaender-1952-1964-latvian-refugees-in-west-germany-and-their-role-in-functioning-of-the-office/> (accessed 23.05.2024).

> **DISPATCH**
>
> S-E-C-R-E-T
>
> **TO:** Chief, SR
> **INFO:** EE, COS
> **FROM:** Chief of Base, Frankfurt
> **SUBJECT:** REDWOOD/AEFLAG — AECANOE 3 Contact Operations
> **ACTION REQUIRED:** See paragraph 4 below
> **REFERENCE:** EGFW 8872, 1 June 1959
>
> **HEADQUARTERS FILE NO.** 74-126-29/1
> **DATE:** 30 July 1959
>
> 1. In accordance with Referenced instructions, a meeting was held with AECANOE 3 on 2 July 1959 in Frankfurt. As expected, he was most cooperative. (The undersigned has had occasional contact with Subject during the past several years.) His organization and it's capabilities were discussed with Subject and it appeared likely that AECANOE 3 could probably carry out the tasks suggested by Headquarters. He was therefore briefed in some detail on the assignments contained in paragraph 3 of Reference. It was emphasized to Subject that a "shotgun" type of approach was not desirable because of the security considerations. Subject was instructed to choose an individual in as many of his organizations chapters as possible and then submit the name and personal history data to us for screening. These individuals are to be chosen on a very selective basis and will serve as confidential personal representatives of AECANOE 3. The rank and file members are not to be informed of this arrangement, but may be utilized as unwitting spotters of Soviet visitors.
>
> 2. AECANOE 3 stated he has several reliable people in mind who he felt would be willing to cooperate. He was instructed to make tentative overtures to them and if he still felt they were suitable, to submit their names and personal history data. We plan to arrange a meeting in the near future and will then inform you what progress Subject has made.
>
> 3. Subject was advanced $1,000. to cover expenses incurred in the course of contact operations. He was told that this money was to be used only for actual expenses and to include receipts in his accountings wherever possible. The payment of bonuses or compensation for work performed was left open, Subject having stated that his contacts would likely be willing to donate their services.
>
> 4. It is requested that fifty copies of the Latvian language "The New Class," by Djilas, be forwarded to FOB. They will be distributed to AECANOE 3 and to any other of his sub-agents who are considered suitable.
>
> **APPROVED:**

Declassified CIA file from 1959 detailing contact with Vilis Janums.

Kangeris writes that during his time at the LCK, he found files marked 'Janums' which contained reports about Communist activity in Latvian groups in West Germany, which identified individuals suspected of being Soviet agents. 'All these messages were sent to the address of an American organisation in Munich,' Kangeris notes. This activity started around 1954–55.

Janums also worked directly for the CIA, with the codename AECANOE 3. He signed his reports to the central office between 1957 and 1961 with the name 'Janis'.

This secret CIA file, dated 30 July 1959 and declassified in 2007, carries details of a meeting with AECANOE-3 on 2 July 1959 in Frankfurt.

> ...as expected, he was most cooperative. (The undersigned has had occasional contact with Subject during the past several years.) His organization and its capabilities were discussed with Subject and it appeared likely that AECANOE-3 could probably carry out the tasks suggested by Headquarters. He was therefore briefed in some detail on the assignments contained in paragraph 3 of Reference [...]
>
> Subject was instructed to choose an individual in as many of his organization's chapters as possible and then submit the name and personal history data to us for screening. These individuals are to be chosen on a very selective basis and will serve as confidential personal representatives of AECANOE-3. The rank and file members are not to be informed of this arrangement, but may be utilized as unwitting spotters of Soviet visitors.
>
> 2. AECANOE-3 stated he has several reliable people in mind who he felt would be willing to cooperate. He was instructed to make tentative overtures to them and if he still felt they were suitable, to submit their names and personal history data. We plan to arrange a meeting in the near future and will then inform you what progress Subject has made.
>
> 3. Subject was advanced $1,000 to cover expenses incurred in the course of contact operations. He was told that this money was to be used only for actual expenses and to include receipts in his accountings wherever possible. The payment of bonuses or compensation for work performed was left open, Subject having stated that his contacts would likely be willing to donate their services.
>
> 4. It is requested that fifty copies of the Latvian language *The New Class* by Djilas be forwarded to FOB. They will be distributed to AECANOE-3 and to any other of his sub-agents who are considered suitable.[9]

Point 4 relates to a book of political theory published in 1957 by Yugoslav intellectual Miloslav Djilas, the son of Montenegrin peasants who became a key figure in the Yugoslav partisan movement in the Second World War and one of Tito's three most important political associates. Its full title is *The New Class: An Analysis of the Communist System*.

---

9   CIA secret file 74-126-29/1 dated 30.07.1959 titled REDWOOD/AEFLAG – AECANOE-3 Contact Operations Declassified 2007. Online at <https://www.cia.gov/readingroom/docs/JANUMS%2C%20VILIS_0054.pdf> (accessed 23/05.2024). AEFLAG (1955–62) was the Latvian arm of a Baltic-wide operation codenamed AEFREEMAN (1953–64) designed to strengthen resistance to communism and harass the Soviet regime in the Baltic countries. Redwood indicates this is action designed for the CIA Soviet Division.

Widely regarded at one time as Tito's successor, Djilas was expelled from the party in January 1954 and jailed for increasingly critical articles arguing against the one-party state and the domination of party officials. He wrote *The New Class* while in jail for criticising Yugoslavia's failure to condemn the Soviet crushing of the 1956 Hungarian Revolution. This critique of the Communist system by one of Eastern Europe's highest-ranking political insiders-turned-dissident led to the book being translated into 40 languages – and earned Djilas another seven years in jail.

In it, he predicted the end of Communist control in countries which had not had a revolution but had the system imposed on them – such as Poland, Czechoslovakia, Hungary, Rumania, Bulgaria and the Baltic states. Djilas writes, 'The Communist East European countries did not become satellites of the USSR because they benefited from it, but because they were too weak to prevent it. As soon as they become stronger, or as favorable conditions are created, a yearning for independence and for protection of "their own people" from Soviet hegemony will arise among them.'

This conclusion would no doubt have had resonance with both the beliefs and actions of Colonel Janums in fighting Communism and his hopes for the restoration of independence in Latvia – which he would never see.[10]

Colonel Janums self-published his memoirs *Mana Pulka Kauju Gaitas* (*My Regiment in Battle*) in 1953 and died in Münster in 1981 aged 87. He was originally buried in the Lauheide cemetery in Münster but in 2007 his body was exhumed and he was reburied in the Braļu Kapi cemetery in Rīga, which was founded for the heroes of the First World War and the Latvian war of independence.

His original gravestone remained in Münster but although there was a strong Latvian population in Germany after the war, the population had by then declined. Latvian returnees from Germany agreed that the best solution would be to repatriate Janums' gravestone, and it was transported back to the Lestene cemetery, where it was unveiled in September 2024.

One of Colonel Janums' legacies has caused recent controversy. In 1952 it was Janums who suggested 16 March as a date to remember fallen Legionnaires. This was not controversial at the time and was treated as a simple commemoration day for the veterans in the diaspora.

The first year the date was observed unofficially in Latvia – 1989 – Soviet militia formed human chains to prevent Legionnaires and their families from attending the commemoration at the Braļu Kapi cemetery. In 1990, after Latvia's declaration of independence from the Soviet Union, 10,000 people attended in the first official commemoration.

The date was made official in 1998 by the Latvian Parliament as a 'remembrance day for Latvian soldiers' but condemned by the Russian State Duma the following year as a 'glorification of Nazism'.

In 2000, as Latvia sought entry into NATO and the EU, the government abolished 16 March as an official commemoration day. During the 2000s, the unofficial

---

10 Djilas, *The New Class: An Analysis of the Communist System* (Frederick A. Praeger, Inc: 1957).

The original headstone from Colonel Janums' grave in Münster, then in West Germany. Picture: Valters Nollendorfs.

commemorations were the scene of protest, counter-protest and some confrontation, and in 2014 the Latvian government banned ministers from taking part in the ceremonies in Rīga. The Ministry of Foreign Affairs website states:

> Since the restoration of independence, the Latvian government has consistently pursued an approach that Latvia commemorates its fallen soldiers on 11 November (Lāčplēsis Day) – the day we remember our heroes.
> As a democratic country, Latvia respects and also guarantees freedom of expression and freedom of assembly. 16 March is not an official remembrance day and people on their own private initiative pay their respects to the fallen soldiers. The senior officials and members of the government do not participate in those commemorative gatherings in the centre of Latvia's capital city.[11]

In recent years 16 March has passed off relatively peacefully and in 2024 an 'unofficial' memorial parade of around 300 people took place in Rīga, which stopped to

---

11 Latvian Ministry of Foreign Affairs website online at <https://www.mfa.gov.lv/en/article/information-concerning-16-march?utm_source=https%3A%2F%2Fwww.google.com%2F> (accessed 2 April 2024).

lay flowers at the Brivibas Monument in the centre. The Latvian news portal lsm.lv reported that one person described as a 'pro-Kremlin activist' was arrested near the Freedom Monument, with a large police presence and monitoring from drones and a helicopter.[12]

Around 400 people commemorated the Legionnaires in the Brethren Cemetery in Lestene on 16 March 2024, during which five Legionnaires whose remains had been exhumed in November 2023 were buried with military honours. In recent years the Brethren Cemetery in Lestene has become the focal point of commemorations organised by Latvian military charities, including the veterans' association Daugavas Vanagi.

---

12 Article dated 16.03.2024 titled *March 16 Events Passed Peacefully* at LSM.lv online [Latvian Public Broadcasting] at <https://eng.lsm.lv/article/culture/history/16.03.2024-march-16-events-passed-peacefully.a545582/> (accessed 25.04.2024).

Bibliography

New interviews

Author interviews with Legionnaires Jānis Čevers, Laimonis Cerins, Žano Mūsiņš, Jānis Urpens, Harijs Valdmanis, Henry Vītols
In Zerbst: Mayor Andreas Dittmann, Juliane Bruder, Professor Dr. Herbert Witte, Andreas Baumgart

Archives

After-action log of 330th infantry regiment, 83rd Division for April 1945, at <https://83rdinfdivdocs.org/units/330th-ir> by Dave Curry, 83rd Division historian

Bušmanis, First Lieutenant Edvins: *The diary of; April to May 1945*. Unpublished, from the archive of the Latvian War Museum in Rīga. Given to the author by, and used with permission of, curator Jānis Tomaševskis, September 2019. Trans. Daina Vītola

CIA declassified files at <https://www.cia.gov/library/readingroom/docs/>

Colonel Janums' Battle Group at Calbe. Film in the collection of the United States Holocaust Memorial Museum at <https://collections.ushmm.org/search/catalog/irn1004700>

CIA secret file 74-126-29/1 dated 30.07.1959 titled REDWOOD/AEFLAG – AECANOE-3 Contact Operations Declassified 2007. Online at <https://www.cia.gov/readingroom/docs/JANUMS%2C%20VILIS_0054.pdf>

Griebel, Eva. *Chronicle Fichtenwalde: 1908–2008*

Library of Congress, George Stevens Jr. Collection, part of the Motion Picture, Broadcasting and Recorded Sound Division. Spring 1945 Special Coverage Unit (SPECOU) film recorded at the Truman Bridge at the river Elbe. Website online at <www.loc.gov/item/2020600757/>

Stadtarchiv Zerbst: pre and post-bombing pictures of Zerbst

War Diary, Latvian Legion 15th SS Division. Microfiche archive held at National Archives, Skolas iela, Rīga, used with permission

Books

Beevor, Antony, *Berlin – The Downfall 1945* (London: Viking-Penguin Books, 2002)
Blank, R., Fings, K. and Echtemkamp, J, *Germany and the Second World War Vol IX–1* (Oxford: Clarendon Press, 2008)
Blumstengel, C., *Zerbst im April 1945* (Extrapost – Verlag für Heimatliteratur, 2009)
Borowski, T., *Last Blood on Pomerania – Leon Degrelle and the Walloon Waffen SS Volunteers, February – May 1945*. (Warwick: Helion, 2016)
Djilas, M., *The New Class: An Analysis of the Communist System* (Frederick A. Praeger, Inc., 1957)
Freivalds, Caunītis, Bērziņš, Kociņš and Hāzners (eds), *Latviešu Karavīrs Otra Pasaules Kaŗa Laikā (The Latvian Soldier During World War Two, volumes 1–9)* (Ziemeļblāzma, Västerås, Sweden, 1970–1979)
Groehler, O., *Anhalt im Luftkrieg* (Anhaltische Verlagsgesellschaft mbH Dessau, 1993)
Guderian, H., *Panzer Leader* (Michael Joseph, 1952, reprinted Middlesex: Classic Penguin, 2000)
Janovskis, G., *Pēc pastardienas (After Doomesday [sic])* Trans. Sarmīte Janovskis-Erenpreiss. (Riga, Latvia: Vesta-LK, 1968)
Janums, V., *Mana Pulka Kauju Gaitas* (*My Regiment in Battle*) (Sweden: Daugavas Vanagi, 1978)
Kalupnieks, Arvīds, *Memoirs: Colonel Janums and his Men in* Leititis (1986). Trans. Mara Walsh-Sinka
Kaufman, Max, *Churbn Lettland – the Destruction of the Jews of Latvia* (New York: Jewish Survivors of Latvia, Inc., 2010)
Koop, G. and Schmolke, K.P., *Pocket Battleships of the Deutschland Class: Warships of the Kriegsmarine* (Barnsley: Seaforth Publishing, 2014)
Leitītis, J., *Pulkvedis Vilis Janums. Raksti, stasti un atminas* (Toronto: Daugavas Vanagi Central Committee, 1986)
Luciuk, L., *The Galicia Division – They Fought for Ukraine* (Kashtan Press, 2023)
Megargee, G. (ed), *US Holocaust Memorial Museum – Encyclopaedia of Camps and Ghettos 1933–1945, Vol I, Part B* (Bloomington and Indianapolis: Indiana University Press, 2009)
Mežgrāvis, Fricis in Freivalds, Caunītis, Bērziņš, Kociņš and Hāzners, (eds), *Latviešu Karavīrs Otra Pasaules Kaŗa Laikā (The Latvian Soldier During World War Two, vol 6)* (Västerås, Sweden: Ziemeļblāzma, 1979)
Neitmann (ed), *Historical Local Lexicon for Brandenburg. Part V – Zauch – Belzig* (2011)
Newton, S., *Panzer Operations: The Eastern Front Memoir of Generaloberst Erhard Raus* (Cambridge, Mass: Da Capo, 2003)
Petersons, A., *Mums Japarnak: Latviesu Karaviri – Pedejie Berlines Aizstavji (We Have to Get Home: Latvian Soldiers, the Last Defenders of Berlin)* (Riga: Aplis, 2003)
Pfleghar, Udo, *Bruckenkopf Zerbst – der Amerikanische Vorstoss uber die Elbe im April 1945* (Dessau: Anhaltische Verlagsgesellschaft mbH Dessau, 1998)
Pogue, Forrest C., *Why Eisenhower's Forces Stopped at the Elbe* in *World Politics, Apr., 1952, Vol. 4, No. 3* (Cambridge: Cambridge University Press, 1952)

Polmar, N. and Allen, T., *World War II: the Encyclopedia of the War Years, 1941–1945* (New York: Dover Publications Inc, 2012)

Rubess, B. and Ikstena, N., *Brīnumainā kārtā: stāsti par Bruņa Rubesa trim mūžiem (The Autobiography of Brunis Rubess)* (Nordik, 1999)

Ručs,K., *Dzīve ar Dievu : prelāts Dr. Kazimirs Ručs, garīdznieks, latgalietis, latvietis trimdā: atmiņas (Life with God Prelate Dr. Kazimirs Ručs, clergyman, Latgalian, Latvian in exile: memories)* (Riga: Madris, 2004)

Silgailis, A., *Latvian Legion* (San Jose, CA: Roger James Bender, 1986)

Witte, H., *Zerbst Ende II – Helle Funken in schwarzer Nacht (Bright Sparks in the Black Night)* (Jena, 2023)

Witte, H., *Zwei Tage im April (Two Days in April)* (Jena, 2020)

Ziemke, Earl F., *Battle for Berlin – End of the Third Reich* (London: Pan/Ballantine, 1974)

Articles

Baumgart, A., Trans. Tania Kibermanis, '1945: The Odyssey of Battle Group Janums', *Zeitung Volksstimme,* 17.06.2022

Beelitz-Heilstätten: Adolf Hitler and Erich Honecker were also in Beelitz, online at <https://www-berliner--zeitung-de.translate.goog/mensch-metropole/beelitz-heilstaetten-auch-adolf-hitler-und-erich-honecker-lagen-in-beelitz-li.51574?_x_tr_sl=de&_x_tr_tl=en&_x_tr_hl=en&_x_tr_pto=sc&_x_tr_hist=true> 16 January 2018

Daugavas Vanagi newspaper reports of Major Alksnītis' funeral, London 1960, at <http://periodika.lv/periodika2-viewer/view/index-dev.html?lang=fr#panel:pa|issue:/p_000_xdav1960n02|article:DIVL478|query:Kelpinas%20mui%C5%BE%C4%81|issueType:P>

'Germany's water dilemma – a swimming lake just outside Berlin is dying' online at <https://www-focus-de.translate.goog/earth/report/in-brandenburg-der-seddiner-see-stirbt-und-zeigt-deutschlands-wasser-problem_id_203136111.html?_x_tr_sl=de&_x_tr_tl=en&_x_tr_hl=en&_x_tr_pto=sc>

Hehne, H. and Kirchner, T., 'Commemoration: Zerbst was destroyed 75 years ago today – contemporary witnesses remember', *Zerbst Actuell,* online at <https://zerbstaktuell.wixsite.com/zerbstaktuell/single-post/2020/04/16/gedenken-heute-vor-75-jahren-wurde-zerbst-zerst%C3%B6rt-zeitzeugen-erinnern-sich> 16.04.2020

Hughes, L., 'The Special Allied Airborne Reconnaissance Force (SAARF)' online at <http://www.insigne.org/SAARF-I.htm> 1993

Kangeris, K., 'Latvian Refugees in West Germany and Their Role in Functioning of the Office', University of Latvia website Büro für heimatvetriebene Ausländer (1952–1964) online at <https://www.lu.lv/en/par-mums/lu-mediji/zurnali/akademiska-dzive/arhivs/56-numurs/buero-fuer-heimatvetriebene-auslaender-1952-1964-latvian-refugees-in-west-germany-and-their-role-in-functioning-of-the-office/>

McGuinness, D., 'Nazi Ravensbrück camp: How ordinary women became SS torturers', BBC, online at <https://www.bbc.co.uk/news/world-europe-55661782> 18.01.2021

Moore, B., 'The British and their Latvian SS prisoners: Zedelhem 1945–46', *The Journal of Slavic Military Studies*, 36 (2), (2023), pp.179–198

Rule, R., 'Leon Degrelle – Traitor of Belgium', *Warfare History Network*, January 9, 2019, online at <https://warfarehistorynetwork.com/article/was-leon-degrelle-a-traitor-of-belgium-or-german-army-hero/> (accessed 02.04.2024)

Silver, J.R., 'Karl Gebhardt (1897–1948) A Lost Man', *The Journal of the Royal College of Physicians of Edinburgh*, 41, (2011), pp.366–71. 10.4997/JRCPE.2011.417

'Truman Bridge Built at Night', *The Thunderbolt*, online at <https://83rdinfdivdocs.org/documents/newspapers/83rd_Thunderbolt_May_5_1945.pdf> (05.05.1945)

'330th Receives Surrender of Nazi Regiment', *The Thunderbolt*, vol. 1, no. 2, online at <https://83rdinfdivdocs.org/documents/newspapers/83rd_Thunderbolt_May_5_1945.pdf> (05.05.1945)

Willmott, L., 'Irma Grese and Female Concentration Camp Guards', *History Today*, online at <https://www.historytoday.com/archive/history-matters/irma-grese-and-female-concentration-camp-guards> (01.06.2015)

Film

Latvian prisoners in Calbe, May 1945: US Army film in the collection of the United States Holocaust Memorial Museum at <https://collections.ushmm.org/search/catalog/irn1004700>

Websites and online sources

Brombergs, A., *Latviju Enciklopedija (The Latvian Encyclopedia)*, Vol 34, Stockholm, (1952), pp.1288–1322. From the Central Intelligence Agency archive, released under the Nazi War Crimes Disclosures Act 2003 online at <https://latvianlegion.org/en/accused/hazners/archives/CIA/VOL1/HAZNERS,%20VILIS%20%20%20VOL.%201_0004.pdf>

384th Bombardment Group archives online at <https://384thbombgroup.com/_content/_pages/mission.php>

Friends of Zerbst Castle website, online at <https://www.schloss-zerbst-ev.de/html/geschichte.htm>

Latvian Ministry of Foreign Affairs website online at <https://www.mfa.gov.lv/en/article/information-concerning-16-march?utm_source=https%3A%2F%2Fwww.google.com%2F>

Periodika.lv online archive for Daugavas Vanagi contemporary newspaper reports, at <http://periodika.lv/periodika2-viewer/view/index/>

Schmerwitz Manor website at <www-gut--schmerwitz-de>

Swinousjcie city website at <https://www.swinoujskie.info/2017/03/10/amerykanskie-bombowce-zrzucily-na-swinoujscie-3218-bomb/>

The 2011 Golm Book online at <https://www.volksbund.de/seite-nicht-gefunden.html>

Traces of War website at <https://www.tracesofwar.com/persons/13430/H%C3%A4mel-Heinz-Waffen-SS.htm>

United States Holocaust Memorial Museum online at <www.ushmm.org>

War History Online at https://www.warhistoryonline.com/world-war-ii/

Warfare History Network website (2019) Rule, R. *Leon Degrelle – Traitor of Belgium*. 09.01.2019 at https://warfarehistorynetwork.com/daily/wwii/leon-degrelle-traitor-or-war-hero/

Wehrmacht.es website at <https://www.wehrmacht.es/en/ss-sleeve-insignia/2347-nsdap-ortsgruppenleiter-armband.html>

Wildenbruch Church webpage online at <https://www.kirche-michendorf-wildenbruch.de/unsere-gemeinde/kirche-wildenbruch>

Zerbst Francisceum website at <https://francisceum.de/>

Index

PEOPLE

Akermanis, Captain Vilis 56, 57, 62, 139, 141, 148, 161–162, 163
Alksnītis, Major Augusts 28, 31, 51, 67, 125,
Arājs, Viktors 211, 212, 220
Ax, Oberführer Adolph 47, 223

Balodis, Alberts 91, 95
Bangerskis, Latvian Legion Inspector-General Rūdolfs 18, 19, 52, 67, 224
Baumanis, Major Valdemārs 36, 48
Baumgart, Andreas 154, 190, 193
Bebris, Cadet Officer Jūlijs 28
Best, Werner 47
Bilmanis, Dr. Alfreds 216
Blumstengel, Claus 179, 182
Bonoparts, Lieutenant Eižens 28
Bruder, Juliane 190, 192, 196
Buls, Corporal Meikuls 28
Bunga, Oļģerts 79
Burk, SS-Oberführer Karl 19, 47, 51, 64
Bušmanis, First Lieutenant Edvīns 48, 55, 57, 65, 68, 75, 77, 82–83, 85, 88, 90, 92–94, 98, 103, 104–107, 112, 114–115, 121–123, 124–130, 137–138, 140–141, 144, 145–147, 151–153, 155, 166, 203, 216–220

Catherine the Great 190
Ceriņš, Laimonis 42
Čevers, Jānis 17
Chuikhov, General Vasily 54
Crabill, Colonel Edwin B. 186
Cukurs, Herbert 212, 220

Degrelle, Leon 20

Dittmann, Mayor Andreas 190, 195, 196
Djilas, Miloslav 227–228
Dukurs, Uldis 81

Edelsheim, General Maximilian von 194
Eisenhower, Dwight D. 175–176, 193–195, 214
Eše, Verners Adjutant Lieutenant 28

Hämel, Hauptsturmführer Heinz 26, 34
Heinrici, General Gotthard 54
Heydrich, Reinhardt 47
Himmler, Heinrich 39, 40–42, 54
Hitler, Adolf 101
Honecker, Erich 101

Gebhardt, Karl 39–40
Gelzenleuchter, Heinrich 188
Geiselhart, Leutnant 146–148, 154, 162, 190
Grese, Irma 40–41
Guderian, Heinz 42, 54

Hāzners, Colonel Vilis 79
Heilmann, Oberführer Nikolaus 213, 222–223
Hunka, Yaroslav 223

Janovskis, Gunars 21–24
Janums, Colonel Vilis 10–14, 19, 28, 31, 45, 47, 57, 60, 61, 62–64, 65, 67, 68–71, 75–82, 83–92, 98, 103–104, 109–114, 115, 124–130, 135, 137–147, 154, 161–163, 166–172, 176, 193, 203–204, 207, 211, 213–214, 218–219, 221–230

Kalupnieks, Arvīds 60–61, 62, 65–67, 85–87, 88–90, 107–109, 115, 138–139, 145, 147, 163
Kangeris, Kārlis 225, 226
Ķīlītis, Major Jūlijs 21, 61, 153
Koenzgen, Oberst Paul 194, 204
Konev, Marshal Ivan 21, 104, 203
Krievs, Pēteris 27
Krīpens, SS-Standartenführer Arvīds 213–215, 218–219
Krūmiņš, Valters 47

Laukers, Captain Arnolds 214, 218, 219
Lazduzieds, Major Jēkabs 28
Leititis, Jekabs 216, 225
Lindenbergs, Corporal Roberts 28
Luciuk, Professor Lubomyr 223

Macon, Major General Robert C. 196
Manteuffel, General Hasso von 54
Meija, Lieutenant-Colonel Osvalds 45, 51, 67
Meyl, Sigrid 31–33
Mežgrāvis, Fricis 25, 34, 63–64,
Moncke, General-Major Wilhelm 64
Montgomery, Field Marshall Bernard 176, 213, 224
Moore, Prof. Bob 212, 215
Moser, Hans 45
Mūsinš, Žano 17–18

Neilands, Lieutenant Atis 47, 64
Neiburgs, Uldis 219

Orlicek, Luise 184–185

Petersons, Aivars 104, 128

Pfleghar, Udo 180–182
Prissjaschnjuk, First Lieutenant Theo 186

Raus, General Erhard von 40–42
Rubess, Brunis 47–48

Ručs, Kazimirs 28
Rokossovsky, Marshal Konstantin 21, 54
Rumba, Leopolds 48

Silgailis, Arturs 18
Simpson, Lieutenant-General William Hood 186
Sipolins, Leopolds 26, 29, 30, 32
Stevens, George 176
Strauts, Lieutenant Aloizs 28

Tomaševskis, Jānis 161

Valdmanis, Harijs 36
Valters, Dr. Miķelis 217, 218, 220
Vītols, Henry 11, 207–210

Walli, SS-Hauptsturmführer Eldon 14, 45–47, 64–66, 78–79, 81, 82, 83–84
Weidling, General Helmuth 54
Wenck, General Walter 75, 79, 119, 128, 193
Wilgress, Dana 223
Wille, Dr. Hermann 188
Witte, Prof. Herbert 186–187, 190–200, 203–204

Zariņš, Kārlis 215, 224, 225
Ziegler, SS-Brigadeführer Joachim 54
Zivier, Ernst 117
Zivier, George 116

PLACES

Altengrabow [Stalag XI A] 195
Apollensdorf 189
Auschwitz 40, 41, 200

Baldenburg (Biały Bór) 42

Barby 155
Beelitz 95, 101, 103, 109, 111, 117, 119, 135, 192, 203

Beelitz-Heilstatten Sanatorium 100–102
Belarus 23
Belzig 119, 125, 203, 204
Bergen-Belsen 40–41
Berlin 13, 14, 20, 34, 44, 47, 52, 62–68, 71, 75, 77, 79, 81–89, 91, 94, 104, 107, 116, 135, 155, 163, 172, 175–176, 193, 215, 224
Bernau 68, 75, 81

Blankenfelde 78, 83, 88, 92, 93, 95, 107
Bublitz (Bobolice) 42
Buchenwald 200
Buhlendorf 148, 161–162, 189

Calbe 155, 166–169
Cherkassy Pocket 20
Cölpin Manor 25–33

Dahlewitz 88–90, 95, 107
Danzig (Gdańsk) 13, 16, 50, 217
Deetz 189
Detmold 217
Distomo 46
Dornburg 193

East Prussia 16
Eichenquast 125–126, 136
Erkner 66, 69–70, 77–82, 85, 155

Feldberg 18, 27, 38, 39, 51
Fenstanton 19
Fichtenwalde 94, 98, 104, 105, 107–108, 111–112, 116–119, 125, 155, 192, 203–204
Freienthal 113–114
Friesdorf 120
Fürstenberg 18, 34, 37–38, 42, 51, 55

Golzow 114, 119, 124, 204
Gorzke 131
Gosen 77–78, 82, 85
Gotenhafen (Gdynia) 16, 50
Grafton Underwood 117
Gross Briesen 120
Güterglück 119, 124, 136–143, 148, 152, 154, 157, 162, 180, 190, 224

Halbe 75
Hangelsberg 69, 70
Herford 216–217
Herzfelde 59, 62–63, 68, 70, 77, 155
Hohenlychen 39–40

Juterbog 75

Kalininko 222–223
Kanin 109

Klein Briesen 119–120
Kleisoura 46
Kol-Saarmund 93
Köpenick 86
Kurzeme 18–19, 36, 50–52, 60–61, 65, 210, 222
Küstrin (Kostrzyn nad Odrą) 52, 54, 61

Lehnin 103–105, 109–113, 203–204
Lestene 228, 230
Lichtenberg 47–48, 60–61, 111
Lindau 129, 139, 143–144, 186, 189, 193, 204
Luckenwalde [Stalag III A] 195
Lychen 18, 37, 39, 51, 61, 65, 67

Mecklenburg 13, 25, 36, 48, 81, 176
Möllendorf 111, 113
Moscow 11, 175, 221
Muncheberg 75

Nauen 92
Neu Zittau 77–78
Neubrandenburg 19, 20, 21, 31, 32–33, 36, 51, 60, 79
Neustrelitz 21, 36, 37, 79, 216

Pomerania 13, 16, 17, 18, 20, 21, 23, 25, 27, 28, 40, 41, 47, 48, 49, 50, 56, 57, 60, 61, 66, 70, 81, 161, 211, 222-224
Potsdam 86, 92, 94, 100, 109, 111, 114, 155, 176, 192, 194
Prague 175, 194

Quast 135

Ragösen 119, 204
Ravensbrück 39–41
Reppinichen 119, 131–134
Rīga 13, 28, 51, 161, 228, 229
Rosslau 176, 189, 193
Rüdersdorf 62, 85
Rumbula 211

Saarmund 95
Schmerwitz Manor 131
Schmöckwitz 79–80, 83–84, 86
Schora 137, 141, 144, 146, 148, 151, 154–156, 162, 165, 190

Schwerin 13, 92, 217
Seelow Heights 54, 75
Spreenhagen 71, 72
Stettin (Szczecin) 20, 54, 75
Swinemünde (Świnoujście) 16–17, 36

Tangermunde 75
Torgau 195
Toruń 18

Usedom 18, 26

Vaiņode 114

Velikaya river 213, 223
Verlorenwasser 107–108, 109–111, 115, 120–123, 124

Werbig 120, 131–132
Wildenbruch 94, 98, 109, 111
Wolin 16

Zedelghem (Camp 2227) 161, 209, 212–214, 218, 224
Zerbst 14, 63, 111, 124, 127, 139, 154, 155, 174–204
Zossen 63, 75

MILITARY UNITS

German
Army Group Vistula 40, 54
Third Panzer Army 40, 54
Ninth Army 54, 75
12th Army 75, 128, 193
9th SS Regiment *Germania* 46
4th SS-Regiment *Der Führer* 46
4th SS *Polizei* Division 46, 47
5th SS *Wiking* Division 46
11th SS Nordland Panzergrenadiers 54
14th SS Galicia Division 223
15th Latvian SS Division
   Fusilier 'Recce' Battalion 13, 47, 55, 57, 61, 62, 64, 66, 69, 81
   32nd Regiment 18, 21, 31, 37, 45, 51, 67, 78, 213
   33rd Regiment 18, 28–30, 51, 61, 162, 217
   34th Regiment 37
   Artillery Regiment 38
19th Latvian SS Division 13, 50, 210
28th SS Grenadier Division *Walloonien* 20
31st SS German-Hungarians 13
33rd SS Charlemagne Division 13
Corps Group Tettau 41
X SS Corps 13, 41
Hitler Youth 38, 45
Panzer Division Holstein 41
Vlasov 36, 195
Volkssturm 38, 62, 68, 86, 176, 179

Red Army
First Belorussian Front 53, 54, 75
1st Ukrainian Front 104, 195, 203
Second Belorussian Front 41, 54
4th Guards Tank Army 104
Eighth Guards Army 54
201st Latvian Rifleman Division 11
43rd Guards Latvian Riflemen Division 12
130th Latvian Rifle Corps 12

US Air Force
9th Tactical Air Force 180
384th bomb group 116
392nd Group 16

US Army
Eighth Armoured Group 11
Ninth Army 186
83rd 'Thunderbolt' Division 163–165
329th Infantry 179, 186
330th Infantry 163, 165, 188
113th Cavalry Group 189
United States Army Signal Corps
Special Coverage Unit (SPECOU) 176

Miscellaneous
16 March commemoration 228–230
AECANOE-3 (Colonel Janums' CIA codename) 227
Anschluss 45
Arājs Kommando 211, 214, 219

Bralu Kapi cemetery, Rīga 228
British Control Commission for Germany 215
CIA 212, 226–227
Courland Pocket 12, 36
Daugavas Vanagi 219, 224, 230
Department VI 46
Deschene Committee Inquiry on War Criminals (1987) 223
European Voluntary Workers' scheme (EVW) 17, 19, 215
Feldgendarmerie 87
Flakhelfer 13
Hague Convention 1907 211
Hussite Wars 133
Janumieši 61, 85, 147
Kristallnacht 45, 46

Latvian Red Riflemen 221
Mexican standoff 146–147, 148–150, 154, 190
Operation Barbarossa 222
Operation Hannibal 16
Operation Violet 195
Reichsarbeitsdienst (RAD) 13, 18
Russian Front 11, 13, 16, 17, 222
St Nikolai Church, Zerbst 183, 185, 195, 200–203
Thirty Years' War 133
The *Thunderbolt* 163, 165
Truman Bridge 163, 164, 177–179
United States Holocaust Memorial Museum 166–170
West Russia Volunteer Army 221
'Year of Terror', Latvia 211